THE
EVERYTHING®
John F. Kennedy Book

Dear Reader,

Undeniably, John F. Kennedy is one of the most interesting people in American history. What is most fascinating is that his simple but powerful call for Americans to serve their country still resonates with people today. For nearly fifty years now, this has become the most stirring memory of Kennedy. It is amazing that this statement, which has had such a lasting appeal, has forever defined his legacy.

For me, partly what is so interesting about Kennedy's life is the time in which he lived. The Cold War, communism, Vietnam, and civil rights were defining points of his presidency, and the way he handled each clearly set the tone for the nation. But more than that, his actions, especially when it came to his desire to slow the nuclear arms race, was a reflection of his idealism. He described himself as an "idealist without illusions," and it was exactly this optimistic yet realistic viewpoint that defined how he led a nation through a turbulent time. Unquestionably, it was Kennedy's actions during this time that make his life an interesting journey in history.

Jessica McElrath

Welcome to

THE
EVERYTHING
PROFILES SERIES ®

Welcome to the EVERYTHING® Profiles line of books—an extension of the bestselling EVERYTHING® series!

These authoritative books help you learn everything you ever wanted to know about the lives, social context, and surrounding historical events of fascinating people who made or influenced history. While reading this EVERYTHING® book you will discover 3 useful boxes, in additional to numerous quotes:

Fact: *Definitions and additional information*
Question: *Questions and answers for deeper insights*
They Said: *Memorable quotes made by others about this person*

Whether you are learning about a figure for the first time or are just brushing up on your knowledge, EVERYTHING® Profiles help you on your journey toward a greater understanding of the individuals who have shaped and enriched our lives, culture, and history.

When you're done reading, you can finally
say you know **EVERYTHING®**!

DIRECTOR OF INNOVATION Paula Munier

EXECUTIVE EDITOR, SERIES BOOKS Brielle K. Matson

ASSOCIATE COPY CHIEF Sheila Zwiebel

ACQUISITIONS EDITOR Lisa Laing

DEVELOPMENT EDITOR Elizabeth Kassab

PRODUCTION EDITOR Casey Ebert

PHOTO RESEARCHER Robin Gordon

Visit the entire Everything® series at *www.everything.com*

EVERYTHING®

JOHN F. KENNEDY
BOOK

Relive the history, romance, and
tragedy of America's Camelot

Jessica McElrath

avon, massachusetts

For my mother, who was inspired by John F. Kennedy's call to serve

An Everything® Series Book.
Everything® and everything.com® are registered
trademarks of F+W Publications, Inc.

Published by Adams Media, an F+W Publications Company
57 Littlefield Street, Avon, MA 02322 U.S.A.
www.adamsmedia.com

ISBN-10: 1-59869-529-0
ISBN-13: 978-1-59869-529-8

Printed in Canada.

J I H G F E D C B A

Library of Congress Cataloging-in-Publication Data
is available from the publisher.

This publication is designed to provide accurate and authoritative information with regard to the subject matter covered. It is sold with the understanding that the publisher is not engaged in rendering legal, accounting, or other professional advice. If legal advice or other expert assistance is required, the services of a competent professional person should be sought.

—From a *Declaration of Principles* jointly adopted by a Committee of the American Bar Association and a Committee of Publishers and Associations

Many of the designations used by manufacturers and sellers to distinguish their products are claimed as trademarks. Where those designations appear in this book and Adams Media was aware of a trademark claim, the designations have been printed with initial capital letters.

This book is available at quantity discounts for bulk purchases.
For information, please call 1-800-289-0963.

Contents

Acknowledgments

Thanks to my mother for her input and
to my husband for his support.

John F. Kennedy's Top Ten Accomplishments

1. John F. Kennedy accomplished what no other American had done—he became the first Catholic president of the United States.

2. To this day, John F. Kennedy's call for Americans to serve their country has remained an inspiring and memorable appeal.

3. Among John F. Kennedy's most notable and long-standing accomplishments was the establishment of the Peace Corps, an organization that is now responsible for sending thousands of American volunteers around the world to help the needy.

4. It was John F. Kennedy's cautious and sensible approach to the standoff during the Cuban missile crisis that ultimately diverted a nuclear war with the Soviet Union and secured the removal of missiles from Cuba.

5. John F. Kennedy was committed to landing a man on the moon, and although it occurred after his death, it was his support of space exploration that helped make it happen.

6. John F. Kennedy's perseverance was instrumental in securing a limited nuclear test ban treaty with the Soviet Union.

7. It was John F. Kennedy's dedication that helped secure the passage of the Area Redevelopment Act, which assisted states that were suffering from high rates of unemployment.

8. Under John F. Kennedy's administration, laws were put in place to end segregation in interstate travel facilities.

9. John F. Kennedy helped promote the arts by holding concerts, plays, and musicals at the White House.

10. John F. Kennedy issued an executive order prohibiting discrimination in the sale or lease of housing that was financed by federally guaranteed loans or owned by the federal government.

Introduction

Amazingly, although John F. Kennedy spent only a thousand days in office, he has become one of America's most admired presidents. He is the subject of numerous books and films, and yet people never seem to tire of hearing his story. The allure of his story and his presidency still appeals to people more than forty years after his assassination.

Some people consider Kennedy one of the most beloved and admirable presidents, while others cast him as a seriously flawed and overrated leader. Nevertheless, what is true about Kennedy is that at a time when a Catholic in the White House was hardly imaginable, he achieved it. Although many of the old suspicions about Catholics still ran rampant, Kennedy convinced Americans that Catholics were no less dedicated to the well-being of the country than Protestants or any other religious persuasion. This, by any account, paved the way for anyone, regardless of race, ethnicity, gender, or religion, to participate in the political system at its highest level.

Kennedy's leadership in regard to the civil rights movement is one of the most controversial facets of his presidency. Although he proclaimed himself a committed proponent of the cause, his immediate actions as president failed to show this dedication. Kennedy did propose civil rights legislation, but only after the world had witnessed egregious acts of violence perpetuated against civil rights protestors. It was Kennedy's stance on civil rights that was certainly his moral failing.

It was not that Kennedy viewed equality as unimportant, but fierce anticommunist sentiments of the time influenced him to put a higher priority on preventing the spread of communism. It was exactly this concern that moved him to support the South Vietnamese government against the communist North Vietnamese. This action would prove to be one of the most momentous of Kennedy's presidency, especially when his successor, President

Lyndon B. Johnson, led the country further into a war that became hugely controversial.

Kennedy had much more success in his policies when it came to peace. The nature of the Cold War fostered an arms race between the United States and the Soviet Union. Kennedy, a World War II veteran, knew exactly the price of war. With this experience in mind, when the Cuban missile crisis nearly brought about a nuclear war, Kennedy handled the situation with caution and calm. This was most notably his shining moment.

Kennedy had visions that reached far beyond his concern over nuclear war. He believed that one of the greatest achievements in space would come when America landed a man on the moon. Although this accomplishment would occur after his death, his push and promotion of the Apollo project was an important step in the end result. But even more than his advocacy for space exploration, it was Kennedy's establishment of the Peace Corps that truly reflects what is most remembered about his legacy—his call for Americans to serve.

This book, while it is a biography about John F. Kennedy's life, is more than that. It is also a look at the history of the time in which he lived. As you explore Kennedy's life, you will come away with a better understanding of a chaotic period when the Cold War, civil rights, nuclear war, and communism all vied for the attention of Americans. The knowledge of these events is important to understanding the country and world we live in today.

Chapter 1

THE FITZGERALDS AND THE KENNEDYS

Driven by the devastating famine that gripped Ireland in the 1840s, John F. Kennedy's great-grandparents fled to the United States. They settled in Boston, amid strong anti–Irish Catholic sentiments. Kennedy's grandfathers set out to better their situation. They paved the way for the family's success in business and politics, but it was his father who would achieve financial wealth and high political office.

The Kennedy Family's Irish Roots

In Ireland, the Kennedy family, like other Catholics, suffered under restrictive penal laws. Without the right to own property, a farmer's fate of tilling someone else's land was essentially set. Patrick Kennedy, John F. Kennedy's great-grandfather, was born in 1823. As the youngest of three sons, Patrick had few options, so he worked on the family farm harvesting and planting crops.

The Journey to America

The potato famine that swept through Ireland between 1845 and 1849 wiped out the primary source of food for much of the Irish population. Hundreds of thousands of people died of starvation and disease, and many farmers were forced to abandon their livelihoods to seek government assistance.

FACT

The emigrants who boarded transport ships in Ireland bound for Liverpool faced a harsh journey. They were forced to remain on the upper deck, where they were exposed to the wind and cold, while food and livestock remained on the lower deck. Often, passengers numbered up to a thousand and had so little space they were forced to stand.

The Kennedy family continued farming, but the family finances suffered. Patrick made the decision to leave Ireland for America in the midst of the famine. It was a difficult decision, especially since the trip itself posed grave danger; at the time, many who traveled to America died on the journey. Thus, before Patrick's departure in October 1848, he visited a priest in order to receive his blessing. His family, well aware of the danger Patrick faced, bade him goodbye as they recited the emigrant's prayer, "May God bring you safely."

Patrick made the journey from Ireland to Liverpool and he secured his passage to the New World on the *Washington Irving* on March 20, 1849. The ship provided a steerage section for Irish emigrants like Patrick. The emigrants remained in cramped, airless quarters in the bowels of the ship, surviving on moldy cheese and stale biscuits. Patrick Kennedy arrived in Boston about a month after his departure from England.

Creating a Life in Boston

Patrick was one step ahead of most emigrants when he arrived in America. He had an Irish friend already in Boston. Months before his journey to America, his friend Patrick Barron had made the same voyage. It is believed that through the help of Barron, who had worked at a brewery in Ireland and had taught Patrick coopering, Patrick obtained a job as a cooper. With his earnings, Patrick secured living quarters at an inexpensive boarding house in East Boston.

Starting a Family

Barron's cousin, Bridget Murphy, was also in Boston. In Ireland she had lived eight miles from the Kennedy farm. According to Kennedy family legend, Patrick and Bridget met on board the *Washington Irving*. However, historians have found no record of Bridget on board the ship. Instead, it is believed that Patrick and Bridget met in Ireland and planned to marry after they met up in Boston. On September 26, 1849, they were married in a Catholic church in Boston.

Patrick continued to work as a cooper, and Bridget earned income as a menial laborer. In 1851, they had their first child, Mary, followed by Johanna in 1852, John in 1854, and Margaret in 1855. Bridget gave birth to the couple's last child, Patrick Joseph Kennedy, called P.J., on January 14, 1858. Cholera struck the family twice. The

HE SAID...

"When my great-grandfather left [Ireland] to become a cooper in East Boston, he carried nothing with him except two things: a strong religious faith and a strong desire for liberty. I am glad to say that all of his great-grandchildren have valued that inheritance."

couple's eldest son died of cholera in 1855, and Patrick Sr. succumbed to the disease on November 22, 1858.

QUESTION

How was cholera contracted and does it still exist today?

Cholera was the result of an inadequate sewage system and contaminated water. It was contracted through contaminated water, food, and through infected feces. Today the risk of cholera in the United States is low, but it still exists in areas of Africa, Asia, and Latin America.

Anti–Irish Catholic Sentiment in Boston

By the time of Patrick's death, Boston had become a haven for Irish immigrants, and the city's population began to reflect the makeup of the new residents. Before the famine, there were fewer than 5,000 Irish immigrants in Boston. In 1855, foreign immigrants represented 53 percent of the city's total population of 136,881; 80.2 percent of this immigrant group—nearly 60,000 people—was Irish. The overwhelming influx of Irish immigrants alarmed staid Bostonians, who reacted with suspicion and outright bigotry. It was common for children of Irish descent born in America to receive the categorization of "foreigner" in the census. In fact, Patrick and Bridget's children were placed in this classification.

The difficulties of being Irish in Boston only increased for Bridget when Patrick died. To make ends meet, she initially worked as a maid and took in boarders. Intolerance to Irish Catholics was rampant in Boston. It was customary for newspaper advertisements to restrict applicants to American or Protestant heritage. Most notorious were the advertisements that spelled out clearly, "Irish Need Not Apply." Finding work as a maid was difficult for Bridget, who was clearly an Irish Catholic immigrant.

The non-Irish upper class, dubbed Brahmins, hoped the Irish would quietly assimilate into society. Public schools drilled pupils in Puritan ethics and American history, but Boston's archbishop promoted the creation of private Catholic schools to counteract the threat to Catholic beliefs. By the 1860s, the wealthy Brahmins fled to the Boston suburbs, where they lived a secluded life away from the Catholic Irish. To further insulate themselves, they enrolled their children in private schools. With the Brahmins gone, the Irish were free to take over politics in Boston.

FACT

Oliver Wendell Holmes Sr., father of the Supreme Court justice, first applied the term "Brahmin" to Boston's upper-class families in an article in the *Atlantic Monthly* called "The Brahmin Caste of New England." He defined the Brahmins as "harmless, inoffensive, untitled aristocracy."

JFK's Grandfather: Patrick Joseph Kennedy

It was in this environment that Bridget Kennedy sought to support her family. She eventually landed a job at a stationery store. As the children grew older, she was able to buy the business and later expand it to include a grocery store. With the money earned from the store, P.J. was sent to Sacred Heart, a Catholic school. P.J. dropped out of school at age fourteen to work full-time as a stevedore.

Financial Success for P.J.

By the time P.J. reached adulthood, he was a large, confident man whose handlebar mustache and big blue eyes distinguished him from Boston's other Irish residents. P.J. followed in his mother's footsteps and took a chance on a business. He dipped into his savings and borrowed money from his mother to buy a floundering saloon in East Boston's Haymarket Square when he was twenty-two years old.

Although P.J. did not drink, many of Boston's Irish laborers did. With such a large clientele, P.J.'s saloon soon became a booming establishment, as he developed a rapport with customers. He was a trusted confidant who provided laborers with tidbits about job opportunities. As his capital grew, he acquired two more saloons and established a retail and wholesale liquor business.

Pursuing a Career in Politics

After his success in business, P.J. entered the political arena. At the time, politics was one of the only avenues of power for the Irish since the Brahmins guarded the world of business. In 1884, P.J.'s popularity among Boston's Irish helped secure his victory for a state-house seat where he served for five years.

THEY SAID...

"From his grandparents on his father's side, he inherited a certain self-possession and dignity of bearing which his father never achieved. Like P.J. Kennedy, John Kennedy commanded respect and attention from all who came in contact with him."

—Doris Kearns Goodwin, *The Fitzgeralds and the Kennedys: An American Saga*

P.J.'s new success opened up his prospects with potential wives. Among his choices was Mary Augusta Hickey. She was the daughter of a Boston contractor who, like P.J., had achieved success despite the anti-Irish environment. Mary was more educated than P.J. since she had attended the Notre Dame Academy, a private Catholic school. Her social standing made her a good match for P.J., who sought to raise his own stature in the East Boston community. Shortly after their marriage in November 1887, Mary gave birth to Joseph Patrick Kennedy on September 6, 1888, and later to two daughters.

In the meantime, P.J. quickly learned that Massachusetts politics was a messy business. He managed to stay out of the limelight of corruption, but ballot stuffing, financial perks, and favors were all part of the business. After serving in the state house, P.J. won a seat in the state senate, where he served for six years.

FACT

The Brahmins did not give up their political clout willingly, but the Irish emerged as a strong political opposition in 1885, when Irish-born Hugh O'Brien was elected Boston's mayor. By 1914, the city's growing Irish population reached 39 percent. It became increasingly difficult for the Brahmins to win an election against an Irish candidate.

Enjoying a Powerful Position in Boston

By the time of his exit from the senate in 1895, P.J. had established himself as a powerful man in the community. From an office in his saloon he arranged job interviews, made recommendations, and once again, dabbled in politics. This time it was at the local level. He was appointed elections commissioner and fire commissioner, served in Boston's Democratic Party Board of Strategy, and secured a position as Boston's Ward Two boss. It was as ward boss that he wielded the most power. Along with other ward bosses for the North and South End and the Charlestown area, he had a hand in choosing candidates for state offices. Political clout also helped ensure P.J.'s financial success. He eventually acquired a coal company and held a notable amount of stock in the Columbia Trust Company, a Boston Irish–owned bank.

Serving alongside P.J. was John F. Fitzgerald, the North End Ward boss, a politician by nature, and a nuisance to P.J. He was everything that P.J. disliked. He was boisterous, flamboyant, he could bellow "Sweet Adeline" at a moment's notice, and his pride was insufferable. His physical stature was just as dissimilar to P.J. as his personality; he was a small man with dark brown hair. P.J. Kennedy, however, would eventually have to learn to tolerate Fitzgerald. Unbeknownst to P.J., their personal lives were destined to intersect.

JFK's Grandfather: John F. Fitzgerald

John Francis Fitzgerald, also known as "Fitzie" and "Honey Fitz," was the son of immigrants. His father, Thomas Fitzgerald, had come to America during the famine in Ireland. He tried his luck as a farmer in Acton, just outside of Boston, but soon found that the city streets of the North End Irish ghetto in Boston offered better prospects. In 1857, he married Rosanna Cox; eventually, they raised nine children together. Thomas Fitzgerald supported his family by working as a street peddler of household goods. He ultimately established himself as a grocer by day and tavern owner by night. His success in business provided him with the revenue to buy and rent out tenements.

The financial security Thomas Fitzgerald achieved provided his children with opportunities for a better life, especially his son John F. Fitzgerald, who was born in 1863. John Fitzgerald attended the Boston Latin School, a well-regarded public institution that had been attended by such notables as Ralph Waldo Emerson and Cotton Mather. His above-average intelligence earned him a spot at Harvard Medical School after receiving his degree from Boston College.

Due to the unexpected death of his father, Fitzgerald decided to forgo medical school after one year of attendance so that he could support his siblings. In 1889, Fitzgerald married Mary Josephine Hannon. Their first child, Rose, was born in 1890.

Embarking on a Political Career

Unlike P.J., Fitzgerald found the unwelcoming nature of business toward Irish Catholics too much to bear. Politics, according to Fitzgerald, was the best way to raise his stature and create more opportunity. He obtained a job as a Customs House clerk for the city and eventually secured a spot as secretary for the North End ward boss, Matthew Keany. In 1891, he officially entered into politics when he was elected to the Boston Common Council. Keany died in 1892, and Fitzgerald, now an old hand at manipulating the political structure behind the scenes, stepped into Keany's place.

With his political charm and power in tow, Fitzgerald set out to win a more desirable position. The same year he ascended to the North End ward boss position, he was elected to the state senate, where he served with P.J. Kennedy. In 1894, he decided to run for the U.S. House seat in the Ninth District of Boston. He did so without the backing of the other ward bosses, who were supporting his opponent, incumbent Joseph O'Neil. Nevertheless, Fitzgerald left no stone unturned on the campaign trail. He held parades and made promises to support public programs. At the age of thirty-one, Fitzgerald's ambitious promises did not go unnoticed. He won the Congressional seat.

HE SAID...

"There seems to be some disagreement as to whether my grandfather Fitzgerald came from Wexford, Limerick or Tipperary. And it is even more confusing as to where my great-grandmother came from—because her son . . . used to claim his mother came from whichever Irish county had the most votes in the audience he was addressing at that particular time."

THEY SAID...

"It is fashionable to-day to cry out against the immigration of the Hungarian, the Italian and the Jew, but I think that the man who comes to this country for the first time, to a strange land, without friends and without employment, is born of the stuff that is bound to make good citizens."

—John F. Fitzgerald, July 4, 1896

Taking a Stand in Congress

Politics, however, failed to protect Fitzgerald from anti-Catholic and immigrant prejudice. In 1896 when a bill was submitted to Congress that would require stringent literacy requirements for immigrants and an understanding of the U.S. Constitution, Fitzgerald appeared to be one of the lone detractors of the bill. Although Fitzgerald railed against it, the bill passed in the House and later in the Senate.

Fitzgerald took his arguments directly to President Cleveland. He arrived at the White House to find the secretary gone and the president alone in his office. Fitzgerald gave the president his best arguments for vetoing the bill. Cleveland did, mere days before his term ended. To Fitzgerald's disappointment, however, Congress was able to override the veto.

A Political Career in Boston

Fitzgerald returned to Boston in 1901, where he continued as ward boss for the North End and purchased a newspaper called the *Republic*. He turned the newspaper on a course to financial success by gearing it toward Irish immigrants and securing advertising.

In 1905, Fitzgerald seized the chance to run for mayor of Boston when Patrick Collins died while serving his term. Fitzgerald ran a tough campaign, making enemies out of his fellow ward bosses when he proclaimed that the people should rule and not the bosses. He also used his Irish heritage to his advantage by accusing his opponents of being anti-Irish. It was with these tactics that Fitzgerald won the election.

THEY SAID...

"From his namesake, John Fitzgerald, Kennedy inherited a driving will, a determination to overcome sorrow and disability through perpetual motion. . . . Kennedy also shared with his grandfather a radiant warmth which he was able to project onto crowds and individuals alike."

—Doris Kearns Goodwin, *The Fitzgeralds and the Kennedys: An American Saga*

Italians, Jews, the French, and even African Americans were welcomed and included in Fitzgerald's city government. He even created a festival in celebration of Boston's immigrants. However, his commitment to all immigrants was also a useful political measure to ensure votes. Fitzgerald lost reelection in 1907 but won it back in 1910 only to lose it in 1914. In 1916, he made an unsuccessful bid for a Senate seat and three years later, after winning a Congressional race, he was forced to resign because of voter fraud.

JFK's Father: Joseph Patrick Kennedy

Joe Kennedy, the only son of P.J. and Mary Augusta, was born in 1888. Determining that her son had a better chance at success as Joseph Patrick Kennedy, Mary broke with Irish tradition and did not give him P.J.'s popular Irish first name, which was bound to quickly identify his heritage.

Mary wanted her son to have more opportunities than a Catholic school could offer. In 1901, when he was thirteen years old, she removed him from the Catholic school Xaverian and sent him to Boston Latin. Academically Joe showed mediocre intelligence, but he excelled in sports. He earned the Mayor's Cup in baseball for having the highest batting average.

Mary hoped that unlike her husband, Joe would pursue a more reputable line of work than politics. She encouraged him to strive for more, urging him to focus on making money. When Joe was twelve years old, Mary sent him off to work. She secured a job for him at a high-end store where his work entailed delivering hats to wealthy Bostonian women. As he grew older, he worked selling candy at the harbor and sold papers at the ferry building.

Joe dabbled in a variety of moneymaking endeavors, including staging plays in the backyard and charging for admission. His greatest achievement came with the creation of a baseball team he named the Assumptions. He acted as coach, manager, and first baseman. He scheduled the games, rented a playing field, bought the uniforms, and collected money from onlookers.

JFK's Mother: Rose Fitzgerald

Rose Fitzgerald enjoyed a privileged life. The family's wealth grew with the success of her father's newspaper, and they moved into a fifteen-room house in Dorchester. The school she attended, Dorchester High School for Girls, and the private lessons in piano, voice, and French all reflected the status of the Fitzgerald family.

Rose also mastered an air of social gracefulness. Her mother was a quiet religious woman who shied away from her husband's political life. In her stead, Rose took on the job of her father's companion. By the time that she was in her early twenties, she had become an important part of her father's success as she accompanied him to political events and on city business.

In 1906, Fitzgerald set his sights on a political alliance with P.J. Kennedy. He invited the Kennedy family to vacation with the Fitzgeralds at Old Orchard Beach in Maine. While their fathers forged a political union, eighteen-year-old Joseph Kennedy and sixteen-year-old Rose Fitzgerald fell in love.

Marriage Unites the Families

Just after the families returned to Boston from their 1906 vacation together, Joe invited Rose to a school dance, but her father refused to allow her to accompany him. John Fitzgerald believed that the son of a tavern owner was not good enough to marry his favorite daughter. Rose and Joe were determined to see each other despite her father's misgivings, and set out on a secret romance. They met at dances, parties, and the city library. John Fitzgerald soon became aware of the romance and intended to put a stop to it, but all of his efforts were unsuccessful.

THEY SAID...

"My greatest regret is not having gone to Wellesley College. It is something I have felt a little sad about all my life."

—Rose Fitzgerald Kennedy, in an interview with Doris Kearns Goodwin in the 1980s

After graduating from high school, Rose wanted to attend Wellesley, but her father, heavily influenced by Boston's Cardinal O'Connell, decided that a Catholic education was more suitable. He enrolled her at the Catholic school, Convent of the Sacred Heart, in Boston. She later attended Sacred Heart in New York and then spent one year at the school in Blumenthal, Prussia, where Fitzgerald was happy to have his daughter far from Joe. At Sacred Heart, Rose developed an intense commitment to the Catholic faith that would endure for the rest of her life.

In the meantime, Joe was determined to become a bigger success than his father and even Fitzgerald. He was accepted into Harvard University in 1908. He lived in Harvard Yard, where his Irish heritage in a privileged Brahmin world was no mean feat. Joe ignored the slurs and the name-calling. He paid more attention to his goal of climbing the social ladder. He attempted without success to join some of the most prestigious clubs and fraternities. After a lot of hard work, he was accepted into the less prestigious but well-regarded Hasty Pudding Dramatic Club.

FACT

At Harvard, Joe invested in a tour bus operation that cost $300. As his friend drove the bus, he pointed out Boston's historic landmarks to the tourists. By the time he graduated in 1912, he had made $5,000 from the business.

After graduation, Joe decided to make his move into the banking business where he hoped to rub shoulders with the wealthy and powerful. To learn the trade, Joe, through the help of his father, secured a position as a state bank examiner. He excelled in the position and soon became known in the banking field for his quick and ambitious nature. In 1913, Boston Irish-owned Columbia Trust found itself threatened by a takeover from a rival Boston bank, but Joe managed to secure funding from Merchants National Bank. Columbia was saved, and Joe was rewarded for his effort. At the age of twenty-five, he became the bank president.

The year 1914 was full of ups and downs for the Fitzgeralds. John Fitzgerald ran for mayor of Boston but withdrew from the race when an opponent, James Michael Curley, indicated he would expose Fitzgerald's most recent extramarital affair with a cigarette girl named "Toodles" Ryan. After Fitzgerald's slip from prominence, Joe's status as a banker made him a somewhat more welcome addition to the family, and Fitzgerald finally gave his consent for Joe to marry his daughter. On September 20, 1914, the couple was married by Cardinal O'Connell.

Chapter 2

JFK'S EARLY LIFE

John F. Kennedy enjoyed a privileged childhood, but his unfulfilled desire for his mother's affection and the frustration of living in his older brother's shadow made for a rocky start. Kennedy struggled with a lonely life at a boarding school, and on top of it all, he battled mysterious medical problems that could not be successfully treated. Nevertheless, he was a Kennedy and he was expected to remain strong.

Enjoying a Wealthy Lifestyle

After they married, Joe and Rose settled into a seven-room, two-and-a-half-story home in a Protestant neighborhood in Brookline, Massachusetts. Their first child, Joseph Patrick Kennedy Jr., was born in 1915.

THEY SAID...

"[H]e is going to be President of the United States, his mother and father have already decided that he is going to Harvard, where he will play on the football and baseball teams and incidentally take all the scholastic honors. Then he's going to be a captain of industry until it's time for him to be president for two or three terms."

—John Fitzgerald, on the birth of his grandson
Joseph Patrick Kennedy Jr.

Creating Family Wealth

On May 29, 1917, John Fitzgerald Kennedy was born in an upstairs bedroom in the Kennedy home. The world at large was in turmoil, and the United States had just entered World War I. Joseph Kennedy Sr., unlike many of his college buddies, decided that it was more beneficial to continue his quest for wealth than to volunteer to serve in the war. Despite the world events, Joe moved ahead with his plan to become a millionaire by the age of thirty-five.

THEY SAID...

"The limits of Jack's knowledge about his Irish relatives was partly the result of his parent's upward mobility and their eagerness to replace their 'Irishness' with an American identity. Rose Kennedy, Jack's mother, took pains to instill American values in the children, ignoring their Irish roots."

—Robert Dallek, *An Unfinished Life*

Joe was more determined than ever for social acceptance and desperately wanted to throw off the label of "Irishman." He was finally able to break through the wall of prejudice at the Massachusetts Electric Company. After a series of rejections in his bid to become a board member, Joe was elected to the company board in 1917. His real step toward wealth came that same year when he left the bank to take a position as the general manager of Bethlehem Steel's Fore River shipyards in Quincy. The annual salary of $20,000 was well worth the expense for the company. Joe increased wartime production substantially and his inventiveness made him indispensable.

John F. Kennedy and sister Eunice, circa 1925, Brookline, Massachusetts, Naples Road.

Photo Credit: John F. Kennedy Library Foundation in the John F. Kennedy Presidential Library and Museum, Boston

After Joe left Bethlehem in 1919, he was hired as a stockbroker by Galen Stone of the investment banking firm Hayden, Stone and Company. His salary was half of what he received at Bethlehem, but his investments more than made up for it. Under the guidance of the firm, Joe learned the art of earning money in the stock market by trading on inside information. For example, when he learned that Henry Ford planned to acquire the Pond Creek Coal Company, he bought 15,000 shares at $16 per share and then sold them for a sizable profit of $45 per share. Insider trading made Joe a rich man. In 1922, Joe opened his own office and expanded his business dealings into real estate and the movie industry. Within six years, Joe had made $2 million.

Joe also acquired his wealth from buying Massachusetts movie theaters and entering the liquor business. During Prohibition, according to Kennedy family legend, he was a bootlegger who worked with mobsters. The real money, however, came from his importation of Irish whiskey and Scotch from England. When Prohibition ended in 1933, he worked as an agent for such companies as Haig and Haig, John Dewar and Sons, and Gordon's Dry Gin.

In 1921, Joe used his growing wealth to purchase a twelve-room home in Brookline and hire a live-in nursemaid for his expanding family. Rosemary was born in 1918, followed by Kathleen in 1920, Eunice in 1921, Patricia in 1924, Robert in 1925, Jean Ann in 1928, and Edward in 1932.

The Kennedy family.

Photo Credit: Miki Ansen/Getty Images News/Getty Images

The Perks of Wealth

The Kennedy family benefited as Joe continued to acquire wealth, especially during difficult economic times. When the Great Depression hit in 1929, the family hardly felt its effects. In 1960, when Jack was asked about his memory of the depression, he stated that he recalled very little about the time except that his family's wealth continued to grow. He remembered his father hiring more servants, the traveling, and the larger homes. The only effect of the depression that he could recollect was his father hiring extra gardeners to help them make ends meet.

FACT
In 1926, Joe Kennedy bought the Film Booking Offices of America, Inc. (FBO). He made a substantial fortune by cutting the cost of producing the already low-quality films and by increasing production to an average of one film per week. In 1928, he bought the KAO theater chain. In nearly three years, Joe had made $5,000,000.

While the family money had sheltered Jack from the effects of the Great Depression, it had also sheltered him from social mores. He developed a habit of carrying very little cash or none at all. Jack, like his siblings, had early on in childhood come to believe that as a Kennedy he was entitled to special treatment. Jack believed that he was good for his debt and it was quite common for friends, store-owners, and restaurants to get stuck with the tab. Nevertheless, more often than not, the debt was later paid.

Seeking Motherly Affection

Money could not buy everything Jack wanted. Having the undivided attention of his mother was one of his greatest desires. His sister Rosemary was intellectually disabled and needed special care, so Rose paid particular attention to her. Rose was at times overburdened by the needs of her nine children. Joe's work often took him away from home, so it was Rose who carried the burden of

" HE SAID...

"I have no firsthand knowledge of the depression. My family had one of the great fortunes of the world and it was worth more than ever then. We had bigger houses, more servants, we traveled more. . . . I really did not learn about the depression until I read about it at Harvard."

childrearing. To counteract the effects of her burdensome life, Rose found comfort in traveling. She traveled extensively throughout the United States and Europe. Sightseeing and shopping were relaxing for her, and it was not uncommon for her to remain away from home for several weeks at a time. While Rose traveled the world, the Kennedy children were under the care of the family maids and nurses.

Jack dreaded his mother's lengthy absences. When he was six years old, a sarcastic Jack told Rose that she was a "great mother" for leaving them all alone. In time, Jack grew to quietly accept his mother's departures, but he never liked them. When his mother was home he became the rebel of the family. He broke the rules, was often late to dinner, dressed improperly, and irritated her with inopportune questions during religious instruction. Rose saw Jack's defiance as an indication of his independence and his desire to do things as he wished.

THEY SAID...

"[H]e was a very active, very lively elf, full of energy when he wasn't ill and full of charm and imagination. And surprises—for he thought his own thoughts, did things his own way, and somehow just didn't fit any pattern. He was a funny little boy, and he said things in such an original, vivid way."

—Rose Kennedy, *Times to Remember*

Jack rarely experienced the warmth, affection, and love he expected from his mother. Rose Kennedy was a strict disciplinarian who required that the children adhere to schedules. As a religious woman, she took great pains to ensure the children received proper religious instruction. Rose took motherhood seriously and viewed it as a profession that required her to take on the challenge with a commitment to fulfill her duty to the best of her ability.

Brotherly Love: Jack and Joe Jr.

Jack's relationship with his older brother Joe Jr. was fiercely competitive. Joe—older, bigger, and stronger—more often than not held the advantage over Jack. This, however, failed to stop Jack from backing down. In one instance, they engaged in a bicycle race and neither would stop. They hit each other head-on. Joe emerged unscathed, but Jack's injuries resulted in twenty-eight stitches.

This type of competition was an ordinary occurrence in the Kennedy home. Bobby Kennedy later remembered being scared and hiding upstairs while his brothers fought downstairs. Joe and Jack faced off in intense wresting matches, where Joe used his size and strength to his advantage. When the boys played football, it was common for Joe to shove the ball into Jack's stomach and look on in amusement as Jack doubled over in pain. Jack, though, successfully learned to use his speed rather than his strength to escape Joe Jr.

Jack was not the only sibling afraid of Joe. With the frequent absence of both parents, Joe Jr. stepped in as the ruler of the home. He sat at the head of the table, made sure his siblings strictly adhered to the rules, and doled out punishment when necessary. Overall, the Kennedy children feared him. Yet Joe Jr. also had a softer side. He played with the younger children, especially Teddy, and attended his siblings' athletic events.

Life at Boarding School

In spite of all of the competitiveness between the brothers, Jack still had developed an intense affinity for Joe Jr. This became especially evident when the family moved out of Boston. In 1927, Joe moved them to Riverdale, New York, a neighborhood in the Bronx.

21

HE SAID...

"[Joe] made the task of bring up a large family immeasurably easier for my father and mother for what they taught him he passed on to us, and their teachings were not diluted through him, but rather strengthened."

A combination of the Irish Catholic prejudice in Boston and Joe's growing success in the film industry led to the decision.

Jack quickly adjusted to his new school, Riverdale Country Day School. When he began sixth grade, Joe Jr. was sent to Choate, a boarding school in Wallingford, Connecticut, and Jack's world became a little more stressful. His academic average reached an all-time low of 75. Jack was soon sent off to boarding school at Canterbury School in New Milford, Connecticut. Although the Catholic rituals provided some amount of familiarity, Jack often felt homesick. His grades, which failed to improve much, reflected his discontent.

THEY SAID...

"I was born here. My children were born here. What the hell do I have to do to be an American?"

—Joseph Kennedy

After only one year at Canterbury, Jack's misery caught the attention of his parents. They sent him to Choate to join his brother in September 1931. There was one potential obstacle. Jack's entrance exam reflected his strong abilities in English and algebra, but he failed the Latin exam. Despite this, Choate was just as anxious as Joe and Rose for Jack to attend the school. The school gave Jack another chance at the exam. After intensive tutoring during the summer, Jack was off to Choate in the fall.

The Kennedy Standard

Jack was happy to be near his brother again, but he soon discovered that it was difficult to hold his own against Joe Jr.'s accomplishments. For the most part, Joe Jr. had managed to live up to his parents' high expectations. He was his parents' pride and joy, and he had the athletic success and the strong academic record to prove it. When he graduated from Choate in 1933, he was awarded the Harvard Trophy for his combined scholastic and athletic accomplishments.

THEY SAID...

"Choate had a highly 'structured' set of rules, tradition, and expectations into which a boy was supposed to fit; and if he didn't, there was little or no 'permissiveness.' Joe Jr. had no trouble at all. . . . But Jack couldn't or wouldn't conform. He did pretty much what he wanted, rather than what the school wanted of him."

—Rose Kennedy, as quoted in *An Unfinished Life*

For Jack, living in the shadow of his brother did little to inspire him. To make matters worse, because of his skinny frame, he earned the less than endearing nickname Rat Face. Although Jack believed he was as smart as his brother and potentially just as athletic, he realized he would always be second.

While Joe Jr. was busy soaking in the praise, Jack had a hard time shaking the feeling of failure. He was falling short of the Kennedy standard. From an early age, the Kennedys were taught to win at all costs. Joe Kennedy instilled in his children that there was only one place that was worthy of Kennedy praise, and that was first place. According to Eunice Kennedy, winning was an expectation, and until she was twenty-four, she believed that she had to win something every day. This win-at-all-costs attitude was reflected in the Kennedy motto: "Finish First."

Joe Kennedy was disappointed and concerned about his careless and disorderly son. Jack was sloppy and often put little effort into his studies. Jack's lack of responsibility became an ongoing concern for Joe. In numerous letters to Jack, Joe expressed his belief that he was capable of more than he put out. He encouraged him to take his studies seriously and to develop a sense of responsibility. Joe was also concerned with Jack's choice of friends. In particular, he was skeptical of Kirk LeMoyne "Lem" Billings, who he considered a bad influence. Lem, however, would remain a lifelong friend.

Medical Problems

Jack's lack of academic distinction was far from the only disappointment for Joe. Jack had long-term medical problems that were a source of concern and frustration for Joe. He wanted his boys to be the best at everything in life. Jack's slight frame and his medical problems were a constant reminder of his son's physical failings.

From the age of two years, Jack's medical troubles had plagued the Kennedy family. When he was nearly three, he came down with a serious case of scarlet fever. He spent two months in the hospital and two weeks at a Maine sanatorium. His parents were almost certain he was going to die. It was such a difficult time that Joe Kennedy put his work aside in order to spend time at church praying for his son's recovery. Joe prayed that if his son was spared death, he would donate money to the church. Jack recovered and Joe did as he promised. However, Jack was soon plagued by numerous other medical ailments.

By the time Jack reached Canterbury, his health was still a problem. An undiagnosed illness caused him to lose six pounds from his already slight frame. He felt tired, dizzy, and weak. On one occasion, he collapsed and was luckily caught by the headmaster.

HE SAID...

"Dad persuaded us to work hard at whatever we did. We soon learned that competition in the family was a kind of dry run for the world outside. At the same time, everything channeled into public service. There just wasn't any point in going into business."—*Time* magazine, Dec. 2, 1957

His condition continued to worsen, and he began to experience abdominal pains, which were diagnosed as appendicitis.

At Choate, his medical condition deteriorated. On several occasions he was confined to the infirmary. It was mostly due to colds, but an unusual urine sample was noted in one instance. By his second and third year, his ailments were marked by common occurrences such as the flu, knee pain, and all-over body pain. Once, Jack was taken to New Haven Hospital, where it was determined that he had hives and was suffering from weight loss. It was also believed that he was possibly suffering from leukemia.

FACT

Spastic colitis is a gastrointestinal disorder that causes abnormal gut contractions. The symptoms include bloating, abdominal pain, diarrhea, and constipation. The condition is characterized by its tendency to disappear and reappear over time. It is treatable with a change in diet, exercise, and medication.

Through all of the medical tests, the hospital stays, and the poking and prodding, there was one thing that Jack learned was expected of him as a Kennedy: he was not to complain. Through it all, even during his junior year at Choate in June 1934 when he was sent to the Mayo clinic and then St. Mary's Hospital in Rochester, Minnesota, he quietly endured the discomfort of his undiagnosed illness and the numerous tests. During this stay, doctors initially believed that he was suffering from peptic ulcer disease but later concluded it was spastic colitis. Jack was placed on a strict diet of rice and potatoes. Despite the new diet, his condition continued to go downhill. Jack spent the remaining school years in and out of the hospital.

Defying the Rules

Jack's lack of effort and his medical problems were just the beginning of his problems at school. The headmaster of Choate, George

St. John, soon found that Jack was just the opposite of his brother Joe.

The Muckers Club

Jack was a troublemaker, and his greatest act of defiance came with the formation of the Muckers Club. St. John's repetitive lectures in chapel about the troublemakers, or muckers as he liked to call them, inspired Jack, Lem Billings, and other friends to organize the club. This was almost the last straw for St. John, who considered the club just another negative mark on Jack's record. When he became aware of the club, he met with Joe Kennedy and Jack in his office. St. John was ready to expel Jack from school, but Joe, although angry with his son, convinced the headmaster to let Jack stay as long as he agreed to dissolve the club.

Following in His Father's Footsteps

It was no secret, not even to Rose, that Joe Kennedy had a long history of extramarital affairs. It was not uncommon for him to invite his newest girlfriend to the Kennedy home, where they innocently dined with the family. The actress Gloria Swanson was among the women who went in and out of the Kennedy home in the 1920s. Rose, just like her own mother, played the polite hostess to her husband's mistress when the woman visited the Kennedy summer home.

It was Swanson, however, who nearly destroyed Rose and Joe's marriage. By the time of the affair, Joe had acquired three studios in Hollywood. He met Swanson at one of the studios during the filming of *Queen Kelly*. Unlike many of his other affairs, Joe became enthralled with Swanson and went to the Catholic Church in hope of attaining the approval to separate from Rose. Once separated, he planned to live with Swanson. When Cardinal O'Connell heard the plan, he made a visit to Swanson and asked her to end the relationship. Shortly thereafter, the affair ended.

Joe's less than secretive behavior had a lasting impact on his children, who knew of and even came to accept Joe's betrayal of their mother. Jack, in particular, came to admire his father's vigorous quest for fulfillment with numerous women. An impressed young Jack hoped that when he reached his father's age, he too would remain a playboy. According to his good friend Lem Billings, when Jack was seventeen he engaged in his first sexual encounter, with a Harlem prostitute.

THEY SAID...

"I was immediately captivated by Jack. He had the best sense of humor of anybody I had ever met. . . . He enjoyed things with such intensity that he made you feel that whatever you were doing was absolutely the most wonderful thing you possible could be doing."

—Lem Billings, as quoted in *The Fitzgeralds and the Kennedys: An American Saga*

In spite of Jack's disobedience of school rules, sexual experimentation, and mediocre academic record, by the time that he graduated in 1935 he had acquired the coveted title of "most likely to succeed." It was an unlikely title for Jack, considering that he graduated 65th out of 110, but there was something endearing about the Kennedy who was witty, fun, and laid back. Even headmaster St. John came to like him. One of the most attractive traits that St. John noticed about him was his ability to think independently. In fact, he found that the more time he spent with the student he had once called a "mucker," the better he liked him. With such a likeable personality and a promising future, it came as no surprise to Jack's classmates, or to St. John, when Jack announced that he was headed for Princeton.

Chapter 3

HARVARD BOUND

If John F. Kennedy had not been the son of Joe Kennedy, attending an Ivy League school with his mediocre grades would have been a fleeting dream. But since he had a familial advantage, he could hardly pass up the chance. College nurtured his emerging passion for national and international politics, which led to his interest and eventual success in a political career. It was the first step to a promising future.

A Detour Before Harvard

Attending Choate had been tough for Jack, but he had high hopes that Princeton would be much different. For starters, he could finally break free from his brother's shadow since Joe Jr. was attending Harvard. Princeton would give him the opportunity to carve out his own path. But once again, Jack was eventually overcome by the nagging feeling that he wanted the same opportunities as his brother. He decided that just like Joe Jr. had done, he too wanted to study in England for a year with socialist Harold Laski at the London School of Economics.

FACT

Harold Laski was a leading socialist in England during the 1930s and 1940s. His views were controversial yet influential. As a Labour party member, he was instrumental in formulating the 1945 party manifesto. That year, the Labour party emerged victorious over Winston Churchill and the Conservatives.

Although Joe Kennedy firmly believed in capitalism, he was unconcerned with the possibility that Jack would return from England a socialist. Joe Jr. had in fact returned espousing the benefits of socialism, but Joe Kennedy felt confident it was a passing phase. Most important to him was for his children to think independently. Early on, Joe made sure that they received plenty of practice. It was common for him to use family dining as a place to groom his children as he quizzed and encouraged them to take a different view from his. Joe prized independent thought greatly.

So Jack, with the blessing of his father, was off to England. He arrived in London in September 1935. Unlike his brother, instead of focusing on his studies with Laski, Jack invested his time in a social life. However, it was short lived. Illness once again held him back. This time, according to Rose Kennedy, he suffered from hepatitis or jaundice. After only one month, he returned to America, where he recovered quickly. Rather than return to England, Jack decided to try to enroll late for the Princeton fall term. His petition was rejected, but Joe was able to arrange his admission in November.

After entering Princeton late in the fall, bouts of illness forced Jack to withdraw in December after he was hospitalized at Boston's Peter Bent Brigham Hospital. He spent some time in Palm Beach, Florida, and in April traveled to Arizona, where his parents hoped the warmer weather would speed along his recovery. While recuperating, Jack made the decision to apply to Harvard. With Joe Kennedy as his father, his admission was a sure thing. Within three days of his application, he was accepted for the fall term despite his mediocre score on the Scholastic Aptitude Test.

A Lady's Man

Again, just like at Choate, Jack found he existed in Joe Jr.'s shadow. Joe played on the varsity football team and was active in school politics. Jack, although dismayed, found he had an advantage over his brother in one particular area. He had an irresistible charm when it came to women. He took immense pride in his conquests and wrote Lem Billings, who was attending Princeton, about his star status as a "Play-Boy." In many detailed letters that ranged from "dirty," "very dirty," and "not so dirty" as described by Billings, Jack recounted his numerous encounters with various women.

THEY SAID...

"The girls really liked Jack. I hated to admit it at the time, but it was true. In fact, he was even more successful with girls than his brother Joe. Though Joe was bigger and better-looking, Jack knew better how to handle girls and they mattered more to him."

—Lem Billings, as quoted in *The Fitzgeralds and the Kennedys: An American Saga*

Jack had finally found something he was proud of and good at. Furthermore, once again, he found the support he needed from his father's example. By this time, he had clearly accepted his father's behavior and spoke amusingly to his friends about his father's sexual liaisons. In one situation, Jack informed a female guest at the Kennedy home to make sure she locked her door when she went to bed since his father liked to "prowl" at night. This was just the beginning of the casualness with which Jack pursued women, and it would remain with him for the rest of his life.

John F. Kennedy with a guest during a birthday party for his sister Eunice in London.

Photo credit: Courtesy Peter Hunger/Magnum Photos

Athletic Endeavors

A social life, sports, and girls appeared to be the only things on Jack's mind. His grades were mostly mediocre, ranging from B's to C's. Social standing and sports went hand in hand. In spite of his health issues and slight frame, Jack was intent on excelling in sports. He joined the swim team and the sailing team and played on the junior football squad.

Even though his health affected his ability in football and swimming, Jack became highly competitive. According to the football coach, he put forth intense effort. He trained hard to get into shape, but his dream of playing football came to an end when he was injured during a scrimmage. In swimming, however, he could be proud. During his freshman year, he and his team enjoyed an undefeated status. His sailing ability was also notable. Under his direction, the team won the intercollegiate championship.

European Tour

As opposed to his father and brother, Jack did show aptitude and interest in foreign affairs. His father, who was serving as the chairman of the Securities and Exchange Commission, was an isolationist and remained unconcerned about world events unless they affected him personally. Jack, on the other hand, had developed an interest in the world. His curiosity was furthered when his father paid the bill for Jack and Billings to travel to Europe during the summer of 1937.

HE SAID...

"[W]hile [the French] all like Roosevelt, his type of government would not succeed in a country like France which seems to lack the ability of seeing a problem as a whole. . . . The general impression also seems to be that there will not be a war in the near future and that France is much too well prepared for Germany."

Exploring France

Jack and Billings arrived in France first. In the convertible sent over on the *SS Washington*, they set out to explore the country. They visited World War I battlefields, churches, museums, and made their way through such cities as Paris, Rouen, Versailles, Amboise, and Cannes.

Jack was intrigued with current events and found that the French were suitable conversationalists on various topics. From these conversations, Jack developed strong opinions about the ideas of the French. He came to believe the French were unconcerned with the potential for another war, and thought the French were unable to see the breadth of a problem.

Jack also developed disdain for certain French behaviors that he found offensive. He was repulsed by their "cabbage breath" and lack of bathtubs. Additionally, he became irritated by the efforts of the French to take advantage of American tourists. In one instance where he had dinner with a French officer, he noted in his diary that the officer had managed to get him to pay for part of the meal. Overall, according to Jack, France was quite primitive.

Taking on Italy

Before visiting Italy, Jack and Billings made a stop in Spain, where they witnessed a bullfight in Biarritz. For entertainment purposes, Jack found it interesting. However, it was the cruelty of the bullfight that convinced him that the appalling stories he had heard about the Spanish civil war were closer to truth than fiction. The Spanish, according to Jack, were "happiest at scenes of cruelty."

Upon arriving in Italy, Jack was impressed with the liveliness of the country, the regimented nature of the children, and the cleanliness. Despite a more positive experience than in France, Jack was turned off by what he described as the Italians' nosiness and their attempts to exploit him. He became irate when settling the hotel bill turned into an attempt by the proprietor to take him for everything he could get.

In Rome, Jack's fascination with international politics led him to visit *New York Times* correspondent Arnaldo Cortesi. Jack became deeply concerned about the likelihood of another war because of what he believed was the competitiveness and intolerance of European nations. He discussed the possibility of war with Cortesi, who believed that war was unlikely and that Europe was ready in the unlikely event that it did happen. Overall, Jack came away from Europe with an understanding that despite the physical divide between America and Europe, European affairs would always impact the United States.

Preparing for a Political Career

After making stops in Germany and England, Jack and Billings returned to the United States in September. Joe Sr. had found further success in the political arena. Not only did *Fortune* magazine publish an article about him, but President Roosevelt appointed him ambassador to Great Britain in December. For Joe Sr., this exciting accomplishment meant doors that had been closed to him because of his Irish heritage would open.

Taking International Affairs Seriously

Jack also benefited from his father's new position. It gave him the opportunity to rub elbows with some of England's most prosperous families, including the royal family. During the summer of 1938, he began work at the U.S. embassy in London. His time in London coincided with Hitler's demand that Prague relinquish the Sudetenland, to which the British acceded in the hope of avoiding a war. These events only intensified Jack's curiosity in foreign affairs that his prior trip to Europe had inspired.

> # THEY SAID...
> "For Jack, the tour was an extraordinary educational experience. Not only did he get the chance to witness the final rumblings of an active continent moving toward war, but his numerous contacts helped in the gathering of information that would make substantial contributions to his thesis on preparedness."
>
> —Doris Kearns Goodwin, *The Fitzgeralds and the Kennedys: An American Saga*

He returned to Harvard for the fall term and arranged to take leave during the spring semester for another trip to Europe. He agreed that during his time abroad, he would gather information for his senior thesis. Jack had to carry a heavy load of six classes to make up for his planned leave of absence in the spring. Although the extra classes added more academic pressure, Jack's genuine concern over foreign affairs earned him higher grades. His professors, especially in the government classes, noted that although he was reserved, he was an active participant in class discussions and was an independent thinker.

Jack sailed for London in February 1939. His father's position as ambassador provided him with opportunities that would not have been available otherwise. He met with King George VI, Queen Mary, and Princess Elizabeth. He went on to Rome at the end of March to witness his youngest brother, Teddy, receive his First Communion from Pope Pius XII. Jack, Joe Jr., and Eunice were given the sacrament in a private Mass by the pope.

Jack's interest in foreign affairs continued to sharpen. He wrote to his father about Germany's plan to take Poland and expressed his thoughts on how Poland would react. "Probably the strongest impression I have gotten," wrote Jack, "is that rightly or wrongly the Poles will fight over the question of Danzig." Jack continued to gather information for his thesis with his travels to Danzig and Warsaw, which gave him the opportunity to speak to Nazi and Polish officials. He also made his way to Kiev, Turkey, Leningrad, Moscow, Bucharest, Beirut, Damascus, Jerusalem, and Athens.

Receiving Special Treatment

As Jack traveled throughout Europe, his father's position opened up far more opportunities than would have been available otherwise. He stayed at several embassies, including the Paris embassy. It was there that he had the opportunity to get to know U.S. Ambassador to France William Bullitt and his aide Carmel Offie. Much of the time he spent at the embassy allowed him to live "like a king," but there were other advantages as well. He had a firsthand look at the operations of the embassy, and as Offie later recalled, Jack was often in his office "listening to telegrams being read or even reading various things." With access to private government matters, this experience most certainly contributed to the fact-finding mission for his senior thesis at Harvard.

In August, Jack encountered a bit of hostility when his father arranged for him to visit Czechoslovakia. By this time the government in Prague was controlled by the Nazis, so this arrangement led to commotion in the U.S. embassy. They resented the idea that Jack, just a student at Harvard and not an official, could learn anything about Prague that was not already known. Despite their protestations, Jack's wishes won out. The tour was a unique opportunity for Jack to view firsthand the Nazi occupied territory at the height of the escalating conflict. The experience, which he viewed as invaluable, contributed to the preparation of his thesis.

At dawn on September 1, 1939, Nazi tanks rolled across the Polish border and decimated the outdated Polish cavalry. Two days later, Jack, Joe Jr., and Kathleen watched from the Strangers' Gallery in the House of Commons as MP Winston Churchill addressed the nation. Churchill, who had long argued against appeasing Germany, eloquently conveyed his pride in his country and his preparation to face the battles to come. Jack was more than impressed; in fact, since he was already a big fan of Churchill's, it was a momentous occasion.

THEY SAID...

"We are fighting to save the whole world from the pestilence of Nazi tyranny and in defense of all that is most sacred to man. . . . It is a war, viewed in its inherent quality, to establish, on impregnable rocks, the rights of the individual, and it is a war to establish and revive the stature of man."

—Winston Churchill, September 3, 1939

Developing an Opinion on World Affairs

Jack returned to the United States confident that he knew the right steps to take to promote peace. In October 1939, in the Harvard *Crimson*, he took an opposing view to the prevailing support for fighting the war. Jack argued that the best course of action was to end the war through negotiation. It was President Roosevelt's obligation, according to Jack, to mediate a settlement. He believed such a feat was possible because England and Germany desired an agreement. In addition, he asserted that if Poland had to be sacrificed to prevent the defeat of Britain and France, then it should be done.

Jack's interest in world affairs continued to blossom. He took numerous classes on contemporary international politics. His courses included Modern Imperialism; International Law; and Comparative Politics: Bureaucracy, Constitutional Government, and Dictatorship. His interests included studying capitalism, Nazism, communism, democracy, and fascism. He became increasingly interested in determining the reasons nations took various actions, and he came to believe that international cooperation was key to success.

Why England Slept

Jack's senior thesis indicated his real interest in international affairs. This 148-page paper was entitled "Appeasement at Munich: The Inevitable Result of the Slowness of Conversion of the British Democracy to Change from a Disarmament Policy to a Rearmament Policy." It took Jack two months to write it with the help of typists, stenographers, and the assistance of the U.S. embassy press secretary James Seymour. Seymour's help was invaluable, and he served essentially as Jack's research assistant. He found relevant books, articles, and political pamphlets that were unavailable in the United States. Joe Kennedy's position also gave Jack direct access to British ambassador Lord Lothian, whom he met with at the family's Florida home in December 1939.

An Impressive Thesis

Drawing from Alexis de Tocqueville's assertion that popular rule does not necessarily create a workable foreign policy, Jack argued that Britain's appeasement policy at Munich was not the result of weak leadership but was the consequence of the failure to arm in the 1930s. Jack asserted that the policy resulted from catering to the pacifists and those who advocated the League of Nations taking greater role in security. This disregard for national security was Britain's true failure, rather than inadequate leadership of prewar prime ministers Stanley Baldwin and Neville Chamberlain. Moreover, Jack believed it was difficult for democratic countries like the United States or Britain to rally support for national security measures until survival was at stake.

Although Jack's instructors noted that his thesis had some organizational problems and misspellings, they considered it a great effort. According to Professor Henry A. Yeomans, in spite of the poor writing quality, the work reflected intelligent thought. Professor Carl J. Friedrich, on the other hand, found fault in Jack's typographical errors, his failure to analyze the premise, and the wordiness and repetitiveness of the work. Nevertheless, despite these shortcomings, Friedrich recognized that Kennedy had put a considerable amount of time into the thesis. The greatest excitement over Kennedy's work came from his thesis advisors Bruce C. Hopper and Payson Wild, who believed the problems within the work were overridden by overall quality.

HE SAID...

"Why, exactly, is the democratic system better? . . . It is better because it allows for the full development of man as an individual. . . . It may be a great system of government to live in internally but it's [sic] weaknesses are great. We wish to preserve it here. If we are to do so, we must look at situations much more realistically than we do now."

JOHN FITZGERALD KENNEDY
Born May 29, 1917, in Brookline, Massachusetts. Prepared at The Choate School. Home Address: 294 Pondfield Road, Bronxville, New York. Winthrop House. *Crimson* (2–4); Chairman Smoker Committee (1); St. Paul's Catholic Club (1–4). Football (1), Junior Varsity (2); Swimming (1), Squad (2). Golf (1). House Hockey (3, 4); House Swimming (2); House Softball (4). Hasty Pudding-Institute of 1770; Spee Club. Permanent Class Committee. Field of Concentration: Government. Intended Vocation: Law.

Photo credit: John F. Kennedy Presidential Library and Museum

Publishing *Why England Slept*

The timeliness of the thesis and the positive assessment it received convinced Jack to try to get it published. With this in mind, he met with Arthur Krock, a columnist for the *New York Times*. Krock helped Jack with revisions and urged him to adopt the title *Why England Slept*. The title was similar to Winston Churchill's *While England Slept*, which chronicled Churchill's attempts to get his country involved in the war. Harper & Brothers and Harcourt Brace rejected Kennedy's manuscript, but publisher Wilfred Funk eventually picked it up.

THEY SAID...

"What seems most important now about Kennedy's thesis is the extent to which he emphasizes the need for unsentimental realism about world affairs. . . . Personal, self-serving convictions are as unconstructive as outdated ideologies in deciding what best serves a nation's interests. Although he would not always be faithful to these propositions, they became mainstays of most of his later responses to foreign challenges."

—Robert Dallek, *An Unfinished Life*

Jack made some changes to the manuscript before publication. In his first version, he had placed the bulk of the blame for disarmament on the British people. After his father passed it around to numerous colleagues, Joe informed Jack that the main criticism the manuscript received was its assessment that the British people were more responsible than the leaders of the country. In response, Kennedy lessened his blame on the public for the failure to rearm. In addition, he made a complete turnaround in his analysis of democracy. Whereas he had originally asserted that democracy was an unreasonable luxury, he instead proclaimed that the preservation of democracy was a noble cause. Lastly, he made the work more appealing by addressing the steps America could take in its goal for national security.

The book was timely, which clearly became evident with its positive reviews and notable sales in Britain and the United States. It quickly climbed to the top of best-seller lists, and Jack enjoyed a celebrity-like status. To promote his book, he enthusiastically gave newspaper and radio interviews and autographed copies. Jack realized that this was a unique opportunity that would help whatever career he sought in the future.

HE SAID...

"We should profit by the lesson of England and make our democracy work. We must make it work right now. Any system of government will work when everything is going well. It's the system that functions in the pinches that survives."

With the success of his book, Jack had finally made his own way. As far as his next move, he was uncertain. After graduating from Harvard in the spring of 1940, he considered law school but ultimately decided to study business at Stanford University. Nonetheless, the courses he took in political science made it clear that his interest remained in the political realm. However, due to his health he only lasted one semester. In addition to the reemergence of his intestinal problems, he suffered from severe back pain. He spent ten days recuperating at the Lahey Clinic where he received lower back support, and then he returned to the East Coast, where he again considered what his life's work would encompass.

Chapter 4

MILITARY SERVICE

John F. Kennedy's medical problems could have easily kept him out of the military, but he decided he wanted to serve his country regardless of his condition. Like many PT boat crewmen who were from wealthy families, Kennedy wanted to serve on board one of the fast, motorized boats stationed mainly in the South Pacific. While death was certainly a prospect he had envisioned, he never expected he would return home a hero.

Navy Life in Washington

As Jack contemplated his future, world events once again intruded. In September 1940, even though the United States had not yet entered World War II, a peacetime draft was implemented, and Jack was among the first draftees that fall. Jack, however, had an easy out. His ongoing health problems could preclude his service. Even if he wanted to join the service, a rejection was certain if his health issues were known. Because of his family's prominence, his failure to qualify due to medical problems would publicly expose his condition.

Joe Kennedy's Blunder

The Kennedy family hardly needed more publicity at the moment, since Joe Kennedy had created a scandal with some disastrous remarks he'd made to the press. Roosevelt had been reelected to a third term on November 5, and Joe Kennedy decided to resign as ambassador, having grown increasingly uncomfortable with Roosevelt's anti-German views. The president requested that he stay on until a replacement was found, and Joe readily agreed.

Days later, a relaxed Joe met with three reporters in his hotel room. As he sat eating apple pie, Joe Kennedy expressed his views on the war in his usual blunt fashion. While he certainly believed America should support Great Britain, he felt strongly that the country should remain out of the war. "Democracy is finished in England. It may be here," he told the reporters. Democracy in the United States would fare badly if the country got into the war, he theorized. By the end of the interview, Joe had also thrown in a few comments about Eleanor Roosevelt and her insistence that he meet with "nobodies."

Joe had assumed that just like on other occasions in which he had spoken with the same frankness, his worst statements would undergo severe editing or would never make it into the article. Although it was Joe's usual nature to speak freely, this time *Boston Globe* reporter Louis Lyons published his statements in their entirety. Suddenly, Joe Kennedy's unabashed statements placed him in an embarrassing predicament. His appeasement stance before the war had placed him on a downward slope, and his defeatist remarks sealed his fate: Joseph Kennedy was no longer politically viable.

THEY SAID...

"It's all a question of what we do with the next six months. The whole reason for aiding England is to give us time. Whatever we give England, we shouldn't think of getting it back. It's insurance. . . . As long as she is in there, we have time to prepare. It isn't that she's fighting for democracy. That's the bunk. She's fighting for self-preservation, just as we will if it comes to us."

—Joseph Kennedy, in remarks made to reporters, November 1940

A Life-Changing Decision

With all of the negativity surrounding his father's misstep, Jack desired to prevent further embarrassment to his family. However, even more than avoiding negative publicity, Jack remained steadfast in his search for a meaningful future. The opportunity to serve in the military was a tempting proposition. While his friends viewed his predicament as humorous due to his medical condition, Jack took his draft notice seriously. In the end, his desire to serve won out.

But Jack needed more than desire. In 1941, Jack failed to pass the physical exam for both the army and the navy, yet he remained determined. He spent the summer getting into physical shape, but he knew he would once again need his father's help. Through the aid of Captain Alan Kirk, an old American embassy friend and the head of the Office of Naval Intelligence (ONI), Joe Kennedy had managed to secure a spot for Joe Jr. in the navy as an officer just months before. Jack hoped for the same arrangement.

The elder Joe contacted Kirk and arranged for Jack to undergo a physical examination. Jack passed his physical exam without the slightest indication noted in the record about his past and present physical problems. According to the report, Jack had endured normal childhood illness and currently abided by a diet without fried food.

THEY SAID...

"Jack had no intention of becoming a career playboy trading on his father's fame and influence. And Joe and Rose believed it inconceivable for any of their children to settle for a sybaritic life. But a life without ambition, without some larger purpose than one's own needs and satisfaction, was never part of the Kennedy ethos. . . . It was impermissible to make frivolity a way of life."

—Robert Dallek, *An Unfinished Life*

Joe's ties secured Jack a spot in the navy on September 25, 1941. In October, he entered as an ensign, and as such, he was commissioned just below lieutenant junior grade. He was assigned to the ONI's Foreign Intelligence Branch in Washington. He was responsible for summarizing reports received from overseas for bulletins.

THEY SAID...

"Yesterday, December 7, 1941—a date which will live in infamy—the United States of America was suddenly and deliberately attacked by naval and air forces of the Empire of Japan. . . . No matter how long it may take us to overcome this premeditated invasion, the American people in their righteous might will win through to absolute victory."

—President Franklin Roosevelt, December 8, 1941

Jack's work was rather simple until the Japanese attacked Pearl Harbor on December 7. Within days, the United States was at war in Europe as well as Asia, and Jack's job suddenly took on new importance. Gone were the days when he worked only six eight-hour days per week. Jack soon found that his new schedule of seven nine-hour days was demanding.

A Controversial Romance

Despite the hardships of his new intense schedule, Jack made sure to find time for romance. One perk of living in Washington was the presence of his sister Kathleen, who was working as a reporter for the *Times-Herald*.

Falling for a Blond Beauty

Kathleen included Jack in her lively social life. It was among Kathleen's friends that Jack met Inga Arvad, a reporter for the *Times-Herald* who wrote the popular feature, "Did You Happen to See?" The feature, which focused on government officials and notable newcomers, had earned Inga a solid reputation as a journalist. The Columbia-educated journalist was also a blond, blue-eyed beauty.

Jack could not help but fall for Inga. There was one problem with the relationship. Inga was married, although she was separated from her second husband. To disguise their relationship, the two double-dated with Kathleen and her boyfriend, John White. Not surprisingly, Joe soon learned of the affair. Although Joe would never condone Jack's marriage to Inga, the playboy in him was pleased that his son was involved with such a beauty. Besides, Joe felt that since it would remain a casual relationship, he could hardly object.

FACT

Joe Kennedy kept close tabs on his children. According to John White, Kathleen Kennedy's boyfriend, it was customary for the Kennedy children to inform Joe Kennedy each time they dated someone new. Once the person was investigated, they were informed about whether the relationship could continue.

A Suspicious Relationship

Perhaps Joe Kennedy was unaware of Inga's past, or maybe he was unconcerned, but the FBI found her residence in the United States suspicious. When Inga began attending the Columbia School of Journalism in 1941, her presence caught the attention of a classmate, who notified the FBI of the presence of a potential German spy. After securing a job at the *Times-Herald*, Inga again caught the interest of the Bureau when a reporter came across a photograph of her and Hitler at the 1936 Olympics in Berlin. When Inga was approached about the suspicious picture, her response displayed at best minimal concern. Inga shrugged off the photo as a fluke of fate. She had been a Berlin correspondent for a Danish newspaper, and she met Hitler while covering the wedding of Hermann Goering. Hitler was struck by her beauty and invited her to watch the Olympics with him.

For Inga, the incident was neither a big deal nor was it something to be concerned about. Nevertheless, from thereafter, her relationship with Jack concerned the FBI. Jack's job in intelligence made it even more important to put the couple under intense scrutiny. Rather than wait to find out whether the allegations about Inga were true, the FBI decided to leak the information to the press. Although Inga thought it was old news, to the press it was new and made a perfect story. Upon receiving the information, Walter Winchell of the *New York Mirror* ran a column about the former ambassador's son and the blond German spy.

Ending the Romance

The January 12, 1942 story was sensational, and it nearly ended Jack's career in the navy. When the assistant director of the ONI heard the story, he was more than ready to dismiss Jack. Although it is unclear, it is possible that Joe Kennedy intervened on behalf of his son. Jack was spared dismissal, but only two days after the news story he received orders to transfer to Charleston, South Carolina.

Up to this point, Jack had successfully kept most of his relationships casual. When he and Inga began dating, they both understood it was nothing more than a short-term romance. While it might have started out that way, when Jack moved to Charleston, the casualness they initially enjoyed in Washington soon became a thing of the past.

THEY SAID...

"You belong so wholeheartedly to the Kennedy-clan, and I don't want you ever to get into an argument with your father on account of me. . . . If I were but 18 summers, I would fight like a tigress for her young, in order to get you and keep you. Today I am wiser."

—Inga Arvad, as quoted in *An Unfinished Life*

Jack missed Inga. They continued to correspond through letters and on the telephone, and on several occasions Inga came to Charleston to visit. Along with Inga came FBI surveillance. The wiretaps revealed that the carefree nature of their relationship had taken on an air of seriousness. In one conversation, Inga expressed her concern about being pregnant and voiced her frustration at Jack's irresponsibility. Jack, however, was unmoved by Igna's outburst. Inga also broached the subject of marriage, but Jack had even less to say. With the increased seriousness of their relationship, Joe Kennedy now urged his son to end the affair. He had approved of a fling with her, but marriage to a divorced non-Catholic was out of the question. In March 1942, Jack and Inga agreed to end their relationship.

Sea Duty for JFK

Without Inga's company, Jack tried his best to settle into his lonely life in Charleston. Throughout March and April, the back pain that he had felt in 1940 emerged with an increased severity. Jack was unable to keep his condition a secret any longer. In April, the pain forced him to seek treatment with a navy doctor. With the diagnosis of recurrent dislocation of the right sacroiliac joint, Jack was declared unfit for duty. He sought other opinions from the navy hospital in Chelsea, Massachusetts, and at the Lahey Clinic. Surgery was discussed, but navy doctors advised against it. By June, although Jack suffered from the same ailments, his diagnosis was changed to a strain of the lower back; he was advised to treat his condition with massages and exercise. It is unclear why the diagnosis was changed so readily, but it has been theorized that Joe may have been behind it. With only a strained back, Jack was fit to return to duty.

On July 23, 1942, Jack received orders that he was bound for combat. Less than a week later, he entered training at midshipmen's school at a branch of Northwestern University in Chicago. For ten weeks he lived in Abbott Hall, a multistory former office building. Although he learned the mechanics of navigation, seamanship, and handling guns, he found the course less than adequate preparation.

Becoming a PT Commander

Training, however, did result in one important decision. Jack decided he wanted to command a patrol-torpedo (PT) boat, a motorized torpedo boat. Jack heard about the opportunity from naval officers John Harlee and John Bulkeley, who were traveling the country in search of recruits. Harlee and Bulkeley had captured their adventures in a best-selling book, which had increased enthusiasm for PT boats. When they stopped by the Northwestern campus, Jack, just like other young men from wealthy families who were familiar with motorboats, became excited at the prospect of manning this boat.

FACT
The British had invented the PT boats, and the United States adopted them during World War II. They were wooden boats eighty feet long with gas engines that could reach speeds of up to forty-one knots. PTs operated mainly at night with the main purpose of interfering with Japanese supply lines in the South Pacific.

Once again, Jack called on his father for assistance. The PT commander position was fiercely competitive, and Jack feared that with his health problems the likelihood of obtaining a spot on his own was doubtful. As it turned out, Jack was one of the lucky ones. A combination of Joe Kennedy's influence and Jack's successful interview with Bulkeley secured his spot. Jack began training in Melville, Rhode Island.

In the meantime, Jack's back problems continued. His condition became so intense that he consulted with his father about whether he should have surgery before he began training. After he learned that his recuperation would take at least six months, Jack resolved to endure the pain. When he began training in Melville, he found it both exciting and painful. He enjoyed the freedom of being his own boss by day, but at night his back problem worsened. Riding in the PT boat all day as the waves pounded it was almost more than his back could take. His only solace at night was the plywood board he slept on.

Going to Combat

Jack wanted desperately to go to combat. He graduated from training on December 2 but soon learned that Bulkeley had other plans for him. Instead of combat, Jack would remain in Melville to train a squadron. Jack was dismayed by the assignment and suspected that his father, who was not the least bit excited about him going to battle, had a hand in arranging it.

Jack called on his grandfather Honey Fitz, who was glad to help him secure an assignment in active combat. He arranged for Jack to meet with Massachusetts senator David Walsh. Jack made a lasting impression on the senator, who readily dispatched a letter to the Navy Department requesting Jack's reassignment to the war zone.

Before going off to battle, Jack was sent to Jacksonville, Florida, in January 1943. When he arrived, he was informed of his assignment to the Panama Canal. It was not exactly what he had in mind, so he did the only thing he could do to change his fate. He contacted Senator Walsh, who quickly sorted out the situation. Jack was given exactly what he wished for—a chance to face combat in the South Pacific.

A Heroic Act

Jack arrived at the Solomon Islands in late March 1943. The Pacific chain of islands east of Papua New Guinea saw some of the most intense fighting of the war, and casualties had been substantial

"HE SAID...

for both the Allies and the Japanese. The Allies had won the two crucial battles of Midway and Guadalcanal by the time Jack arrived, but that didn't mean all the action was over—not by a long shot.

When Jack arrived in the Solomons, he was in for a surprise. If he had really thought he would spend his days relaxing on the beach, as he had wrote to Inga, he soon learned his vision was far from the truth. His first taste of combat came the moment he arrived, when the captain of his boat was killed during a Japanese air raid. Jack was shocked by the incident.

The glamour of combat soon vanished as Jack came to comprehend that for those on the front lines, death was a great possibility. Soon after arriving in the Solomon Islands, Jack visited the grave of George Mead, a friend who had been killed in the Battle of Guadalcanal. "The whole thing was about the saddest experience I've ever had and enough to make you cry," he wrote in a letter.

Commanding a Crew

Jack was assigned to command *PT 109*. According to his letters to his family, the glamour of commandeering a PT was less than thrilling. The night patrols out on the rough water were uneventful. However, Jack's monotonous life on the island soon came to an end. The Allies were preparing to invade the Japanese-controlled New Georgia Islands, and the PTs were given the responsibility of preventing the Japanese from reinforcing their stronghold with new supplies.

Lt. John F. Kennedy aboard the *PT 109* in the South Pacific, 1943.

Photo credit: John F. Kennedy Presidential Library and Museum, Boston

On August 1 at 6:30 P.M., Jack's *PT 109* was among the fifteen boats sent to the Blackett Strait to engage a Japanese convoy, which included four destroyers. The PTs were equipped with a total of sixty torpedoes, enough to inflict severe damage on the Japanese ships. That was not to be the case.

The Japanese convoy passed the PT boats without sustaining any damage. The PTs that had used up all their torpedoes went back to port, while *PT 109* and at least two other boats stayed in the strait to wait for the convoy's return journey.

Escaping Death

As Jack and his crew sat with only one of the three engines running, a large dark figure materialized out of the pitch black. It was the Japanese destroyer *Amagiri*, and it was coming directly at *PT 109*. Jack was at the helm and tried desperately to maneuver the boat to safety, but the *Amagiri* rammed the PT, splitting it in half. Less than a minute had passed since the crew had first spotted the destroyer.

Jack was thrown against the cockpit, landing on his back. Several members of the crew were flung into the water and three sustained serious injuries, but Jack and ten members of his crew survived the collision. Two men were missing and presumed dead. After Jack assessed the situation and determined the PT boat was not in danger of exploding, his first plan was to get the crew back onboard. Jack and two crew members swam out to the stranded men, and Jack towed the seriously burned Pat "Pappy" McMahon back to the boat.

At first, Jack believed their rescue was imminent. However, the collision had been seen from the base, and officials assumed that all the men were dead. What was left of the PT boat was taking on water, so Jack made the decision that the crew should swim to Plum Pudding Island, a small mass of land three miles away. Once again, he clenched the ties of McMahon's life jacket in his teeth and towed the injured man.

FACT

Robert Ballard, the explorer who found the remains of the *Titanic*, also located the wreckage of *PT 109* in 2002. Working with the National Geographic Society, Ballard's teams used sonar to locate the boat. They took photos but did not remove or disturb the wreckage, which Ballard said he considered a grave.

The island was positioned off the normal route for PT boat patrols, so Jack had little hope of rescue. With just thirty minutes' rest, Jack swam back out to Ferguson Passage, where he waited for a passing PT. The PTs, however, were patrolling west of Jack's location that night. He set out again for Plum Pudding Island, stopping on a different island long enough to nap and regain some energy. He returned to Plum Pudding at noon the next day, much to the surprise of his crew, who believed he was dead. A crewmember repeated Jack's journey that night, August 3, but with no more success.

Jack determined the best course of action was for the entire crew to leave the 70-yard-wide Plum Pudding for nearby Olasana Island, which might provide more food and water—and a better chance at being rescued. Unfortunately, Olasana Island was a disappointment, and Jack and another crewmember, Barney Ross, set out the next day for Cross Island. There the two men stumbled upon candy, fresh drinking water, and a one-man canoe. They also startled two native islanders, who fled despite Jack's attempts to make contact with them.

Jack took the canoe on another unsuccessful attempt to flag down PT boats in Ferguson Passage that night, and the next day he left Ross on Cross Island to take the supplies they'd found back to the crew on Olasana. Upon his arrival, Jack found that the men had been discovered by the two islanders he and Ross had seen. The men turned out to be Allied scouts, and Jack asked them to deliver a message carved on a coconut: "Native knows pos'it he can pilot 11 alive need small boat Kennedy." One day later, four islanders returned with a letter from a New Zealand lieutenant, which instructed Jack to come to him while he arranged for their pickup. All of the remaining members of the *PT 109* crew were rescued on the morning of August 8, six days after their ordeal began.

A Hero's Welcome

It did not take long for the press to seize upon the story about the former ambassador's son whose heroic actions saved his crew. Jack's family—except for Joe Kennedy, who learned of his disappearance through military sources—was unaware of Jack's predicament while he was missing. However, news of his rescue quickly alerted them to the situation. The *New York Times* ran a story entitled "Kennedy's son is hero in Pacific as destroyer splits his PT boat." The *Boston Globe* ran its story under the headline, "Kennedy's son saves 10 in Pacific; Kennedy's son is hero in the Pacific."

By most accounts, Jack was a hero. He had led his men out of the water to safety and had ensured their rescue. Joe Kennedy was proud of his son and basked in the letters of praise he received from friends. There were critics who stated the obvious. Had the boat remained out of the path of the destroyer, the crew wouldn't have needed to be rescued in the first place. Jack remained modest about his hero status, and he explained in a letter to Inga that the real heroes were the men who died in combat, not those who returned. Years later, Jack was asked to expound upon his heroism. He replied simply, "It was involuntary. They sank my boat."

THEY SAID...

"Jack's heroism spoke to larger national mores: he was a unifying example of American egalitarianism. His presence in the war zone and behavior told the country that it was not only ordinary G.I.s . . . risking their lives . . . but also the privileged son of a wealthy, influential father who had voluntarily placed himself in harm's way and did the country proud."

—Robert Dallek, *An Unfinished Life*

Medical Ailments Disrupt Military Service

Joe Kennedy was ready for Jack to return home, and he set out to make it happen. He feared the next time his son disappeared during the war, it would be for good. Jack, on the other hand, was ready for combat. He remained embarrassed by the destruction of his PT, but more than anything, he wanted to avenge the deaths of his two crew members. After receiving nearly two weeks to recuperate, Jack was back on the water. This time, he commanded a new kind of boat that had guns instead of torpedoes. On board the *PT 59*, Jack had his opportunity to seek revenge and engage in military combat.

After six intense weeks of battle, Jack was drained. He wished to go home. His back and stomach pain increased. Rather than bring his ailments to the attention of navy doctors, Jack tried to get sent back to the United States by feigning less severe problems. He discovered that minor aches and pains were far from enough to get him off the island. On November 23, the severity of his medical problem became clear to navy doctors when severe stomach pain landed him in a navy hospital. The results from the x-rays showed that he suffered from an ulcer crater, which indicated the development of a duodenal ulcer.

Jack's condition warranted his return to the United States. He arrived in January 1944 and checked into the Mayo Clinic, where doctors quickly determined that he should have surgery on his back. Jack, though, was determined to get some rest and visit with his friends and family before reporting for duty as an instructor. Jack put off the doctor's recommendation only to find that his back pain persisted. He received a second opinion at the New England Baptist Hospital in Boston, which also recommended surgery.

Jack was determined not to let his back pain interfere with his navy duties. He reported for duty at the PT base in Miami, Florida. Unlike the grueling nature of his experience in the South Pacific, Jack enjoyed a light workload that often required little more than relaxing with his feet up on his desk. Meanwhile, his back pain continued to worsen. On June 11, it was discovered that he had a ruptured disk. The only avenue he had left was to go ahead with the back surgery.

FACT

A duodenal ulcer, also referred to as a peptic ulcer, is a result of erosion in the lining of the stomach. The cause is usually the product of a bacterial infection in the stomach. The other conditions that raise the likelihood of an ulcer include the usage of ibuprofen or aspirin, smoking cigarettes, and alcohol abuse.

On June 23, 1944, at New England Baptist, Jack underwent surgery. Doctors discovered that, rather than a ruptured disk, Jack's condition was a result of unusually soft cartilage. Shortly thereafter, Jack's doctors revealed that he suffered from fibrocartilage with degeneration. Jack's recovery from surgery was slow, and his doctors advised him it would take six months for him to return to navy duty. At first, he experienced muscle spasms when he attempted to walk, and his stomach began acting up again. As the end of his six-month leave neared, doctors determined he was permanently unfit for duty and recommended that he retire from the navy.

❝ HE SAID...

"In regard to the fascinating subject of my operation, I . . . will confine myself to saying that I think the doc should have read just one more book before picking up the saw."

When Jack entered the navy, his prior medical problems with his stomach and back had remained out of his file. Jack's appearance before the retirement board sparked questions about his prior condition before entering the navy. His restricted diet now became an indication to Dr. B.H. Adams, the medical bureau's chief, that Jack had a preexisting condition. However, other board members believed that Jack's statement that his current abdominal condition began while in the Solomon Island was a correct assessment and quickly overruled Adams's curiosity. After interviewing Jack on December 27, it was determined that he was permanently incapacitated. Jack's retirement became official on March 1, 1945.

Chapter 5

FINDING HIS WAY

Jack returned to the United States after his health forced him to leave the South Pacific, but Joe Jr. remained in Europe, where he was serving as a navy pilot. On August 12, 1944, Joe Jr.'s plane exploded, killing him. Joe's death was devastating for the entire Kennedy family, and Jack found that he had to rediscover his purpose. Up to that point in his life, the competition with his brother had been a guiding force, and without an opponent Jack was unsure about his future. However, his father determined that he would take his brother's place and embark upon a political career. With his family's support, Jack ran for Congress.

A Devastating Time: Joe Jr.'s Death

Joseph Kennedy Jr. fought as a navy pilot during World War II, patrolling the English Channel. He was scheduled to return home after completing thirty missions, but he decided to stay on. He volunteered for a dangerous mission that required him to fly a navy PB4Y Liberator bomber containing 22,000 pounds of explosives to a German launch site on the Belgian coast. Joe and a copilot were supposed to eject themselves from the plane after activating the remote control guidance and arming system. But their plane exploded before they even reached the English Channel.

The Kennedy family was devastated. Joe Sr.'s worst fear had come true. Worse, the navy couldn't provide much in the way of an explanation. Officials believed the accident had occurred as a result of an electrical detonation, which was triggered by a stray radio frequency signal.

FACT

In 2001, a new theory emerged regarding the cause of Joe's death. According to a British Royal Electrical and Mechanical Engineer veteran, the accident was a result of the failure of American officials to notify England with instructions to turn off their radars. As a result, the radar signals interfered with the radio controls of Joe's plane and caused the explosion.

For Joe Sr., however, the death of his eldest son was compounded by the death of his dream of Joe becoming America's first Irish Catholic president. Joe Jr. had encapsulated all that was expected of the Kennedys, and now that his eldest son was dead he questioned how his goal would come true. Jack soon realized that the fate of the family rested on his shoulders.

A Stint as a Journalist

Jack was gravely affected by his older brother's death. Out of his grief came a grouping of essays that paid tribute to his brother. Jack titled the book *As We Remember Joe*. The book was a reminder to Jack that Joe Jr. had had a promising future ahead of him. Jack wasn't sure what his own future held now. In the past, Joe's accomplishments drove Jack, and their brotherly competition had defined Jack's identity. In addition, he realized that Joe's death would cement their father's image of Joe Jr. as the superior son. Jack felt he was shadowboxing a shadow he could never beat.

FACT
During this time, Jack expressed his disillusionment about war and peace to a navy friend. Jack thought war had not yet become bad enough for people to develop an opposition to it. War, wrote Jack, would exist until the conscientious objector received the same status as the war hero.

As Jack came to grips with the death of his brother, he delved into a writing career. Money was not a concern at this point in his life; his father had set up trust funds for all of his children. In fact, Joe Sr.'s fortune was more than enough to sustain the family for generations. When Joe arranged a position for Jack as a correspondent for the Hearst *Chicago Herald-American* for the April 25, 1945, United Nations Conference in San Francisco, Jack jumped at the opportunity. This time, it was more than his father's influence that led to the break. Jack was a war hero and a successful author in his own right.

From April 28 to May 28, Jack wrote seventeen 300-word stories. He wrote about his observations of the tension between the Americans and the Soviets and about the ineffectiveness of the United Nations.

The Hearst Company was pleased with Jack's work. They decided to send him to London to cover the British elections in June. Jack quickly summed up the preelection situation. On June 23, in his first dispatch, he predicted Prime Minister Churchill would lose the election due to the people's desire for change. Jack anticipated the Conservatives were bound to lose their reigning hold on the government; however, he still admired Churchill, so on the day of the election he modified his first prediction. This time he predicted the election would be close, but that the Conservatives would win. He was incorrect; the Labour party won by a landslide.

Considering a Political Career

Jack was content with his work for the *Chicago Herald-American*. His father, on the other hand, began to develop big plans for his son. In the meantime, Jack traveled to Potsdam and Germany with U.S. Navy secretary James Forrestal, who hoped Jack would join the Navy Department staff. Jack made the most of his opportunity with Forrestal. He viewed the war-damaged cities in Germany and had the opportunity to meet with Dwight Eisenhower, who had served as Supreme Commander of the Allied Forces during World War II.

THEY SAID...

"Joe used to talk about being President some day, and a lot of smart people thought he would make it. He was altogether different from Jack—more dynamic, sociable and easy going. Jack in those days . . . was rather shy, withdrawn and quiet. His mother and I couldn't picture him as a politician."

—Joseph Kennedy Sr., as quoted in *The Fitzgeralds and the Kennedys: An American Saga*

Transferring Ambitions

After Jack returned to the United States, he came to the realization that he had benefited from his father's focus on Joe. While Joe's future was intensely scrutinized, Jack had been free to do as he wished. Joe Jr. had made it clear that he intended to become president, and Joe Sr. felt certain that his social and easygoing eldest son was perfect for the job. With his death, however, Joe took a second look at Jack. Never before had he envisioned a future for

Jack in politics; he had been sure Jack was destined for a career in writing or teaching. Now he slowly began to see Jack in a new light. Joe was proud of Jack's work for Hearst and with the prospect of his son securing a position in the Navy Department.

For the first time, Joe realized that his quiet, less personable son might be able to take Joe Jr.'s place. In spite of his own ambition, Jack was quickly swept up into his

HE SAID...

"One politician was enough in the family, and my brother Joe was obviously going to be that politician. I hadn't considered myself a political type, and he filled all the requirements for political success. . . . I didn't even start to think about a political profession for more than a year later."

father's plan. While his father was developing confidence that Jack would make a superb politician, accounts by those familiar with his personality were surprised that he would consider a career in politics. According to politician and family friend Mark Dalton, Jack was shy and not very affable. Another friend noted that when speaking in public, he seemed ill at ease and embarrassed.

Deciding on Politics

Although Jack's personality appeared less than suitable for a political career, his interest in and knowledge of politics were a perfect match. His good friend Lem Billings felt that Jack was well suited for a political career and believed Jack would have entered politics even if Joe Jr. had lived. In the end, Jack's decision to enter politics was influenced more by pressure from his father than anything else. As Jack later recalled, it was an understatement to say that his father "wanted" him to enter politics; instead, he "demanded" it. Although Jack was initially reluctant, he would eventually become an impassioned and willing participant.

Seeking a Congressional Seat

For the most part, Joe Kennedy was insecure about Jack's political wherewithal. To balance the scale in Jack's favor, he set out to prepare the way for his son. He determined that Massachusetts was the best place for Jack to seek office, but it was still unclear what he would run for. Joe's first step was his acceptance of Massachusetts Governor Maurice Tobin's offer for a chairmanship over a planning commission assigned to survey the state's economy. In this position, Joe was able to rub elbows with powerful people in government and the media.

Developing Speaking Skills

In the meantime, Jack set out on his own campaign to gain visibility. Among the various public speaking opportunities was an American Legion meeting on September 10, 1945. The speech, which focused on postwar Europe, was a huge success. It was played on the radio and he received numerous requests for copies.

However, not all of Jack's speeches were as successful. Often, according to observers, he was wooden and serious, and he stuck closely to his prepared text. By all accounts, his public speaking ability was poor, especially when it came to extemporaneous speeches on local issues. Jack found that he was most comfortable when speaking about international politics.

> ## THEY SAID...
> "Many a night when he'd come over to see Daddy after a speech, he'd be feeling rather down admitting that the speech hadn't really gone very well. . . . I can still see the two of them sitting together, analyzing the entire speech and talking about the pace of delivery to see where it had worked and where it had gone wrong."
>
> —Eunice Kennedy, as quoted in *The Fitzgeralds and the Kennedys: An American Saga*

As was often the case after a bad speech, Jack lamented his failure. Even so, his father was often by his side afterward to build him up. It was common for Jack and Joe to ruminate over the speech. They discussed all aspects of the address, from the delivery to the content. According to Jack, his father had confidence in his abilities and provided encouragement. Joe Kennedy used a combination of subtle criticism and positive reinforcement to direct Jack.

Jack's quiet style differed from the usual Boston politician. His grandfather John Fitzgerald was a prime example of the style of old Boston politics. His boisterousness and Irish charm had taken him a long way. Jack lacked this same type of charm and was noted for his aloofness. Often, instead of staying around to meet voters, Jack was one of the first to leave after a speech. His shyness was sometimes interpreted as snobbishness.

Candidacy Attacked

Initially, Joe desperately wanted Jack to run for lieutenant governor, but Joe listened to advice from his cousin Joe Kane. Kane pointed out that Jack's youth—he was only twenty-eight years old—would expose him to questions about his lack of experience in a run for lieutenant governor. On the other hand, a run for Congress in a democratic district would protect him from these types of questions. Kane also observed that as a Congressman Jack would be asked to give speeches and would remain in the public eye. In the position of lieutenant governor, Jack would essentially remain ignored.

In late April 1946, Jack and his father finally decided that he should seek election to the open congressional seat in the Eleventh District. In fact, Joe had already paved the way. James Michael Curley held the seat in the Eleventh District, but he had recently been convicted of fraud for his participation in mailing wartime government contracts. Joe Kennedy was able to convince him not to seek reelection by helping Curley pay off his debt with a generous donation of $40,000. Curley decided to run for mayor of Boston, and Joe Kennedy's contributions to that campaign set him back another $100,000.

Jack was happy with the choice. He still preferred national and international politics over local issues. Regardless of his preference, he soon learned that winning the election was going to take a lot of work. Joe Kane was wrong about one thing: as a congressional candidate, Jack still became the target of attack. He was running against nine other candidates in a district that included Boston, Charlestown, Somerville, and Cambridge, all of which were working-class areas. Jack had two things going against him. He was the son of a millionaire, and he had never lived in the Eleventh District except in his early childhood and college years.

FACT

James Michael Curley dominated Boston politics during his four stints as mayor. He ran for mayor ten times and won four of those elections. He never held two consecutive terms. Curley's first term lasted from 1914 to 1918 and his last from 1946 to 1950. Unlike John Fitzgerald and other Irish mayors who attempted to breach the cultural divide, Curley openly pitted the Irish and non-Irish against one another.

His opponents could hardly forgive Jack for these failings. Even before he announced his candidacy, Dan O'Brien, an influential Cambridge undertaker, warned Jack he would lose, precisely because he was a carpetbagger. Other opponents pointed out that Jack was a rich kid who lived at a hotel, lacked political experience, and knew nothing about the needs of his potential constituents.

Even the newspaper the *East Boston Leader* had an opinion about Jack. In one column the newspaper declared: "Congress seat for sale—No experience necessary—Applicant must live in New York or Florida—Only millionaires need apply." According to one columnist, Jack was a "rich kid," had established a "phony" residence, and had done nothing that entitled him to win any votes. Jack was dismissed as an opportunist who sought to win based on his family connections.

QUESTION

What is the origin and meaning of *carpetbagger*?

A carpetbagger was a Northerner who went to the South after the Civil War to make money during Reconstruction. The term originated from the carpetbags they used to carry their possessions. It has come to refer to an outsider who becomes involved in politics for personal benefit.

Support from the Catholic Church

There was some truth to the press statements. Joe Kennedy had maintained close ties to Boston's Catholic church, especially Bishop Richard Cushing. Just as Joe knew how to work the political system, he was no stranger to getting exactly what he wanted from the church. Cushing hoped to be a cardinal one day, and he hoped Joe's contacts with the papacy might help him secure the position.

When Jack decided to run for Congress, Joe Kennedy knew he had Cushing's support. Over the years, financial donations to the church had paved the way for this type of sponsorship. In August 1946, the Catholic newspaper featured a photo of Jack and his mother handing a $600,000 check to Cushing for the construction of a hospital in Joe Jr.'s memory. Over the course of the congressional campaign, the Kennedys made more donations to various Catholic foundations that included St. Mary's Hospital, Christ Child Society, and the League of Catholic Women. Cushing invariably shared his favorable opinion about Jack when asked.

Canvassing for Votes

Jack's competitive spirit emerged and carried him through the campaign. He put aside his discomfort about speaking in public and interacting with strangers and set out to win the primary.

Recruiting Volunteers

With Joe Kennedy working behind the scenes, the first campaign strategy was to secure the support of volunteers in each district. Jack first needed to gain the support of prominent locals. In uncharacteristic fashion, he personally approached potential recruits. Dave Powers, a Charlestown resident, recalled what happened one night when he answered a knock at the door. Before him stood a tall, thin young man who stuck out his hand and introduced himself as John Kennedy, a congressional candidate. Kennedy proceeded to explain that he hoped that Powers would help him in his campaign. When Powers explained that he was acquainted with one of his opponents, Kennedy, undeterred, continued to seek his assistance. Within a few days, Kennedy won Powers's support.

Winning Over Voters

Jack also used his charm to win voters. While he had previously struggled to connect with his audience, his run for the House energized him. When Powers accompanied Jack to a meeting of the Gold Star Mothers, he witnessed Jack's budding charisma. After Jack had finished speaking to the women about the war and its toll on the men and their families, he concluded by telling them that he knew how they felt since his mother was a Gold Star Mother. Jack's ability to relate to his audience formed a bond with them. After the speech, he stayed around and greeted the women instead of reverting to his old habit of leaving immediately.

FACT
Gold Star Mothers was originally created as a local group in Washington, D.C., during World War I. Its purpose was to comfort mothers who lost sons during military service and to provide support to injured veterans. In 1928, it became a national organization. The name originated from the gold star that families hung in their window to honor a deceased veteran.

Jack decided that just as his grandfather Honey Fitz had done, he too needed to place himself at the center of the hustle and bustle of Boston's community. Jack no longer displayed discomfort as he made rounds to restaurants, pool halls, saloons, and barbershops. He talked to everyone he could, including stevedores, mail carriers, and factory workers. Despite his back pain, his early morning schedule began at 7:00 A.M. He waited in front of factories and docks, where he made sure to shake hands and talk to as many workers as possible.

After greeting the early-morning workers, Jack went door to door, where he introduced himself to housewives. Fire stations and police stations were next on his agenda, and in the afternoon he returned to the docks to greet the workers he had missed in the morning. Jack's enthusiasm made Joe Kennedy proud. One day in East Boston, Joe looked on as his son spoke to voters. Until that day Joe had never thought Jack was capable of such behavior and had believed that the odds were stacked against him.

THEY SAID...

"The challenge of politics, as young Kennedy saw it, was to build that sense of participation in peacetime, to make people recognize they were as dependent upon each other in civilian life as they were in war, to get people mobilized into a common effort."

—Doris Kearns Goodwin, *The Fitzgeralds and the Kennedys: An American Saga*

By the time of Jack's campaign, World War II had been over for about a year. War veterans were considered heroes, and Jack was not an exception. Joe commissioned some polls, and based on the results he decided to focus the campaign on Jack's service in the war. Jack was still uncomfortable with being a hero, so instead he placed the focus on the courage of injured crewmate Pappy McMahon, who had sustained severe burns. Jack also used his friendship with McMahon as an opportunity to highlight the comradeship soldiers developed during war. This was an effective strategy. Dave Powers noted that Jack's veteran status was appealing to many men; it showed he had guts and men tended to respond to that.

HE SAID...

"The temper of the times imposes an obligation upon every thinking citizen to work diligently in peace as we served tirelessly in war. . . . Everyone who is able should do his utmost in these days of world and national progress to contribute his talents in keeping with his abilities and resources."

Although the war was an uncomfortable topic for Jack, his campaign advertising reflected his status as a war hero. In one advertisement, a war veteran was depicted with his son as he pointed at a picture of Jack and remarked, "There's our man, son." Joe also arranged for the reproduction of *New York Times* reporter John Hersey's article about *PT 109,* which had been published shortly after the incident. A press release was included with the 100,000 reprints of the story. In it, crewmate William Johnston attested to Jack's bravery and leadership during the crew's struggle to survive.

Appealing to the Working Class

Once he had gotten the voters' attention, Jack held it with his position on issues. He addressed jobs, Social Security, and the housing shortage for veterans. In the beginning of his campaign it had appeared that his status as a rich kid could hurt him, but he put the issue to rest by simply admitting that it was true. He confronted the money issue head on during a meeting where all of his opponents spoke about growing up poor. He acknowledged that he was the only one not brought up in a "hard way." He would later address the issue in a feature article about him in *Look* magazine. When asked why with all of his wealth he was interested in running for Congress, he responded that because he was the son of a rich man, he was motivated by his obligation to help those less fortunate than he was.

A Family Affair

While Joe worked in the background, Eunice and Pat Kennedy helped by directly appealing to voters with house parties. Jack's sisters were instrumental in securing volunteers to host the parties. They provided enough food, plates, and utensils for each hostess to entertain twenty-five to seventy-five guests in her home. The sisters visited each party, and Jack came shortly thereafter. Typically he gave a short speech and answered questions. Jack felt the most comfortable at these parties because of their quaint, informal setting.

During the last few weeks of the campaign, Rose Kennedy arrived to give her support. Having grown up the daughter of a politician, Rose was a veteran at campaigning. Her elegance and charm were great assets. At the parties, the women were treated to Rose's firsthand accounts of the king and queen of England.

Joe Kennedy's influence was all but invisible to outside observers, but Jack and others who were closely associated with the campaign felt his presence intensely. The staff quickly realized that Joe Kennedy, not Jack, was in charge of his bid for Congress.

While Joe purposely stayed out of the limelight, he did make one public appearance. During the last days of the campaign, in spite of the critics who called the event tasteless, the Kennedy women began planning a formal reception. Thousands of engraved invitations went out, inviting women to meet the Kennedy family at a hotel in Cambridge. On June 15, 1,500 women in formal evening gowns arrived at the reception, where they were greeted by all of the Kennedys—except for Kathleen, who was in England—in a receiving line.

Winning the Election

On June 18, Jack enjoyed his first political victory. It had taken some $250,000–$300,000 to win, but he emerged victorious in the Democratic primary with 40.5 percent of the votes. He won 22,183 votes; his closet rival received 11,341 votes. In November 1946, Jack won the House seat over his Republican opponent by 69,093 to 26,007 votes.

Chapter 6

CONGRESSMAN JOHN F. KENNEDY

When Jack Kennedy entered Congress in January 1947, he was in for an unwelcome surprise. The Republican Party had successfully secured a majority in the House and the Senate. Kennedy, however, took his minority position and freshman status in stride. He knew that just like the other new Democratic House members, his influence was minimal, yet he was content. Public service, as he liked to call it, seemed right. In fact, Congressman Kennedy could envision a political future beyond the House.

Representing His Constituents

As a new member of the House, Kennedy's first priority was setting up his office. He was assigned a two-room office suite at the Old House Office Building. He hired Ted Reardon as his head of staff and veteran Mary Davis as secretary; Bostonian Billy Sutton, who Kennedy referred to as "the court jester," served as his aide. Sutton was the perfect match for Kennedy. While Kennedy cringed at the idea of meeting with constituents, Sutton embraced the opportunity. Moreover, he was sociable and extremely capable when it came to getting to know the inner workings on Capitol Hill. It was a comfortable fit, and Jack welcomed Sutton's desire to take the lead in matters that required social skill.

Taking a Stand for His Ideals

Once Jack's office was up and running, his focus turned to working for the voters. At the forefront were domestic issues. This, of course, was far from where his interest lay. His passion still rested in international affairs. Nevertheless, the prospect of an unbalanced budget caught his attention. It frustrated the fiscally conservative Kennedy, who, unlike his colleagues, was uncomfortable with the idea of an unbalanced budget. When the Republicans set out to pass a bill giving tax cuts, Kennedy objected. He believed it was unfair to lower-income citizens, and he became increasingly concerned that the bill would lead to economic insecurity. Nevertheless, Kennedy held only one vote in Congress, and his freshman status held little sway over other members.

HE SAID...

"I wasn't equipped for the job. I didn't plan to get into it, and when I started out as a Congressman, there were lots of things I didn't know, a lot of mistakes I made, maybe some votes that should have been different."

Kennedy also took seriously Congress's failure to protect the poor. He became concerned when the House failed to act on important social welfare issues, such as a provision to address the housing shortage. Kennedy responded to the fact that World War II veterans bore the brunt of the shortage. He was further outraged when the House refused to act on the housing shortage until an investigation was conducted. It was a stalling tactic, but Kennedy lacked the political clout to press for immediate action. Kennedy's passion for the issue, however, won favor with his constituents, especially veterans who viewed his stance as courageous.

FACT

Among the other freshman congressmen who took their oath of office for the first time on January 3, 1947, was a young Republican delegate from California by the name of Richard M. Nixon.

For the most part, Kennedy found himself on the side of the aisle that responded to the needs of his working-class district. Nevertheless, the labor unions did pose a unique problem. Kennedy believed the unions were just like big business in their ultimate concern for their own interests without regard for the larger needs of the country. In addition, communist leanings in the unions had put him in an awkward position. So Kennedy made the decision to vote on union issues according to what was best for the country and for those he represented. On the issue of communist infiltration, he supported the perjury charges brought against the leaders of the United Electrical Workers and the United Auto Workers. On the other hand, Kennedy stood firm for the interests of his districts when he voted against a bill that would have weakened the right to strike.

There was also the issue of providing federal aid to schools. As a representative of a largely Catholic constituency, Kennedy felt the pressure to support the position of government aid for parochial schools. For the most part, he agreed with the position of many Americans. Forty-one percent of those polled favored federal aid to parochial schools. Jack too felt that if money was given to public schools, religious schools were also entitled. However, Kennedy's desire for a balanced budget won out. Overall he felt that unless absolutely necessary, the states should rein in and bear the costs of their own educational systems.

THEY SAID...

"He wished to be known as a public servant whose judgment rested not on narrow ideological or personal prejudices, and little mattered to him more during his term in the House than making clear that he operated primarily in the service of national rather than more limited group interest."

—Robert Dallek, *An Unfinished Life*

A Risky Decision

There was one issue to which Jack hesitated to lend his support, despite the attention it received in his district. In June 1947, Boston Mayor James Michael Curley was finally sentenced for his fraud conviction. Curley, while serving his fourth term as mayor, was sent to federal prison in Danbury, Connecticut, to serve his six- to eighteen-month sentence.

Curley, however, did not go quietly. After ranting and raving about his diabetes and high blood pressure, he had the Boston public on his side. It was a true testament to his political viability and connection with Boston's citizens that he could garner their support in spite of his criminal conviction. With the backing of the community, Curley sought clemency. Amazingly, 172,000 Boston supporters, one quarter of the city's population, signed a petition requesting freedom for their mayor. To help the cause, John McCormack, the Democratic whip, passed a petition through the House in support of Curley's pardon.

It was not long before Kennedy was presented with the petition. Although Curley was the mayor in one of his districts, Kennedy was torn on the issue. All of the other Massachusetts representatives had quickly fallen into line with McCormack's request, but Kennedy was a holdout. One reason was an old family wound. Curley had forced Kennedy's grandfather out of the 1914 mayoral race, and Honey Fitz was still fuming over the loss. Honey Fitz was certain that he had been destined to become Boston's powerful and adored leader, but

Curley had snatched the title from him. On the other hand, Kennedy was concerned that if he chose not to sign the petition for a man in poor health, he was bound to lose voters in any subsequent election. Moreover, a refusal to support McCormack was politically unwise.

After weighing all of the consequences, Kennedy made the difficult decision not to sign the petition. He had done a follow-up on Curley's health with the surgeon general and learned that Curley's condition could be treated in prison. So although it was a risky political decision, Kennedy decided it was better to remain distant from a controversial figure like Curley even at the cost of his political viability.

At the time of his decision, Kennedy was certain that Curley was politically dead. However, Curley was pardoned and released from prison five months later. He immediately returned to his post as mayor with all the vigor of a healthy man. The media zeroed in on the story and criticized those in the Boston community who had signed the petition to keep him out of prison because of his supposed poor health. Jack's potentially perilous decision had ended well.

Joe Kennedy's Influence

Although it was Jack who was in office, Joe Kennedy was still lurking behind the scenes. Not only was he responsible for paying for his son's staff, which exceeded the allowance he received as a representative, he was also busy preparing the way for the political future. Joe was instrumental in Jack's inclusion among the top ten outstanding young men by the U.S. Junior Chamber of Commerce in 1947, alongside Pulitzer Prize-winning author Arthur Schlesinger Jr.

Joe continued his quest to further Jack's political career by promoting favorable news stories about him in the *New York Times*, the *Boston Globe*, and on the radio. The stories, however, were useless without Jack moving up the ranks in the House, so Joe used his connections to secure Jack an appointment to the House Education and Labor Committee and the Veteran's Affairs Committee.

At all times, though, Joe realized the importance of keeping a low profile. Joe's stance as an isolationist and the perceived image of him as an anti-Semite threatened to hurt Jack rather than help him.

FACT

Arthur Schlesinger won a Pulitzer Prize in 1945 for his historical work *The Age of Jackson*. He was later known for his 1966 Pulitzer Prize–winning account of the Kennedy presidency, *A Thousand Days*. He also wrote *Robert Kennedy and His Times*, which won the National Book Award, and other books on American history, the presidency, and his own life.

Although Joe influenced his son in many ways, they parted company when it came to international politics. In early 1947, when Joe publicly exposed his isolationist view that America should remain uninvolved in preventing the spread of communism throughout Europe, Jack's independence on international politics became evident. Jack supported U.S. involvement in helping Greece and Turkey prevent a communist takeover. The congressman viewed this as essential in establishing security and peace. If anything, he viewed his father's opinion on the matter as one that placed personal interest above national interest.

A Bachelor Lifestyle

Overall, Jack found that being a House member left him with lots of time to have a bustling social life. He lived in a townhouse on Thirty-first Street in Georgetown with Billy Sutton and his twenty-six-year-old sister Eunice, who worked as an executive secretary on the Juvenile Delinquency Committee of the Justice Department. According to Sutton, with the number of people coming in and out of the home, it was like a Hollywood hotel.

Kennedy's charm, likeability, wit, and youthful good looks remained his most endearing qualities. It was a good thing, since his casual style of dress of khaki pants, sneakers, and wrinkled shirts were unlikely to win over any new friends among his congressional colleagues. It was only on the special occasions in session in the House that he sported an expensive suit.

Kennedy's informal style of dress reflected the nonchalance with which he engaged in romantic relationships. His close friends recalled his one-night stands with numerous women. Quite a few were airline stewardess and secretaries, but he also had relations with actresses, models, and a tennis player. Kennedy was a charming man, and women found him irresistible.

THEY SAID...

"I once asked him why he was doing it—why he was acting like his father, why he was avoiding real relationships. . . . He took a while trying to formulate an answer. Finally he shrugged and said, 'I don't know really. I guess I just can't help it.' He had this sad expression on his face. He looked like a little boy about to cry."

—Priscilla Johnson, as quoted in *An Unfinished Life*

Kennedy's cavalier attitude toward sex and relationships has been widely discussed. Biographers have formulated various theories for Kennedy's attitude. Peter Collier and David Horowitz speculated it was a result of narcissism, and Doris Kearns Goodwin explained that Kennedy had great difficulty with intimacy. It has even been asserted that the precariousness of Kennedy's health was the cause. His friend Priscilla Johnson gave a simple explanation—it was the excitement of the chase. Whatever the reason, at the age of thirty, Jack's behavior clearly reflected that he was not ready to settle down.

Visiting Ireland

On August 31, 1947, while Congress was in recess for the summer, Jack traveled to Ireland to visit his sister Kathleen. His trip was a combination of business and pleasure. He was part of a congressional commission charged with exploring labor and educational conditions in Western Europe and the Soviet Union. Jack decided to visit Kathleen prior to proceeding on his fact-finding mission.

When he arrived in Ireland, he found his recently widowed sister in good spirits. Her late husband, William Cavendish Hartington, had been the heir of the Duke of Devonshire. He was from one of the wealthiest and most powerful families in England. He was also a Protestant, which did not sit well with Rose Kennedy. When they wed in May 1944, Joe Jr. escorted Kathleen down the aisle at her wedding. After spending only a month together, Billy went off to war and was killed in Belgium in September 1944, one month after Joe Jr. died.

Upon the urgings of her in-laws, Kathleen decided to stay in England. They treated her kindly and allowed her usage of the family property. Jack arrived in Ireland and went to the Devonshire's Lismore Castle in County Wexford. There he met Kathleen's other invited guests, Parliament member Tony Rosslyn, British High Commissioner in Australia Charles Johnson, prominent politician Anthony Eden, and Pamela Churchill, who was Winston Churchill's former daughter-in-law. Jack enjoyed the relaxing time at the castle and got along especially well with Eden, who would become prime minister in 1955. But it was Pamela Churchill that Jack chose to accompany him on a journey to find out more about his Kennedy roots in County Wexford.

One day while the rest of the group was enjoying a game of golf, Churchill and Jack set out in Kathleen's large imported American station wagon. Five hours later, they arrived in New Ross, where they quickly discovered that Jack's relatives lived on the edge of town in a small white house. When they arrived, they were greeted by a woman and her many children. Once her husband came in from the field to greet the strangers, they sat down and discussed their shared family heritage. It was unclear at the time, but Jack later came to believe that they were third cousins. After enjoying a cup of tea with butter and eggs, Jack gave the excited children a ride through the village in the station wagon.

An Astonishing Medical Diagnosis

Immensely content after seeing his sister and the countryside of their ancestors, Jack left for London. His health, which had continuously troubled him, worsened. He collapsed as a result of acute nausea and low blood pressure. He recuperated at the London Clinic, where his doctors made a startling diagnosis: Addison's disease, a hormonal disorder.

QUESTION
What are the causes of Addison's disease?
Addison's disease is caused by the failure of the body to produce a sufficient level of cortisol or aldosterone. Cortisol is a hormone that regulates the body's response to stress. Aldosterone is responsible for maintaining blood pressure and balancing the body's water and salt intake.

Jack's general condition was consistent with the symptoms of the disease, which included nausea, vomiting, weight loss, and muscle weakness. The disease impaired the body's resistance to fight off infection, and before the 1930s the fatality rate was high. With the introduction of a new drug treatment, the chances of survival increased. However, a doctor told Pamela Churchill, "That young American friend of yours, he hasn't got a year to live."

Jack, unaware of the doctor's prediction, returned from London in September aboard the *Queen Mary*. It was a difficult trip since the symptoms of Addison's disease still plagued him. When he reached the states, a priest gave him last rites while he was still on board the ship. Boston newspapers quickly got the news of Jack's condition, but they only noted it was the result of malaria.

The Death of Kathleen Kennedy

Jack managed to recover quickly. During his visit with Kathleen in Ireland, she had confessed to an affair with Lord Peter Fitzwilliam, a war hero, wealthy Protestant Englishman, and married man. Jack was supportive, but when Kathleen informed their parents that Peter planned to get a divorce and marry her, Rose Kennedy threatened to disown her.

Joe was also displeased with the relationship, but he gave in to his daughter's pleading and agreed to meet with Kathleen and Peter in Paris on May 15, 1948. On May 13, Peter and Kathleen set off in a private plane for a short getaway to Cannes. After stopping for fuel in Le Bourget, they lunched for a few hours with Peter's friends. They returned to the airport and resumed their trip, despite warnings of dangerous weather conditions along their flight path. The plane ran into a thunderstorm as it reached the Rhone Valley. The pilot and copilot were unable to control the plane, and it crashed into a mountainside.

The news reached Jack in Washington as he was enjoying a relaxing evening at home. He was devastated. He had developed a close relationship with Kathleen, and he was shocked and heartbroken. According to Lem Billings, he was plagued by depression and insomnia after Kathleen's death.

THEY SAID...

"For Jack, losing Joe and Kathleen was losing a part of his past, his common experiences, his identity. . . . The only thing that made sense, he decided, was to live for the moment, treating each day as if it were his last, demanding of life constant intensity, adventure and pleasure."

—Lem Billings, as quoted in *The Fitzgeralds and the Kennedys: An American Saga*

For Jack, Kathleen's death was a reminder of his own mortality. He predicted that he would not live past forty-five and developed a constant obsession with death. On one occasion, he asked Ted Reardon how he preferred to die. When Reardon responded that old age was his preference, Jack countered that war was the best way to go.

Political Aspirations Beyond the House

As Jack lived for the moment, he finally came into a sense of just what his future could be. He had never considered the House a stopping point, and of course, neither did his father. As he continued to grieve for Kathleen, he considered the possibilities. He was certain now that he wanted a career in public service, and he settled on a run for state office; the governorship especially appealed to him. To that end, Jack set out on a campaign across Massachusetts to test the waters. His weekend treks during the spring and early summer months of 1948 took him to 39 cities and 312 towns, where he spoke at Elk clubs, PTAs, and Communion breakfasts. It was a grueling schedule that took a toll on his back. By the end of a long day, it was common for Jack to spend hours soaking in a warm bath.

The Kennedy family in Hyannis Port around 1948.

Photo Credit: John F. Kennedy Presidential Library and Museum, Boston

Jack's effort failed to produce the kind of results he hoped for. In June 1948, a Roper poll showed that Governor Robert F. Bradford held a lead of 43.3 percent to Jack's 39.8 percent. In addition, Jack was tied with Democratic opponent Maurice Tobin. However, what put an end to his bid was a survey of the poll's voters, which showed that overwhelmingly they had little knowledge about his position on policies. Jack settled in for two more years in the House and won an unopposed election.

Jack carried on despite his disappointment. His health had improved since he started receiving cortisone to treat his medical condition. It came just in time, since Jack would need the strength to deal with another loss. His grandfather Honey Fitz died in October 1950, and Jack was heartened by the compassionate response of Boston's residents. More than three thousand people came to pay their respects at John Fitzgerald's funeral service. Jack came away with a new outlook. According to Billings, he realized that there was a tremendous impact a politician could have on ordinary citizens. It solidified Jack's determination to run for statewide office in the future.

Developing a Stance on Communism

In the meantime, Jack turned his attention to his work in Congress and the issue of communism. Eastern European countries were turning to communism, and U.S. foreign policy was becoming more aggressively opposed to the spread of communism. In 1947, President Truman announced the United States would take an active part in containing Soviet expansion. The United States committed $400 million to assist Greece and Turkey in their fight against communism. In addition, it allocated funds for the redevelopment of democratic countries in Europe.

Jack became an impassioned crusader against the communist threat. It went along with his interest in foreign policy, and he figured if there was any issue that could help his career, it was communism. In 1947, he supported giving financial aid to European countries to combat the spread of communism. However, when China's democratic government fell in 1949, Jack stood apart from his Democratic colleagues. He blamed his fellow Democratic Party member President Truman for the failure to involve America in world affairs.

Jack made further comments about the president and his policies regarding communism at a November 1950 Harvard Graduate School of Public Administration seminar. According to Jack, President Truman's failure lay partly in his veto of the McCarran Act. The act required the registration of communists and allowed for their internment should the nation experience a national emergency. Jack had voted for the act and believed the president's failure to support it was a reflection of his lack of attention to the communist issue and his faulty leadership in foreign relations.

HE SAID...

"If one thing was bored into me as a result of my experience in the Middle as well as the Far East, it is that Communism cannot be met effectively by merely the force of arms. The central core of our Middle Eastern policy is . . . the export of ideas, of techniques, and the rebirth of our traditional sympathy for and understanding of the desires of men to be free."

Jack initially supported Republican senator and family friend Joseph McCarthy of Wisconsin. McCarthy's accusations of communist infiltration in the government got Jack's attention and increased his concern. When McCarthy began his effort to root out communists within the government, Jack was a loyal supporter. Just like McCarthy, he too was ready to limit civil liberties for what he believed was the greater goal of protecting the country. Yet he did not support some of McCarthy's more aggressive tactics, and he soon distanced himself from McCarthy's zealous anticommunist hunt. By 1951, Jack had his sights set on advancing beyond the House of Representatives, and he argued that communism in the government no longer existed. This paved the way for his next move.

Chapter 7

SENATOR JOHN F. KENNEDY

Kennedy's political career was finally on track. He decided that his next move would entail running for the Senate, and he anticipated that once in office he would receive the boost he needed to run for president. Once he did win, he was certainly correct about receiving national attention. However, as he would learn, the press reported the good and the bad. Marrying Jacqueline Bouvier garnered the right kind of press, but it was the negative stories about his nonvote on the condemnation of Joe McCarthy that he wished would disappear.

An Enthusiastic Campaign

In the spring of 1951, Kennedy contemplated whether to run for governor of Massachusetts or for the Senate. He preferred the Senate since his real interest was in international affairs. He quickly ruled out a run for governor, but one barrier stood in the way of his final decision to run for a Senate seat. Massachusetts Governor Paul Dever was also considering the Senate. If Dever entered the race, Jack would have to take him on in the primary, which would very likely weaken his position against incumbent Henry Cabot Lodge II. Jack waited patiently for Dever's decision, which came in April 1952, when the governor announced that he had decided to run for reelection instead.

FACT

Henry Cabot Lodge was a Harvard graduate, a journalist, and a war veteran. At the age of thirty-four, he won his first bid for the Senate when he defeated James Michael Curley. He served three terms in the Senate, successfully defeating two other popular Irish opponents.

Preparing for a Senate Campaign

Although this cleared the way for Jack, he was at a substantial disadvantage. Lodge had name recognition with 68 percent of Massachusetts voters compared to Jack's 35 percent. Joe Kennedy became involved in the campaign full-time. He moved to an apartment on Beacon Street a few blocks from Jack's residence.

Once again, Joe Kennedy took control of the campaign, bringing in a team of trusted aides. Jack tried to take a stand on running his own campaign. He brought in Mark Dalton, an attorney who had managed his previous House campaign as an unpaid volunteer. This time, Jack intended to hire him as the full-time paid manager, but Joe Kennedy found the selection intolerable. When Jack prepared a press statement regarding the appointment, Joe stood in the way of its release. Dalton continued to work in the campaign while awaiting the formal announcement, but his presence came to an abrupt end when Joe Kennedy could no longer stand him. One afternoon, he yelled at Dalton, telling him that he had accomplished nothing but spending Kennedy money. Dalton left and never returned.

Bringing in Bobby Kennedy

It became clear that Joe Kennedy had gone too far. With a leaderless staff, the prospect of Jack's victory appeared grim. Jack's advisor, Kenneth O'Donnell, called Robert Kennedy and asked him to step in as campaign manager. Bobby was hesitant at first, especially considering that he was working in New York for the Justice Department. He enjoyed his job and had never anticipated running a political campaign. O'Donnell knew that Bobby was a good balance for Jack and convinced him that his leadership was necessary.

Bobby brought some essential qualities to the campaign staff. He provided the operation with organization and focus. His unwavering and blunt way of dealing with people quickly earned him a reputation as Jack's hard-nosed brother, and it left little question that Bobby would never allow his brother's candidacy to fall victim to incompetence or interference. Governor Dever soon learned this lesson.

One of Bobby's first actions was to get rid of the governor. Dever was seeking to join forces with Jack in a dual campaign, but Jack wanted no such shared effort. Bobby, in his usual abrupt manner, told Dever that a joint effort was out of the question. Dever, like the many others who crossed paths with Bobby, noted the pain of feeling Bobby Kennedy's wrath.

Outspending Henry Cabot Lodge

Overall, Kennedy and Lodge had few differences when it came to policy. Both wanted a balanced budget, supported labor unions, and believed in less government when it came to domestic issues. What it came down to was money. Campaign finance laws restricted a candidate to spending no more than $20,000 in personal funds and limited individual contributions to $1,000; there was no limit on the usage of state party funds. To maneuver around these restrictions,

Joe set up several political committees so that a donor could make multiple donations to all of the committees. Joe's wealthy friends eagerly contributed to the "Improvement of the Massachusetts Fish Industry," "Improvement of the Shoe Industry," "Improvement of the Textile Industry," and the "Citizens for Kennedy and a More Prosperous Massachusetts."

The money was spent on billboards and media ads and financed local campaign offices throughout the state, as well as Kennedy teas. Once again, women received invitations to attend elegant teas where they heard Rose Kennedy tell interesting stories about her family, her travels, and her life. Thousands of women also had the unique opportunity to meet all of the Kennedys as they passed through a receiving line. The teas were so popular and well attended that even Henry Lodge later raved that it was a brilliant vote-getting maneuver.

THEY SAID...

"John Kennedy spoke directly to the past, arguing that his grandfather had lost to mine by only fifty thousand votes in a close election which could have gone the other way if women had been allowed to vote. But now they could vote, he concluded, and this election could well turn on their decision. What a great pitch!"

—Henry Cabot Lodge II, as quoted in *The Fitzgeralds and the Kennedys: An American Saga*

Perhaps the biggest expense came when Joe Kennedy made a $500,000 loan to *Boston Post* owner John J. Fox. Fox, a millionaire oil and gas speculator, had been left with little cash after purchasing the paper the year before. So when Joe approached Fox with a request that he endorse Jack rather than Lodge as he had planned, he readily complied. The paper's large circulation was expected to generate 40,000 votes. Several years later, Fox disclosed that the loan was made during the campaign. Joe viewed it as nothing more than a business transaction.

Winning the Ethnic Vote

When election day arrived, Jack was positioned to win. While it would come as a shock to Lodge, Jack won by 70,737 votes. A contributing factor was his ability to capture the ethnic vote. Jack initially had a hard time winning Jewish voters. His father's lingering reputation as an anti-Semite influenced the response he often received from Jewish voters. For example, during the campaign when he spoke at the Boston Club dinner meeting to 300 Jewish people, he was met with a less than enthusiastic response. Jack was perceptive of the crowd's mood and confronted the doubt head on. He bluntly stated that he was running for Senate and not his father. It was this approach that opened the door in the Jewish community. From thereafter, he spoke at other Jewish organizations and met with prominent Jewish leaders.

In addition to winning over the Jewish voters, Jack received the support of the Albanians, Canadians, Greeks, Finns, Poles, Portuguese, and Scandinavians. Overall, voter turnout increased in the ethnic districts. While Lodge in the previous 1946 election had secured a significant number of votes in ethnic areas, his support significantly decreased.

Setting Up an Office

In 1953, Jack began his term in the Senate as one of the forty-seven Democratic members. The Republicans comprised the majority with forty-nine members, so Jack's prospect of moving any desired agenda forward was hopeless. First, if he wanted to get anything done it was necessary to set up his office. He kept on Ted Reardon as his administrative assistant in Washington and Frank Morrissey remained in charge of his Boston office. For his Washington office, he hired two new staff members: Evelyn Lincoln as his personal secretary and Theodore C. Sorensen as his legislative assistant.

The twenty-four-year-old Sorensen proved to be a capable assistant. He had worked as an attorney at the Federal Security Agency and for Congress on railroad retirement legislation. Sorensen grew up in an activist non-Catholic family, so he had developed strong political views. His father had been an attorney general and a Senator, and his mother, a Russian Jew, was a women's suffrage proponent. Sorensen, who was a member of the Americans for Democratic Action, had great aspirations when it came to civil rights and pacifism.

FACT

The Americans for Democratic Action is a liberal lobbying organization that was formed in 1947. The founders of the ADA included Eleanor Roosevelt, Hubert Humphrey, theologian Reinhold Niebuhr, and historian Arthur Schlesinger Jr. It is still in existence today, and promotes democratic action and encourages members to lobby their representatives in Congress.

When Jack Kennedy met with Sorensen during two five-minute interviews, he was almost immediately convinced that Sorensen was right for the job. He was young, ambitious, and passionate about what he believed. Sorensen, on the other hand, was not so easily convinced that he wanted Jack as an employer. While he was impressed with Jack's easygoing and modest nature, he was unsure about his stance on important political issues. Sorensen questioned Jack about his opinion on the Catholic Church and Joe McCarthy. In the end, Sorensen was pleased when Jack told him that his opinions were not yet fully developed since he had been under his father's influence thus far. As time would tell, Sorensen and Jack would develop a highly compatible working relationship that would continue during Jack's term as president.

Marrying Jacqueline Bouvier

After Jack settled into the Senate, he had time to renew a romance with Jacqueline Bouvier that had begun when they first met in 1951 at a dinner party. They immediately clicked. They had a lot in common, considering that Jackie, just like Jack, had an air of loneliness about her. She was the daughter of John Bouvier III and Janet Lee Bouvier. Her father's philandering had led to the eventual divorce of her parents when she was nine years old. As a child she was moved back and forth between her father's home and her mother's new home with her wealthy, socially prominent stepfather, Hugh Auchincloss. Although she enjoyed a privileged life, she found her greatest comfort and happiness in solo activities such as riding horses, reading, and listening to music.

THEY SAID...

"He saw her as a kindred spirit. I think he understood that the two of them were alike. They had both taken circumstances that weren't the best in the world when they were younger and learned to make themselves up as they went along. . . . Even the names—Jack and Jackie: two halves of a single whole."

—Lem Billings, as quoted in *An Unfinished Life*

Introducing Jackie to the Family

Now that Jack was in the Senate, he needed a wife. Jackie's charming nature was appealing. Jackie was more intelligent than Jack's other girlfriends, and her social status was evident by her natural charm and class. Joe Kennedy admired her independence. That was a hard feat, especially when she visited the richly competitive environment of the Kennedys' Hyannis Port estate. This became evident during the family's touch football games where winning meant everything. On one occasion, Jackie succumbed to the pressure to play, but quickly became content to just watch after she broke her ankle. It was during this time, as Joe and Jackie watched the others play, that Joe grew to appreciate her outspoken and independent nature.

THEY SAID...

"Anticipate that each Kennedy will ask you what you think of another Kennedy's (a) dress, (b) hairdo, (c) backhand, (d) latest public achievement. Be sure to answer 'terrific.' This should get you through dinner. Now for the football field. It's 'touch,' but it's murder. . . . Run madly on every play, and make a lot of noise. Don't appear to be having too much fun, though. They'll accuse you of not taking the game seriously enough. Don't criticize the other team either. It's bound to be full of Kennedys too, and the Kennedys don't like that sort of thing."

—David Hackett, *Rules for Visiting the Kennedys*

While Joe and Jack found Jackie's charm and independence appealing, Rose Kennedy cared little for such traits. For Rose, Jackie's independence was at odds with her own carefully structured life. Rose still required mandatory participation in meals, so when Jackie failed to appear for several meals while staying at the Kennedy home, Rose was irritated. She quickly informed Jackie that such behavior was intolerable.

Tying the Knot

Regardless of Rose's displeasure with Jackie, Jack decided that they were well matched. He asked her to marry him by telegram in the spring of 1953. They were married on September 12 at St. Mary's Roman Catholic Church in Newport. The wedding was attended by family, friends, and nearly 3,000 people who were intent on getting a glimpse of the event that would put an end to Jack Kennedy's bachelorhood. Jackie, well aware of the rumors regarding Jack's promiscuity, had hoped that Jack would become a dedicated and faithful husband. She soon found out that Jack was intent on continuing his philandering despite the feelings of his lonely wife, who often waited patiently for him to come home. According to Lem Billings, as time went on, Jack became indiscreet with his extramarital affairs. It was most embarrassing to Jackie when the couple went to parties together. It was not uncommon for Jack to leave Jackie all alone as he disappeared into another room with his latest sexual partner.

A Rocky Start for the Newlyweds

Jackie soon found that for the most part, she was destined to live a life without her husband. His duties in the Senate and his travels throughout Massachusetts kept him away from home. It was especially difficult for her on the weekends when she was alone. Jack remained unconcerned about his absences and looked to his parents' long-standing marriage as evidence that his could survive. Jackie, on the other hand, was miserable. She soon found comfort in decorating and shopping. This got Jack's attention when he realized that her spending was quickly decreasing his net worth. Jack tried to rein her in with instructions that she restrict her spending to either traveling or eating well.

Seeking National Attention

While Jackie was at home alone, Jack was still pressing forward in his political career. It was the presidency that he now aimed for. He decided that in order to place himself in the national spotlight, he had to take a position on issues from a national perspective rather than from the limited view of state interests.

Supporting a Contentious Proposal

To that end, the St. Lawrence Seaway river transit system provided him with the perfect opportunity. This proposed transportation system between Canada and the Great Lakes was a controversial issue for a Massachusetts politician to vote in favor of. For twenty years, the project had remained a point of contention in Congress. It threatened to put a damper on the economy of Boston, but at the same time, the Midwest was positioned to benefit. Jack decided he would do what no other Massachusetts senator or representative had done before. He would stand in favor of the measure.

In January 1954, he made a speech in support of the controversial bill. It was a dangerous position, but he was well prepared with a reasonable explanation for his stance. He spoke about the bigger picture. He pointed out that his decision was a combination of factors, among them the importance of America sponsoring the project jointly with Canada in order to ensure that it maintained control. In addition, he pointed out that there would be an indirect economic gain for the Boston community and that, on any account, the benefit to the nation should take precedence over any state considerations.

Although it was a risky position, Jack won some allies. Two Massachusetts congressional members voted with him in support of the waterway, and a Massachusetts newspaper was even persuaded by his arguments. However, Jack wanted more than votes in favor of the project, and when he appeared on the nationally televised NBC program *Meet the Press* in February 1954, he got exactly what he wanted. It was not support for his position that he wanted so much as the national attention he would receive.

An Accurate Prediction about Indochina

Kennedy's opinion about the situation in Indochina brought him more national attention. Indochina, a French colony, was comprised of Cambodia, Laos, and Vietnam. During World War II, France moved toward the federation of Indochina. Cambodia and Laos went along quietly, but the colonies of Annam, Tonkin, and Cochin China wanted to form the independent territory of Vietnam. By December 1946, the tensions between Vietnamese nationalists and the French erupted in the French Indochina War. The nationalists, some of whom were communists, also became a concern for the United States. In 1950, France requested U.S. aid. By 1954, America was financing well over 50 percent of the war.

FACT
In March 1946, France agreed to the establishment of the free territory of Vietnam within the French union and the Indochina federation. The dispute erupted when the parties differed on whether Cochin China was part of Vietnam. The French wanted it to form an independent state while Vietnam wanted it incorporated.

The Indochina war was the perfect opportunity for Jack to show his knowledge about international politics. He quickly got to work studying the issue. During the summer of 1953, he came up with a solution. He advocated that since the war was going badly and the French only provided limited autonomy to Cambodia, Vietnam, and Laos, the United States should make aid to the French contingent upon French promotion of freedom and independence. Jack reiterated his opinion about the French Indochina War on *Meet the Press* in February 1954. When asked whether he believed that the United States should strip control from France, he emphasized that since victory was elusive, the only solution was for the French to promote independence and to orchestrate winning the war by bringing in local leaders and more manpower.

HE SAID...

"No amount of American military assistance in Indochina can conquer an enemy which is everywhere and at the same time nowhere, 'an enemy of the people' which has sympathy and covert support of the people."

Jack's ideas brought him respect and support. Three months after his television appearance, France was defeated. At the Geneva Conference, it was decided to split Vietnam at the Seventeenth Parallel. On one side was North Vietnam, which was under the control of the communist government of Ho Chi Minh and on the other side was the French-controlled government in South Vietnam, which was lead by Bao Dai. Months later, the French regime was replaced with a government led by Ngo Dinh Diem, a regime approved by the United States, France, and Great Britain. As Kennedy had forecast, France lost. His accurate and timely prediction earned him a burgeoning reputation as a senator with a good sense regarding foreign affairs.

Undergoing a Life-Threatening Surgery

As Jack worked hard to get his name into the limelight, his medical condition became worse each day. He needed the use of crutches when he walked from his Senate office to the chambers. In the late spring of 1954, Jack's back pain became worse than at any other time. He returned to the Lahey Clinic in August where X-rays revealed that his fifth lumbar vertebra had buckled under pressure. The only remedy was a dangerous surgery that could leave him paralyzed if it was not successful. His Addison's disease was an additional complication; it left him more prone to infection.

Jack was determined to undergo the surgery despite the risks. He told his father that he would rather be dead than remain in pain and on crutches. Joe Kennedy and his doctors, though, were hesitant to proceed immediately. On October 10, 1954, Jack arrived at the New York Hospital for Special Surgery ready for his operation. Surgeons determined that they would try a special treatment first. On October 21, after the surgery had been postponed three times, Jack finally underwent a three-hour operation in which a metal plate was inserted in his spine.

Jack emerged from the surgery in stable condition, but within three days he developed a urinary tract infection. Antibiotics were ineffective, and Jack's condition deteriorated. He fell into a coma. When the doctors told Joe Kennedy that Jack was expected to die within hours, a distraught Joe called a priest to deliver last rites. Amazingly, just days later, Jack triumphed over his condition.

THEY SAID...

"Jack was determined to have the operation. He told his father that even if the risks were fifty-fifty, he would rather be dead than spend the rest of his life hobbling on crutches and paralyzed by pain."

—Rose Kennedy, as quoted in *The Fitzgeralds and the Kennedys: An American Saga*

By December, his recovery was so slow that his doctor recommended that he move into the family's Palm Beach home. Progress was still slow two months later. Jack was in pain and still unable to walk. It was determined that he had an infection and would need an operation to remove the plate. It was removed on February 15, 1955. Jack recovered within three months and returned to the Senate to a warm welcome by his colleagues. His surgery had failed to escape the watchful eye of reporters, but Jack caught a lucky break. It was reported that his condition was a result of the injuries he had suffered during his service in the war.

HE SAID...

"My brother was working for Joe. I was against it, I didn't want him to work for Joe, but he wanted to. And how the hell could I get up there and denounce Joe McCarthy when my own brother was working for him? So it wasn't so much a thing of political liability as it was a personal problem."

Failing to Condemn Senator McCarthy

When Jack returned in May, he could finally concentrate on the important matters in Congress. Jack's friend Senator McCarthy and his anticommunist crusade had begun to take on a negative view with his fellow senators and the public. For years, McCarthy had been a dedicated warrior in the effort to rid the country of communists. He brought in government officials, radicals, communist party members, and military officers.

Americans and Congress were becoming more and more opposed to McCarthy's anticommunists tactics. Senate majority leader Lyndon B. Johnson led the crusade against McCarthy. He allowed the military hearings conducted from April through June 1954 to be televised. In addition, he led the effort in securing the sixty-seven majority votes in favor of condemning McCarthy. Kennedy, in a decision he would come to regret, did not vote on the initiative.

Kennedy's reason for failing to condemn McCarthy had nothing to do with agreeing with the other senator's policies. In fact, in February 1954, Kennedy publicly proclaimed that McCarthy's actions were extreme and unnecessary. Months later, in July,

HE SAID...

"The courage of life is often a less dramatic spectacle than the courage of a final moment; but it is no less a magnificent mixture of triumph and tragedy. A man does what he must—in spite of personal consequences, in spite of obstacles and dangers and pressures—and that is the basis of all human morality."

Kennedy was prepared to vote in favor of censuring McCarthy. However, partly because his brother Bobby had been appointed to serve as counsel to McCarthy's investigative subcommittee in early 1953, he decided to take a middle path and abstain from voting. Unfortunately, he failed to consider the political ramifications of his nonvote.

Later, when Jack was asked about his nonvote, he gave several different reasons for his decision. First off, he stated that it was a hard decision considering that his brother Bobby was working on McCarthy's subcommittee. In another explanation, he stated that he was unable to identify with the people being questioned. Lastly, he explained that he was in the hospital undergoing back surgery and was unaware of the condemnation. In spite of Jack's reasons, he would come to realize that it was a hard decision to live with.

Writing *Profiles in Courage*

When Jack Kennedy was asked in 1954 about his experience as a senator, he responded that it was the "most corrupting job in the world." According to Jack, the constant concern over reelection often determined a senator's vote on an issue. Rather than making a decision on principle, senators were burdened with the fear of losing their seat and voted according to survival rather then conscience.

Jack most admired courage, but he failed to display it in the McCarthy issue. It was a hard failure to swallow, considering that he believed this type of moral courage could and did make a difference in the world. From Jack's beliefs about political courage emerged the idea to write a book about eight senators who made controversial decisions for the national welfare even though they were at odds with public opinion. The book was titled *Profiles in Courage*, and it relayed the actions of John Quincy Adams, Daniel Webster, Thomas Hart Benton, Sam Houston, Edmund G. Ross, Lucius Quintus Cincinnatus Lamar, George Norris, and Robert A. Taft.

When the book was published in 1956, it immediately became a bestseller. However, once again his father interfered. He launched a campaign for the consideration of Jack's book to the Pulitzer Prize board. The book had already aroused suspicion over Jack's sole authorship, and Joe's action only furthered the negative publicity. Columnist Drew Pearson alleged that the book was ghostwritten, and John Oakes of the *New York Times* believed that Jack was not the author. Nevertheless, columnist Arthur Krock spearheaded the campaign in favor of the book, and Jack Kennedy was awarded the prize in 1957.

Jack was angered by the allegations. It was true that he had had the assistance of Ted Sorensen, who helped research the book and drafted portions of it along with a professor at Georgetown University, but Jack was the final editor and had written much of it. There is evidence that Kennedy did in fact write at least some of the book. Tapes of him dictating the book to his secretary are housed in the John F. Kennedy Presidential Library and Museum.

Chapter 8

THE ROAD TO THE WHITE HOUSE

Kennedy's congressional experience brought the presidency within reach. In 1956 he was considered a prime Democratic vice presidential candidate, but he lost the nomination to Estes Kefauver in a bruising battle at the Democratic National Convention. It was the first time much of the country had heard of the young senator from Massachusetts. Thereafter the press took more notice of his record in the Senate, and by 1960 Kennedy was poised to represent his party as the presidential nominee.

An Unsuccessful Bid for the Vice Presidency

Former Illinois Governor Adlai Stevenson headed the Democratic ticket in the 1952 presidential election, and as the 1956 elections drew closer it appeared there was a strong possibility he would do so again. Kennedy was eager to be considered for the vice presidency, and Stevenson was open to considering him. In anticipation, Kennedy secured control of the Massachusetts Democratic delegation over Representative John McCormack, who had not forgotten about Kennedy's refusal to sign the petition to grant clemency to Mayor James Michael Curley back in 1947.

Positioning Himself for a Vice Presidential Bid

Kennedy sent out feelers to the Stevenson camp. Stevenson viewed Kennedy as one of the most promising of the younger generation of Democrats, but his staff worried that Kennedy's Catholicism might alienate voters. Without making any promises, Stevenson asked Kennedy to submit his name for the vice presidential nomination at the Democratic National Convention in Chicago.

Joe Kennedy was opposed to his son's bid for the vice presidency. He believed Eisenhower was certain to win reelection, and it was politically risky for Jack to run on a ticket that was sure to lose. Furthermore, Joe feared Democrats would blame the inevitable loss on Jack's Catholicism, and his hopes for a presidential run would be seriously hurt.

Despite his father's concern, on August 12, 1956, Jack arrived in Chicago for the Democratic national convention with only a slight glimmering hope of winning Stevenson over. The next night, Jack's narration in a film about the history of the party received widespread praise at the convention. His good looks and charm positioned him well, and the *New York Times* compared him to a "photogenic movie star." The hotel lobby filled with crowds of adoring people who hoped he would become the vice presidential nominee.

The first part of the convention went as planned. Kennedy introduced Stevenson to the assembled delegates, who duly nominated

Stevenson as their presidential candidate. What happened next was not entirely anticipated. Instead of selecting his own running mate, Stevenson decided to let the delegates choose one for him. Taken by surprise, the vice presidential hopefuls scrambled to round up support.

THEY SAID...

"[T]he personality of the Senator just came right out. It jumped at you on the screen. The narration was good, and the film was emotional. He was immediately a candidate. There was simply no doubt about that because he racked up the whole convention."

—Dore Schary, as quoted in *The Fitzgeralds and the Kennedys: An American Saga*

Kennedy and his team met to decide how to handle the situation. Kennedy himself wasn't convinced he should fight for the nomination, but when he heard the Georgia delegation was behind him, he exclaimed, "By God, if Georgia will vote for me, I must have a chance. I'll go for it."

His excitement, however, temporarily subsided when his father received the shocking news of his plan by phone. It was a rare occasion, especially in regard to politics, that Kennedy made such a big decision without his father's assent. But this time, Kennedy decided to move forward with or without his father's support.

Battling for the Nomination

Kennedy knew that a win was a long shot. Tennessee senator Estes Kefauver was popular among the delegates, and Minnesota senator Hubert Humphrey had a core of support. Nevertheless, a chance at the vice presidency would position Kennedy for the presidency in 1964. In spite of the odds, Kennedy supporters put out an all-night effort printing banners, placards, noisemakers, and leaflets. In addition, Jack and Bobby Kennedy spent many hours in and out of hotel rooms trying to gain the support of delegates.

> ## THEY SAID...
> "Texas proudly casts its vote for the fighting sailor who wears the scars of battle."
>
> —Senator Lyndon B. Johnson, announcing the
> Texas delegation's support for Kennedy

The late-night rally to move Kennedy into position appeared to have paid off when the first ballots were cast the next day. Kefauver received 483½ votes to Kennedy's 304. The second ballot looked even more promising; Kennedy was in the lead with 648 votes to Kefauver's 551½. Amazingly, Jack had needed only 38 more votes to win, but the third round ended Jack's bid. Kefauver was the first to receive a majority. He won 755½ votes to Jack's 589.

Although Kennedy lost, the television networks carried live coverage of the nomination process, and it caught the attention of the American public. Kennedy, with his endearing smile, was suddenly thrust into the public limelight. His gracious concession speech earned him respect, and he walked away from the convention as an upwardly mobile politician. Even Joe, who had disagreed with his run, was pleased with the result. According to Joe, the convention had propelled Jack into the perfect position. Arthur Schlesinger Jr. was also elated. In a letter to Jack he remarked: "Your general demeanor and effectiveness made you in a single week a national political figure."

Campaigning for Adlai Stevenson

Kennedy's popularity with the public was more than a fluke. When he set out across the country to campaign for Adlai Stevenson that summer, his charm, wit, and humor left audiences clamoring for more. He saw clearly that Stevenson was likely to lose the election by a landslide, but he realized that stumping for Stevenson was an effective way to boost his own recognition across the country. Kennedy traveled to twenty-four states and gave about 150 speeches before the November election, which went, as expected, to Eisenhower. For Kennedy, the intensity of campaigning for Stevenson was a learning experience that gave him a glimpse of what his own future campaign would entail.

QUESTION

How are delegate votes determined at a party's national convention?
Democrats award delegates according to the proportion of votes a candidate received at a state primary or caucus. Depending on the state, the Republicans award delegates by using the proportional method or by awarding all the state delegates to the candidate who received the most votes during the state primary or caucus. In 1960, the Democratic Party delegates voted according to directives from state party bosses and not the candidates their constituents urged them to support.

Advancing Presidential Ambitions

On November 25, 1956, Thanksgiving Day, Jack and Joe Kennedy finally sat down and discussed the prospect of Jack's running for president in 1960. The one great barrier, as Jack saw it, was his religion. Joe argued that times had changed and the country was no longer the Protestant's "private preserve." Furthermore, Joe felt strongly that the new generation, the offspring of immigrants, would gladly vote for a Catholic.

The Personal Side of Public Life

That was all that Jack needed to convince him. Although he was only thirty-nine years old, he dreamed that in spite of his youth and inexperience he could win the nomination over older and more seasoned contenders. His confidence rested partly in his awareness that the public liked him. If anything, his public appeal lay in his celebrity-like status. He was from a rich and prominent family, and Americans could not help but wonder about the life of this wealthy Kennedy.

Shortly after his bid for the vice presidency at the Democratic convention, he glimpsed just how powerfully a politician could affect the sentiments of ordinary people. While Jack was sailing off the coast of Elba with his brother Teddy and a friend, Jackie went into premature labor and gave birth to a stillborn daughter. The family was unable to reach Jack for three days, but he flew home immediately upon hearing the news. The details of the tragedy had already reached the newspapers, and the public responded to Jackie and Jack's loss with sympathy. They received numerous letters from ordinary people expressing their sorrow, each one a testament to just how much Jack Kennedy had become a beloved politician in the eyes of many Americans.

THEY SAID...

"After dinner, Jack and his father went into the little study off the living room to talk about the future. Their conservation started with Jack presenting all the arguments against his running in 1960, knowing that his father would break them down. I remember thinking it was like a minuet with each partner anticipating the steps of the other."

—Rose Kennedy, as quoted in *The Fitzgeralds and the Kennedys: An American Saga*

Committing to Algerian Independence

Kennedy returned to the Senate after the election. His strength still lay in his knowledge of foreign affairs, and he was anxious to show the American public just how much he knew. In January 1957, he was appointed to the Senate Foreign Relations Committee—no small feat.

In his bid for the appointment, he went up against former vice presidential nominee Kefauver. Kennedy had an advantage—the support of Senate majority leader Lyndon B. Johnson—but it did take a bit of convincing, especially since Kefauver had four years' seniority over Kennedy.

Kennedy drew attention to himself with his unconventional opinions on Algeria's struggle for independence from France. The war had started in 1954, and by 1957 hundreds of thousands of French soldiers had been deployed to extinguish the conflict and bring the unruly colony back into line. The Eisenhower administration staunchly backed the French, but Kennedy was troubled. He meticulously researched the conflict, talking to people involved in all aspects of the dispute, and drew his own conclusions.

On July 2, 1957, Kennedy took to the Senate floor and challenged the Eisenhower administration's position. Kennedy argued that America's ideals conflicted with its actions; it advocated freedom and democracy, yet it helped the European nations keep the colonies from gaining independence. These policies risked alienating the colonies. Kennedy asserted that the United States should chart a course against imperialism, and he advocated helping the French and Algerians reach a settlement for Algeria's independence.

Kennedy's remarks caused an uproar. Secretary of State John Foster Dulles insisted the United States should keep out of the conflict, President Eisenhower reiterated his commitment to staying the course, and the French defense ministry was beside itself. The press seized the story. Editorials from the *New York Times* to *Time* magazine lambasted Kennedy's speech.

Kennedy was worried about the harsh reaction, but his father's response was reassuring. "You lucky mush. You don't know it and neither does anyone else, but within a few months everyone is going to know just how right you were on Algeria," Joe Kennedy told him, and he was right. Politicians and press alike took a second look at Kennedy's remarks and decided the senator had a point. Kennedy published an article on the subject in the October issue of *Foreign Affairs* and chaired the Africa Subcommittee of the Foreign Relations Committee in the Senate.

HE SAID...

"I've learned that you don't get far in politics until you become a total politician. That means you've got to deal with the party leaders as well as the voters. From now on, I'm going to be a total politician."

Failure to Support Civil Rights

Once again, Kennedy had proven his strength lay in the foreign policy arena. While Kennedy spearheaded the call for freedom for Algeria, he was slower to embrace civil rights legislation in his own country. His political pragmatism led him to try to please those on both sides of the issue.

FACT

The Civil Rights Act of 1957 was intended to provide a way to enforce existing voting regulations that guaranteed all U.S. citizens the right to vote, regardless of race or ethnicity. It gave federal prosecutors the authority to bring charges against anyone who interfered with another person's right to vote.

Senate Majority Leader Lyndon B. Johnson led the way in securing the bill's passage, but political wrangling gutted it of any real power. Kennedy voted to keep a part of the bill that would have granted the attorney general expanded authority to go after civil rights violators. That provision did not make it into the final bill, but Kennedy's support earned him points with civil rights proponents. Much to their chagrin, however, Kennedy also voted for an amendment to the bill that would require a trial by jury in criminal cases; this provision was essentially useless since Southern white juries were sure to excuse violators.

Kennedy failed to anticipate just how much flack he would receive from civil rights activists and liberals. Roy Wilkins of the National Association for the Advancement of Colored People (NAACP) publicly and privately criticized Jack for his vote. Other widely publicized criticism focused on his lack of moral courage. According to a senate colleague, Jack should "show a little less profile and a little more courage." Although the criticism died down in time, the subject reemerged during his presidential campaign.

FACT

According to Roy Wilkins, Kennedy's vote reflected his interest in "rubbing political elbows" with southern segregationists. Privately, Wilkins told Kennedy that it was exactly that type of vote which gave a clear indication that with him as president, civil rights advancement would remain stagnant.

Taking a Stand Against Union Bosses

While Jack was in Congress, Bobby Kennedy served as chief counsel for the McClellan Committee, which was in charge of investigating labor unions' connections with organized crime. Jimmy Hoffa, the leader of the Teamsters union, was the committee's number one target. His connection with the Mafia and the mishandling of the union's pension fund caught the committee's attention.

Bobby was committed to justice for union members even if it hurt Jack's run for president in 1960. Not even the potential wrath of his father could dissuade Bobby from taking up the cause. Jack, although extremely hesitant at first, joined Bobby in his crusade against the union. In March 1958, Jack introduced a bill in the Senate that threatened to put a damper on improper union expenditures. The bill, however, failed. Nevertheless, his stance against union corruption cast him as an honest and caring crusader working toward the benefit of the people.

HE SAID...

"If we are to secure the friendship of the Arab, the African, and the Asian . . . we cannot hope to accomplish it solely by means of billion-dollar foreign aid programs. We cannot win their hearts by making them dependent upon our handouts. . . . No, the strength of our appeal to these key populations . . . lies in our traditional and deeply felt philosophy of freedom and independence for all peoples."—Kennedy's address to the Senate, July 2, 1957

Gaining Popularity

Although the bill's failure was a disappointing blow, Jack managed to create the positive image of a presidential hopeful who cared about ordinary citizens. It helped that the media found Kennedy's charm appealing. Both Jack and Bobby became the subject of numerous articles, such as the *Look* magazine feature called "The Rise of the Brothers Kennedy" and the *Saturday Evening Post* article entitled "The Amazing Kennedys," by Harold Martin. Martin, like various other journalists, anticipated that the Kennedys were the next great family to churn out politicians like the Lodges. They predicted that Jack would become the first Kennedy to serve as president. *Time* magazine ran a cover story in December 1957—three years before the presidential election—lauding him as a probable Democratic nominee.

THEY SAID...

"Jack is the greatest attraction in the country today. I'll tell you how to sell more copies of a book. Put his picture on the cover. . . . He can draw more people to a fundraising dinner than Cary Grant or Jimmy Stewart. Why is that? He has more universal appeal. That is why the Democratic Party is going to nominate him."

—Joe Kennedy, as quoted in *The Fitzgeralds and the Kennedys: An American Saga*

The journalists' predictions were a reflection of the popularity that Jack had secured with the public. When he ran for reelection for his Senate seat in 1958, not a single Republican opponent challenged him. He won 874,608 votes out of 1.32 million votes cast— 73.6 percent of the total vote. Joe Kennedy supplied $1.5 million of his money. It was well worth it considering that the senator received hundreds of weekly requests to speak. In 1957, he spoke in forty-seven states, giving a total of 144 speeches. It was clear that Jack was a rising political star, and it appeared that just as journalist Marquis

Childs predicted, he would defy the odds of a Democratic senator being selected as a presidential nominee.

Announcing Candidacy for President

Although many in the press were convinced that Kennedy was the next Democratic nominee, his youth, inexperience, and Catholic faith were a concern. Kennedy was only forty years old, and in November 1957 he had just become the father of his first child, Caroline Bouvier Kennedy. His youth, however, was less troubling to Democratic voters, who in 1959 placed him in a tie with Adlai Stevenson as their preferred presidential nominee. Nevertheless, he was disheartened that he placed fourth behind Lyndon B. Johnson, Adlai Stevenson, and Senator Stuart Symington in a poll of congressional Democrats.

Trying to Become a Liberal Democrat

Jack was not as popular among more liberal Democrats. His failure to vote for the condemnation of McCarthy and his weak stance on civil rights made him a troubling contender. Eleanor Roosevelt, who was no fan of Joe Kennedy, took up the charge against Jack. Her opinion of Jack had changed little since the 1956 Democratic convention, when she openly opposed his nomination as vice president. In a magazine article, she criticized Kennedy's failure to take a stance on the McCarthy issue. Furthermore, in her opinion his failure to display the type of courage he championed in his book demonstrated his lack of readiness for the presidency.

In addition, during one of her television appearances,

HE SAID...

"Several nights ago, I dreamed that the good Lord touched me on the shoulder and said, 'Don't worry, you'll be the Democratic presidential nominee in 1960. What's more, you'll be elected.' I told Stu Symington about my dream. 'Funny thing,' said Stu, 'I had the same dream myself.'"

she confidently stated that Jack's father was responsible for spending a massive amount of money throughout the country to promote his candidacy. Jack was deeply offended and asked for a retraction. Although she complied, the truth was that by July 1959, Joe Kennedy had already spent $1 million and had secured a private plane through a Kennedy company for Jack to use as he traveled throughout the country.

In 1958, Jack set out to win over liberals. In a March television interview, he identified himself as a Democratic liberal. In other interviews, he stated that he was independent from the Democratic Party and emphasized his record of supporting liberal causes. What he said, however, mattered little to most liberals, who believed otherwise. His voting record countered his assertions. Nevertheless, Kennedy insisted that he represented a new kind of liberalism. Jack needed the help of historian and liberal Democrat Arthur Schlesinger to define just what kind of liberal he was.

Ignoring the Religious Issue

The Catholic issue posed the greatest threat to Jack's campaign. Although anti-Catholic sentiments had lessened since Al Smith's unsuccessful run for the presidency in 1928, a May 1959 poll revealed that 24 percent of Americans refused to vote for a Catholic presidential candidate. The Church was still considered by many—especially progressive Democrats—as a closed-minded religious institution that threatened individual freedom.

THEY SAID...

"True, there was now a new generation, and religious tolerance had grown. But how much, how far, and how effectively was debatable. There were strong feelings, and in some cases strong convictions, among Catholic as well as Protestant and Jewish leaders that Jack's Catholicism would prove to be too severe a handicap. Political leaders dislike backing losers."

—Rose Kennedy, *Times to Remember*

Once again, Eleanor Roosevelt weighed in. She believed that the country was ready for a Catholic president as long as the church and state remained separate. She did not believe Jack Kennedy was able to do this. Jack was unmoved by the negativity. Becoming vice president with the prospect of running eight years later was hardly an option. He decided that he would rather take his chances. On January 20, 1960, he officially announced his candidacy for the Democratic nomination at a press conference in the Senate Caucus Room.

On the Campaign Trail

Jack was in for a tough battle. With the hesitancy over his youth and Catholic faith, and his sporadic support for liberal causes, winning favor with state party bosses who controlled many of the convention's state delegates would prove an amazing feat. There were only sixteen state primaries, so making contact with state leaders was essential. This was clearly different from his other campaigns, so plotting a course of action would take the organizational aptitude of Bobby Kennedy.

Kennedy needed the support of state leaders such as Chicago's Mayor Richard J. Daley, California Speaker Jesse Unruh, and Pennsylvania Governor David L. Lawrence, but he also needed support from primary voters. So Jack did what he had grown accustomed to doing over the past few years. He traveled. First he stopped in New Hampshire where the primary was scheduled for March 6, 1960. This New England territory was a certain win, since Adlai Stevenson and Stuart Symington had little hold on the state. Jack won 85 percent of the vote.

Campaigning in Wisconsin

Jack was also expected to win Indiana and Nebraska, but the Protestant state of Wisconsin posed a real challenge. This time, Kennedy had a challenger: the personable and well-liked Hubert Humphrey. Jack, however, had paved the way the year before with a sixteen-day tour of the state. Although the cold wreaked havoc on his back, for six weeks he walked the streets meeting and greeting the voters, many of whom gave him an unenthusiastic welcome. In the end, Jack's vigor paid off. On April 5, he narrowly beat Humphrey with 56.5 percent of the vote.

Proving his Viability in West Virginia

Although Wisconsin was a victory, there were still doubts about Kennedy's ability to win non-Catholic votes. The six districts he won in Wisconsin were composed mainly of Catholic voters, while Humphrey won the Protestant districts. In a sense, this was a defeat for Kennedy since it failed to prove his viability among non-Catholics in a national race. On the religious issue, the press turned out to be more of a hindrance than a help; they commonly mentioned his religion in news stories. This was frustrating to Jack, but he carried on. He hoped to put the issue to rest once and for all when he arrived in West Virginia, where only 4 percent of the state was Catholic. This time, Jack expected to enjoy a decisive victory over Humphrey and prove he had what it took.

Jack decided to address the religious issue head on. His first stop in West Virginia was in Charleston. From the steps of the post office, he openly discussed the issue. This was an important decision, considering that Humphrey was using the religious issue to his advantage. Humphrey had aptly adopted the theme song "Give Me That Old Time Religion," and warned listeners that voting for a Catholic would mean a partnership with the pope. Jack, although frustrated, assured voters that church and state would remain separate under his leadership.

Jack needed all the help he could get. Jackie came along but campaigned for only a short time due to her pregnancy. Her mannerism and style of dress were impressive to voters, who

HE SAID...

"I am a Catholic, but the fact that I was born a Catholic, does that mean that I can't be President of the United States? I'm able to serve in Congress, and my brother was able to give his life, but we can't be president."

viewed her as a type of American queen. Also on the campaign trail with Jack were his brother Ted, long-time friend Lem Billings, and brother-in-law Sargent Shriver. In a stroke of genius, Joe, working on the campaign from Hyannis Port, recommended that they send Franklin D. Roosevelt Jr. to campaign for Jack in West Virginia.

The state was surrounded by monuments memorializing FDR, so the presence of his son was a winning strategy. During Roosevelt's personal appearances, he praised Jack and contrasted Jack's heroic service in World War II with assertions that Humphrey was a draft dodger who had sought military deferments during the war. Humphrey was irate that the statements were not retracted after he informed Jack that physical disabilities had prevented his service. To the public, Jack made it clear that he had never approved the statements, but it was too little too late. The damage had been done to Humphrey's image.

Jack outspent Humphrey $34,000 to $25,000—significant considering that votes were essentially for sale. Voters cast their votes according to the approved list of candidates named on their slate. The county boss, who determined the slates, backed the candidates who paid the most money. Jack could afford to pay, but Humphrey could not. On May 10, Kennedy won West Virginia by 60.8 to 39.2 percent.

Winning the Democratic Nomination

West Virginia was the decisive victory that he needed. The Catholic issue had proved beatable. Jack moved on to Nebraska, Maryland, and Oregon, where he won decisive victories. In June, he picked up Pennsylvania, which gave him a solid backing. The campaign became a little complicated when Lyndon B. Johnson announced his candidacy on July 5, six days before the Democratic convention in Los Angeles. Although Jack's health problems were a family secret, Johnson went public with claims that Kennedy had Addison's disease. Jack responded with a press statement that he was in good health and not suffering from what was "classically" known as Addison's disease.

FACT

The statement was technically true because Jack had never undergone testing to determine for certain whether he had Addison's disease. In fact, since he had refused testing, it was never for certain that he was suffering from the disease. However, according to biographer Robert Dallek, he most likely had a secondary form of the disease.

Jack arrived at the convention with the belief that he would win the nomination, but with the realistic feeling that anything could happen. He was right. When Stevenson arrived on July 13, he received an emotional reception as Eugene McCarthy put his name into the running for the nomination. Stevenson's glory was short lived, and his home state of Illinois cast fifty-nine and a half votes for Kennedy and only two for Stevenson. The real battle was between Johnson and Kennedy.

It was an intense time, and even Joe Kennedy was worried. Although he was in Los Angeles, he decided to remain absent from the convention that night as the rest of the family, including Rose Kennedy, went to the Sports Arena. On the first ballot, Kennedy had twice as many delegates as Johnson. At the end of roll call, Wyoming cast its fifteen votes for Jack, giving him the majority required to win the nomination. A smiling Jack and an intensely satisfied Bobby walked together into the convention hall. The Kennedy family's long-awaited victory had finally come.

HE SAID...

"Of course I want Lyndon Johnson. . . . The only thing is, I would never want to offer it and have him turn me down; I would be terrifically embarrassed. He's the natural. If I can ever get him on the ticket, no way we can lose."

John F. Kennedy accepting the nomination at the 1960 Democratic Convention.

Photo Credit: Cornell Capa/Magnum Photos

Choosing a Running Mate

With the nomination behind him, Jack needed to select a vice presidential running mate. He had already thought long and hard about his choices. Humphrey, Johnson, Stuart Symington, and Stevenson headed his list of potential vice presidents. He quickly eliminated Humphrey and Stevenson, whose lack of support was enough to remove them from the running. Kennedy liked Symington and believed his popularity in the Midwest would help the campaign. Nevertheless, Kennedy could not overlook his youth. Two young running mates were bound to draw attention to their age rather than the important issues they ran on. Thus, the wise choice was Texas senator Lyndon B. Johnson.

Kennedy figured Johnson's roots in the South could help the ticket. At 2 A.M., Dave Powers called Johnson at his hotel room to give him the news. Johnson was already sleeping, so the proposition was put on hold until the next morning. In the meantime, there was one potential snag in the plan. Through an intermediary, Jack had promised labor leaders and civil rights groups that LBJ was not a contender. If he selected LBJ now, he threatened to lose their backing. Jack awoke the next day with this new dilemma at the forefront of his mind. An angry group of labor leaders arrived at his suite at 11 A.M. Kennedy tried his best to assure them that his selection of Johnson was in their best interest. Kennedy rationalized that by making Johnson his right-hand man, he could keep tabs on him. Labor leaders were unconvinced and warned that they would block Johnson's nomination if forced to do so.

There was little Jack could do to appease labor leaders other than select a more liberal vice presidential nominee. He wavered on making a final decision on Johnson since it appeared that he was going to face a fierce battle against the liberals. By this time, Johnson knew that he was in the final running. Jack, therefore, had to play his hand wisely; he did not want to alienate anyone, especially considering that Johnson would remain the Senate majority leader if he were not selected as vice president. Thus, Jack delayed in giving a final confirmation to the Johnson camp regarding his decision.

FACT

In 1937, three years after he married Claudia "Lady Bird" Taylor, Lyndon Johnson was elected to the House of Representatives. In 1948, he made his way into the Senate, where, five years later, he became the youngest minority leader in the history of the Senate. In 1949, when the Democrats took control of the Senate, he became the majority leader.

But Jack had not realized just how much Johnson wanted to be vice president. Late that afternoon when Bobby met with Johnson in his suite and asked him to withdraw, he was confronted with an emotional LBJ. According to Bobby, a shaken Johnson responded with tears in his eyes that he wanted to be vice president and was willing to help Jack fight for his nomination.

That was all Bobby needed to hear. He responded to the emotionally charged Johnson with the affirmation that Jack wanted him if he wanted to be vice president. Minutes later, Jack confirmed the decision with a Johnson aide by phone. When he was up for nomination at the convention, Johnson did as he promised. The fight was not Jack's alone. Once Johnson agreed to support the civil rights agenda, liberal and labor opposition dissolved. The delegates swiftly nominated Johnson as the vice presidential nominee.

HE SAID...

"[T]he problems are not all solved and the battles are not all won; and we stand today on the edge of a New Frontier—the frontier of the 1960s, the frontier of unknown opportunities and perils, the frontier of unfilled hopes and unfilled threats. . . . . The New Frontier is here whether we seek it or not."

A New Frontier

With the issue of a running mate settled, Jack made his televised acceptance speech to 80,000 people at the Los Angeles Coliseum. His performance was one he wished he could forget, but the content of his speech was memorable. With the help of Ted Sorensen, he composed a message that tackled the religious issue, war, economic stability, and social justice. Most of all, it emphasized the future and the need for the American people to meet it as one. Jack called it the New Frontier.

The Democratic nominee cautioned against complacency, and he warned the country that the New Frontier was "not a set of promises; it is a set of challenges." This was an idea that Jack himself was still formulating. The exact wording would be crystallized in his inaugural speech: "Ask not what your country can do for you. Ask what you can do for your country." But that was still a long six months away.

Chapter 9

THE PRESIDENTIAL ELECTION

The presidential race of 1960 would prove to be momentous. Having promised a New Frontier, Kennedy had to deliver a tangible plan—and address persistent doubts about his religious faith and his stance on civil rights. Kennedy took advantage of the relatively new medium of television to advance his presidential ambitions. Kennedy won the presidency over Richard Nixon, but his margin of victory—0.2 percent of the popular vote—was the narrowest in the nation's history up to that point.

Overcoming the Doubts and Rumors

Jack was happy yet exhausted when the convention was over. He took a short break at the Kennedy home in Hyannis Port, but he returned to the campaign two days later.

Winning Over Critics

First on the agenda was securing the support of the Democrats who had been his loudest opposition. He quickly won Stevenson over and dispatched him to California to rally his supporters. Stevenson warned Kennedy that he would fall behind in his knowledge of foreign affairs during the campaign and recommended he have a plan to be brought back up to speed after the election. Kennedy readily agreed and put Stevenson himself in charge of the foreign policy report.

Harry Truman, who had expressed his concern at Jack's youth, preferred Jack over Republican nominee Vice President Richard Nixon, who had called him a communist. Lastly, Jack's feistiest critic, Eleanor Roosevelt, was also soon on board. It was Jack's openness to new ideas, his ability to learn, and his interest in "helping the people of his own country and mankind in general" that convinced Eleanor Roosevelt to give her support. She now had a certain amount of respect for Jack.

Securing the support of his most ardent critics was an easy task compared to winning over the American public. Immediately after the Democratic convention ended, Kennedy sailed ahead with a 17 to 22 percent lead over Nixon in California, Illinois, New York, Pennsylvania, and Texas. But by September, Jack trailed with only 47 percent support to Nixon's 53 percent.

A Harmful Exposure

Kennedy needed to build a base of support, but he was concerned that his womanizing might cause trouble in the campaign. In June 1959, the FBI, along with thirty-five reporters, received letters and a photograph regarding Jack's untoward behavior. Also in the FBI files was the notation that Jack had engaged in relations with an airline stewardess.

It is unclear whether Jack knew specifically about the FBI file or that journalists had received information about his womanizing, but he certainly realized that the publication of the scandalous information could wreak havoc on his campaign. In 1960, a revelation in the mainstream press about his extramarital affairs could have ruined his chance of winning the presidency. In fact, this information was so detrimental that Joe Kennedy was poised to take action if necessary. According to Missouri's Democratic Congressman Richard Bolling, Joe was ready to air information about Nixon's own extramarital affairs should Nixon reveal information about Jack's philandering. It seemed that it was only a matter of time before the information was revealed.

THEY SAID...

"[M]ost of the stories about his private life seem to date from 1955 and before. My view, therefore, is that such rumors are out of date and largely unsubstantiated. And I must add even if they were true they would hardly seem to be crucial when the alternative is Nixon!"

—Adlai Stevenson, as quoted in *An Unfinished Life*

When Adlai Stevenson heard the stories, he quickly dismissed them, believing that when Jack's back problems improved, he had settled down. The rumors also failed to get much attention from the newspapers. None of the thirty-five reporters who received the information reported the story. In that era, stories about the sexual lives of politicians rarely made it into the mainstream newspapers. This type of story was considered beyond the realm of appropriate publication.

Taking On the Catholic Issue

Despite his best attempts to convince voters that his Catholic religion would not influence his actions as president, the issue would not go away. On September 7, 150 ministers from the National Conference of Citizens for Religious Freedom issued a statement challenging Kennedy's ability to lead the country as a Catholic. It made the front page of the *New York Times,* and Kennedy campaign staff reported that voters all over the country were suspicious of the candidate's faith. Kennedy knew he would have to respond.

FACT

The Kennedy campaign received letters during the campaign expressing concerns about Kennedy's religion, and it fell to James Wine, Kennedy's special advisor on religious issues, to answer most of them. They now take up eleven boxes at the John F. Kennedy Presidential Library. In addition to answering letters, Wine was instrumental in appealing to Protestant leaders to oppose attacks against Kennedy's religion.

Kennedy hoped to put the issue to rest once and for all. He accepted an invitation to speak to the Greater Houston Ministerial Association on September 12. Jack conferred with Catholic scholars John Courtney Murray and John Cogley to prepare for the speech, which he drafted with Ted Sorensen.

When Jack arrived at the televised event at the Houston Rice Hotel Crystal ballroom, he was well prepared. His speech, unwavering in its commitment to put to rest the "so-called religious issue," showed just how badly he wanted to be president; his father's dream had become his own. Without detracting from his opponents' concerns, he calmly put matters into perspective. The religious issue was a secondary one, and it would not affect his ability to be president—"for war and hunger and ignorance and despair know no religious barriers." Nevertheless, Kennedy continued, he realized that the public were concerned about his Catholic faith. He outlined the differences between himself as an individual and the presidency as an institution. He made it clear he was running for president as a Democrat, not as a Catholic.

It was a turning point in the campaign. Kennedy had faced a largely suspicious audience with poise and maturity, and he had articulately made a case for his place as a Catholic in high political office. The applause he received was far from thunderous, but there were no more blaring statements from Protestant ministers questioning his faith and his candidacy. The issue was closed for Kennedy himself, and he prepared to confront Richard Nixon face-to-face.

The Great Debate

Finally, Kennedy's faith was no longer at the forefront of the election and he was free to take on issues of substance. Kennedy needed to carve out positions for himself to differentiate his views from Richard Nixon's. Both Nixon and Kennedy had entered Congress the same year and there was only a four-year age difference between the two, but Nixon's eight years as vice president made him seem older and more experienced. Television network executives proposed a series of debates—the first ever televised debates between presidential candidates—and Kennedy jumped at the opportunity. Nixon was already well known, but television could provide Kennedy with a forum to get his name out to millions of Americans.

Television History

Nixon and Kennedy met for the first of four debates at the CBS studio in Chicago on September 26, 1960. Kennedy looked relaxed, tanned, and healthy in a dark suit. Nixon, on the other hand, looked haggard due to his recent hospitalization for a serious knee injury. He'd lost twenty pounds, and his gray suit was

HE SAID...

"I am the Democratic Party's candidate for President who happens also to be a Catholic. I do not speak for my church on public matters—and the church does not speak for me. . . . [I]f the time should ever come . . . when my office would require me to either violate my conscience or violate the national interest, then I would resign the office."

too big for him; worse, it blended in with the gray background. CBS anchor Howard K. Smith served as moderator, and a panel of four reporters led the questioning.

FACT

A month before the first debate, Eisenhower answered a question about his vice president's contributions to the administration by replying, "If you give me a week, I might think of one." Nixon was stung by the remark, and he spent precious time in the first debate trying to address it.

The Debate Begins

Before a television audience of 70 million, the debate began with the opportunity for each candidate to give an opening statement. Kennedy was well prepared. He had spent the day going over important facts and had written an opening statement. In a confident, even-keeled manner, Kennedy addressed the American people about important issues. A gaunt-looking Nixon used his opening statement to contrast the differences between the candidates and defend the current administration.

The debate centered around domestic affairs, but the answers themselves mattered less than the candidates' attitudes to the debate. Kennedy used the television cameras to speak directly to the audience and engage them. Nixon debated Kennedy; he seemed more concerned with his opponent than with the millions of Americans watching him from their living rooms.

And the Winner Is . . .

By the time it was over, those who watched the debate on television had been struck by Kennedy's charisma. But for those listening on the radio, Nixon was the perceived winner. Radio listeners were unable to see Nixon's pale complexion and sickly looking frame. In any case, Kennedy had accomplished what he set out to do: he had put himself on level ground with Nixon. No longer could the vice president claim Kennedy was young and inexperienced. It was this win that gave him the boost he needed, and a confident Kennedy debated Nixon again on October 7, 13, and 21.

THEY SAID...

"I watched Jack last night on the debate, praying through every sentence. . . . He looked more assured than Nixon and looked better physically. Jack seemed to have all the initiative and once or twice rose to inspiring heights of oratory. . . . Jack really looks, sounds, and acts like young Lincoln. . . ."

—Rose Fitzgerald Kennedy, *Times to Remember*

Securing the African American Vote

The debates failed to win over one crucial pocket of constituents: African American voters. Civil rights was a tricky issue. If Kennedy supported the movement, he risked losing support from white southern segregationists. Yet he needed the support of liberals and African Americans; if he failed to support a civil rights agenda, he risked losing their vote. Kennedy based his decision on politics and not morality. He decided not only to adopt the Democratic civil rights platform, but to add to it.

Backing Civil Rights

Upon the urgings of Harris Wofford, Kennedy's advisor on civil rights, Kennedy set up a civil rights division of his campaign. He hired black publisher Louis Martin to court the media, paid congressman Adam Clayton Powell $50,000 to give ten speeches endorsing him, and made Frank Reeves, who was closely aligned with the NAACP, a traveling companion. Kennedy traveled throughout the country speaking at black conventions about the immorality of segregation. He emphasized that unlike Eisenhower, who had failed to change the injustice of the system by the simple "stroke of a pen," he would support civil rights legislation.

Martin Luther King's Endorsement

Kennedy wanted the endorsement of the Southern Christian Leadership Conference's (SCLC) Martin Luther King Jr. His first meeting with King in June had not gone well. King not only refused to endorse him but questioned Kennedy's stance on civil rights. Kennedy's vote for the weakened 1957 civil rights bill had come back to haunt him. Although Kennedy expressed his support of civil rights, especially voting rights, King was not convinced. At their second meeting in September, however, Kennedy impressed King with his increased knowledge on civil rights. Now King was on the fence, neither siding with Kennedy nor Nixon.

King, however, felt that as a civil rights leader he should remain nonpartisan. Nevertheless, Harris Wofford, a long-time friend of King's, worked out an agreement with King that if Kennedy met with him in the South, he would give a public statement approving of Kennedy's commitment to carrying out the Democratic civil rights platform. They decided to meet in Miami, but Kennedy called it off after King mentioned that he planned to invite Nixon.

HE SAID...

"There are no Federal District Judges—there are 200-odd of them; not a one is a Negro. We have about 26 Negroes in the entire Foreign Service of 6,000, so that particularly now with the importance of Africa, Asia, and all the rest, I do believe we should make a greater effort to encourage fuller participation on all levels, of all the talent we can get—Negro, white, of any race."

It was a disappointing conclusion, but the saga wasn't over. In late October, King was arrested for participating in a sit-in protest at a department store in Atlanta. All of the other protesters were released, but King was sentenced to four months of hard labor for violating probation. His probation had resulted from a traffic ticket, and he planned to contest it, but the judge dismissed his attorney's protests and sentenced him anyway.

Coretta Scott King, six months pregnant with the couple's third child, feared for her husband's life. Coretta King appealed to Harris Wofford, who in turn called Sargent Shriver, Kennedy's brother-in-law and head of the campaign's civil rights section. Shriver went to Kennedy's hotel in Chicago and urged the candidate to consider Wofford's proposal to call Mrs. King. Without consulting any of his advisors, Kennedy picked up the telephone. He told Coretta King that he shared her concern and offered to help in any way he could.

THEY SAID...

"Senator Kennedy . . . was running for an office, and he needed to be elected, and I'm sure he felt the need for the Negro votes. So I think that he did something that expressed deep moral concern, but at the same time it was politically sound. It did take a little courage to do this; he didn't know it was politically sound."

—Martin Luther King Jr., *The Autobiography of Martin Luther King Jr.*

It was a risky move. When Bobby Kennedy heard about the call, he was irate. He was afraid the act had alienated key voters less than two weeks before a close election, but he quickly redirected his wrath as he mulled over the situation. As an attorney, he knew the judge's actions were unjust. He called the judge from a pay phone in New York, told him that his actions were in defiance of the law, and requested that he release King.

The next day, King was released on a $2,000 bond. Several days later at a press conference, King thanked Kennedy for his concern. Although it fell short of an endorsement, Martin Luther King Sr. publicly switched his support from Nixon to Kennedy. "Because this man was willing to wipe the tears from my daughter[-in-law]'s eyes, I've got a suitcase full of votes, and I'm going to take them to Mr. Kennedy and dump them in his lap," the elder King announced. It was exactly the kind of result Kennedy had wished for.

Winning the Election

At this point, King's statement was more than Kennedy had expected. It was helpful, especially with the presidential race so close. Eisenhower had finally gotten behind Nixon and was actively campaigning for him. Harris Wofford got right to work. He set out to take advantage of the situation with King. Wofford decided that the best course of action was to advertise the fact that Nixon had declined to comment or help King when he was in prison. Immediately flyers were distributed throughout black communities around the country with the headline, "'No Comment' Nixon versus a Candidate with a Heart, Senator Kennedy: The Case of Martin Luther King."

Senator John F. Kennedy and wife Jackie campaign for the presidency, October 1960.

Photo credit: Lee Lockwood/Time Life Pictures/Getty Images

In mid-October, Kennedy held a lead of 51 to 45 percent, but three days before the election Nixon had closed the gap substantially: a Gallup poll showed that Kennedy led with 50.5 to Nixon's 49.5. The election was just as close, and Jack went to bed at 3:30 A.M. with only a slight advantage over Nixon. When he awoke the next morning, he was pleasantly surprised that he had won Pennsylvania, Missouri, Illinois, Minnesota, Michigan—and the election.

Kennedy had won 303 electoral votes to Nixon's 219. However, he had only won the popular vote with a narrow margin of 118,574—49.72 percent. Nonetheless, it was a victory for Kennedy, and of course, for his father as well. So for one of the few times in Kennedy's political career, he shared the excitement of his win with his father, who was by his side as he made a statement to the press.

Preparing for the Presidency

As Jack settled down after the exhilaration of the election, he was faced with the fact that his defeat of Nixon had been one of the smallest since 1884, when Grover Cleveland had won by only 23,000 votes. Jack, however, had no choice but to neutralize his doubts, questions, and feelings regarding his victory and focus instead on preparing to become president.

A group portrait of John F. Kennedy, surrounded by his family after the news that he won the U.S. presidential election, Hyannis Port, Massachusetts.

Photo credit: Hulton Archive/Getty Images

Meeting with Eisenhower

On December 6, 1960, Kennedy and Eisenhower met. During the meeting the two men discussed Algeria, Laos, Latin America, Cuba, and nuclear testing. Kennedy appreciated Eisenhower's appealing personality, but he was surprised that Eisenhower knew less about the topics than he had expected. Eisenhower, on the other hand, came away with a new impression of Kennedy. During the latter part of the campaign, he had become much more vocal about his support for Nixon due to his belief that Kennedy was too young and inexperienced for the presidency. Eisenhower left the meeting with a complete change in opinion. Although Kennedy was the youngest man elected to the presidency, he saw that Kennedy was bright and competent.

Weeks later, Kennedy had another meeting with Eisenhower. For forty-five minutes the men tackled some of the issues that most concerned Kennedy, among them the civil war ravaging Laos. What concerned Kennedy most was the prospect of a communist takeover, and he was intensely interested in the current policy on intervention. Furthermore, Kennedy was concerned about Cuba and had heard rumors of U.S. assistance to anti-Castro guerrilla forces. Concerns about Castro's Cuba, however, would have to wait. Overall, it was Laos more than Cuba that Jack worried about. He hoped a resolution of the Laos conflict would be determined before he took office.

Choosing a Cabinet

In addition to getting up to speed on important issues, Jack had to decide who would help him run his administration. His long-time companions who had assisted him in his Senate career and in his campaign for president were to be duly rewarded with offices in the West Wing near the Oval Office. Dave Powers would serve as his special assistant, Pierre Salinger the press secretary, Larry O'Brien was to become the legislative liaison, O'Donnell the appointments secretary, Sorensen a special counsel, and the newly recruited Arthur Schlesinger was appointed special assistant, operating out of the East Wing.

After the appointments of his important supporters, Jack faced some tougher decisions. He wanted the best and the brightest in his administration, but he knew few possible candidates. Thus, to the disappointment of some Democrats, he was not opposed to moderate Republicans serving in his administration. He made this decision in part because his margin of victory in the election had been so slim. He also had an affinity for new ideas. For Kennedy, it mattered less who he appointed and more what the outcome of his policy was.

THEY SAID...

"In particular, he was little acquainted in the New York financial and legal community—that arsenal of talent which had so long furnished a steady supply of always orthodox and often able people to Democratic as well as Republican administrations. This community was the heart of the American Establishment."

—Arthur Schlesinger, *A Thousand Days*

Kennedy planned to take an active role in guiding his secretary of state, so he did not much mind who occupied the position. He believed that the compliant Dean Rusk, the president of the Rockefeller Foundation, was perfect for the position. He asked Adlai Stevenson, who had hoped to head the State Department, to serve as the U.S. Ambassador to the United Nations. Kennedy appointed liberal Republican C. Douglas Dillon to the post of secretary of treasury and Walter Heller as chairman of the Council of Economic Advisors. He recruited the president of Ford Motor Company, Robert S. McNamara, as secretary of defense.

Appointing Bobby

Jack's next dilemma was what position to appoint his loyal brother Bobby. Bobby, however, wanted some independence and was turned off by the idea of working in the White House directly under the control of his big brother. Jack favored the position of attorney general for Bobby. Bobby was not so sure, considering that he had never practiced law. He was also fearful that the appointment would lead to charges of favoritism.

To counter such charges, Jack, Bobby, and Joe devised a scheme. Jack told family friend Clark Clifford that Joe was forcing him to appoint Bobby attorney general. Joe confirmed the story. Bobby played his part by expressing his hesitance to accept the appointment. Early one morning, Bobby and Jack sat down to breakfast with John Seigenthaler of the *Nashville Tennessean*. Jack and Bobby put on a convincing dialogue about Bobby's resistance to serve as attorney general. The end result of the early morning show was no surprise; Jack finally convinced Bobby to accept. Seigenthaler's presence was insurance that the story of Bobby's hesitancy would make the news. Kennedy had finally chosen all of his Cabinet members and was ready for one of the biggest and most important days of his life—the inauguration.

Chapter 10

THE FIRST HUNDRED DAYS

John F. Kennedy was the youngest president ever to take office and the first president to be born in the twentieth century. As the seventy-year-old Eisenhower relinquished the presidency to his successor, a new generation came of age—in Kennedy's words, a generation "born in this century, tempered by war, disciplined by a hard and bitter peace, proud of our ancient heritage." Kennedy's powerful inaugural address set the tone for his new presidency. A Gallup poll taken shortly after the inauguration showed an approval rating of 72 percent for the man who had squeaked into the Oval Office by the barest of margins in the November elections. But behind all the promise of the new administration loomed the threat of the Cold War.

A Memorable Inaugural Address

A heavy snowstorm wreaked havoc on Washington, D.C., the night before the inauguration. Kennedy intended the inauguration to be an unforgettable ceremony supplemented with spectacular events and celebrations.

THEY SAID...

"He understood the importance of pageantry in tying the nation together. He recognized that even as the people would reject a king, their hearts tugged for the inauguration with pomp and ceremony. For that reason, he deliberately decided to invest his inauguration with pomp and ceremony."

—Lem Billings, as quoted in *The Fitzgeralds and the Kennedys: An American Saga*

The Inaugural Ceremony

At noon on January 20, 1961, Joe, Rose, Bobby, and Jackie Kennedy strode across the Capitol steps to the platform where Jack would take the oath of office. Once all the dignitaries and guests had taken their seats, the president-elect emerged and took his seat between Eisenhower and Johnson. After an eight-minute invocation by Boston's Cardinal Cushing, Marian Anderson's strong voice led the singing of "The Star-Spangled Banner."

FACT

During his blessing, Cardinal Cushing noticed smoke drifting up from underneath the platform and feared it was a bomb. He slowed his speech in the hope that he could stay at the podium long enough to absorb the bomb blast for Kennedy. The source of the smoke turned out to be a faulty wire, which was remedied without incident.

Anderson's stirring performance was one of Kennedy's efforts to incorporate the arts into his inauguration. Kennedy also invited Robert Frost to read a poem, and the revered poet stepped up to the podium after Lyndon Johnson had taken the vice presidential oath of office. Frost intended to read a new poem, "Dedication," which he had written specifically for the occasion. After a few false starts, the eighty-six-year-old Frost realized he couldn't read the speech amid the glare of the sunlight on the snow. Instead he beautifully recited "The Gift Outright" from memory.

The New President's Address

Frost's pitch-perfect recital set the stage for Kennedy's inaugural oath and address. Kennedy had worked tirelessly on the speech for months, writing and rewriting each sentence until it suited him. Influenced by Abraham Lincoln's powerful Gettysburg Address, Kennedy set out to make the greatest possible impact with the fewest possible words. He focused on his specialty—foreign affairs.

Kennedy laid out a promise to the nation and the world and infused his message with a tone of hope and optimism. Freedom,

HE SAID...

"In the long history of the world, only a few generations have been granted the role of defending freedom in its hour of maximum danger. I do not shrink from this responsibility—I welcome it. I do not believe that any of us would exchange places with any other people or any other generation. The energy, the faith, the devotion which we bring to this endeavor will light our country and all who serve it—and the glow from that fire can truly light the world. And so, my fellow Americans: ask not what your country can do for you—ask what you can do for your country. My fellow citizens of the world: ask not what America can do for you, but what together we can do for the freedom of man."

asserted Kennedy, was of foremost importance to the United States. He pledged to promote the cause of freedom and help eradicate poverty anywhere in the world. He extended an offer to the Soviet Union to "begin anew." If the two superpowers could work through their differences, Kennedy reasoned, they could work together to accomplish positive goals, such as exploring space and promoting arts and commerce.

The end of the speech, Kennedy's call to civic duty, was most memorable. National duty required Americans to act against tyranny, poverty, disease, and war. The thirty-fifth president of the United States ended his inaugural address with a call to Americans to sacrifice for the greater good.

Embracing the Press

Kennedy's relationship with the press and his ability to spark national interest in his press conferences boosted his public appeal. Kennedy liked what the press could do for his presidency, and during his first few months in office he used it to his advantage. Kennedy made it a policy to be as open with the press as possible and encouraged his staff to talk to reporters.

President Kennedy at a news conference.

Photo credit: Abbie Rowe, White House/ John F. Kennedy Presidential Library and Museum, Boston

His frequent live press conferences were his most effective tool in winning over the public. The conferences were broadcast on television and radio. To all who watched or listened, Kennedy's relaxed style and knowledge on important issues, especially foreign policy, made him seem a master statesman. Viewers often witnessed Kennedy's wit and confidence, as well as his superior knowledge on many topics. His press conferences were widely popular, and almost three out of every four adults had either viewed or heard one.

It took time, however, for Kennedy to prepare for each press meeting. He poured hours into his preparation for each press conference. Pierre Salinger was charged with gathering potential questions and answers from government officials and with presenting them to Kennedy at the press conference breakfast.

Tackling Civil Rights Issues

Kennedy was painfully aware that he had been voted into office with only 49.7 percent of the popular vote. He feared that even though the Democrats held the majority in the House, getting progressive bills through Congress could prove tricky, especially with a sizable population of Southerners in both parties. Kennedy decided not to pursue the civil rights agenda he had proposed during the campaign. Instead of congressional legislation, he intended to use executive orders to confront the issue. He told Harris Wofford, his special assistant on civil rights, that he felt racial discrimination was "nonsense," but he knew it was useless to attempt to pass anything through Congress.

THEY SAID...

"The fact of the matter is that the time when President Kennedy started televised press conferences there were only three or four newspapers in the entire United States that carried a full transcript of a presidential press conference. Therefore, what people read was a distillation. . . . We thought that they should have the opportunity to see it in full."

—Pierre Salinger, John F. Kennedy Library Oral History Interview

Next, Kennedy created a new organization, the Committee on Equal Employment Opportunity, to address the issue of the meager number of blacks working in government. The committee promised to punish businesses that discriminated against blacks by denying them government contracts. Kennedy appointed Lyndon Johnson to chair the committee.

THEY SAID...

"It is not surprising that the President had an inadequate sense of the breadth and depth of the problem. Prejudice and discrimination were irrational, he felt, but many immigrant groups had overcome similar barriers, and he was sure Negroes would do so too, in due course, with appropriate help."

—Harris Wofford, *Of Kennedys and Kings*

If his prior actions had failed to prove his commitment to civil rights, Kennedy expected that these next measures would garner him support. He supported the renewal of the Civil Rights Commission, which was responsible for assessing the progress of civil rights around the nation, ordered the inclusion of blacks in the coast guard and other branches of the armed forces, and appointed African Americans to important posts in his administration. However, civil rights leaders felt let down. They believed Kennedy was delivering less than he had promised during the 1960 election.

Taking On the Domestic Economy

Kennedy turned his focus to matters he felt he could control. The economy had gone into a recession in the last year, and Kennedy was hard pressed to figure out a solution. A tax cut, public works programs, and lowering the interest rates were ineffective solutions, according to Kennedy. Instead, he focused on getting control over what the federal government could do to improve the economy. The plan, which he proposed to Congress on February 2, included dispersing tax refunds and farm subsidies more quickly, building highways, and getting urban renewal programs underway.

FACT

In his first month as president, Kennedy appointed Robert C. Weaver as the administrator of the Home Finance Agency. Southern Democrats grumbled about the appointment of an African American to such a high position, but they approved it. However, Congress blocked Kennedy's attempts to create a Department of Urban Affairs in 1961 and 1962, partially because some legislators feared Kennedy would elevate Weaver to a cabinet-level position.

Initially, the economy remained stagnant, but it began to improve steadily with the assistance of Congress's enactment of the Area Redevelopment Act, which promised to assist ten states with high unemployment rates. In addition, the minimum wage was raised to $1.25 and Social Security benefits were increased. By April, the public felt that the economy was on its way toward renewal. Fifty-eight percent of Americans polled were optimistic about the economy, compared with a meager 34 percent a month earlier. It was good news for Kennedy, who enjoyed a 72 percent approval rating.

Establishing the Peace Corps

Kennedy's belief in serving one's country came to life with the establishment of the Peace Corps. In 1951, he had envisioned the creation of a charitable organization that would serve the underprivileged in the Middle East. He revisited the idea in an impromptu speech on the steps of the Michigan Union at the University of Michigan during his presidential campaign. He encouraged the students to serve their country by helping the underprivileged in poor countries. Once

"HE SAID...

The Area Redevelopment Act "will help make it possible for thousands of Americans who want to work, to work. It will be of special help to those areas which have been subjected to chronic unemployment for many months, and in some cases for many years. In this free society we want to make it possible for everyone to find a job who wants to work and support their families, and this bill is an important step in that direction."

he became president, a more well-developed proposal from Senator Hubert Humphrey spurred the idea along. On March 1, 1961, Kennedy issued an executive order establishing the Peace Corps on a trial basis.

The plan for those serving in the organization included no salary and only a minimum stipend for necessities. They were to live among the native people in disadvantaged countries, where they would train and help the needy. Volunteers were mainly charged with assisting and training in such projects as village development, health care, and sanitation development. The Peace Corps was restricted from acting in any way as a tool for spying or promoting propaganda. Kennedy's brother-in-law, Sargent Shriver, was appointed as the director. More than 5,000 people applied for the program, and the first batch of fifty-one Peace Corps volunteers served Africa from 1961 to 1962. The program expanded, and today's Peace Corps has more than 7,000 volunteers in seventy-seven countries.

President Kennedy and Peace Corps Director
R. Sargent Shriver welcome Peace Corps volunteers
to Ghana and Tanganyika.

*Photo Credit: Abbie Rowe, White House/John F. Kennedy
Presidential Library and Museum*

The U.S.-Soviet Rivalry

There was another benefit to the Peace Corps. It was a way to show
the benefits of freedom to developing countries and keep them
from turning to communism. This was especially important to
Kennedy since the arms race with the Soviets was at the forefront
of his concerns. When he was running for office, a U.S. patrol plane
had been shot down by Russia while flying over the Barents Sea.
Two crew members survived and were taken into Soviet custody.
For six months, Eisenhower made negligible headway in securing
their release. However, a few days after Kennedy became president,
the men were released.

Kennedy trained his focus on the arms race between the Soviets
and the United States. During his campaign he had argued that
America should increase its development of missile technology to
catch up with the Soviet Union, but in February 1961 McNamara
announced that there was no missile gap, and in fact, the U.S. was
far more armed than the Soviets.

QUESTION
When and why did the Cold War begin?
The Cold War began after World War II when the Soviet Union set up communist governments in Albania, Bulgaria, Czechoslovakia, Hungary, Poland, and Romania. The United States set out to limit the expansion of the Soviets' communist influence. It led to an arms race, but the two superpowers never went to war directly. They did, however, take opposing sides in strategic conflicts, including the Middle East.

Kennedy sought to rein in the arms race. He was afraid that other countries would obtain nuclear weapons if nuclear testing was not banned, and he put his efforts into negotiating a test ban treaty to end the nuclear buildup. A temporary suspension on nuclear testing already in place had begun in November 1958, but Kennedy hoped for a more permanent agreement. The Soviets, on the other hand, saw it differently. The United States was already a stronger nuclear power, and the test ban treaty would benefit only the Americans.

HE SAID...

"[W]e propose to complete the revolution of the Americas, to build a hemisphere where all men can hope for a suitable standard of living, and all can live out their lives in dignity and in freedom. . . . Our Alliance for Progress is an alliance of free governments, and it must work to eliminate tyranny from a hemisphere in which it has no rightful place."

Without a permanent agreement with the Soviets, Kennedy began to feel intense pressure from military personnel and U.S. allies for the renewal of testing. By the end of March 1961, Kennedy increased the defense budget. Additionally, he authorized a threatening show of military force. He ordered ten new Polaris submarines to supplement the nineteen already in operation and commissioned missiles with longer range. Kennedy also increased his arsenal of Minutemen ballistic missiles to 600, hoping it would serve as a deterrent to the Soviets; he did not want to have to use the weapons.

The Wide-Reaching Threat of Communism

There was more to worry about than just the arms race with the Soviet Union. The threat of communism was an ever-growing danger. Kennedy was particularly afraid that communism would take root closer to home in Latin America, where Cuba's Fidel Castro encouraged liberation from U.S. influence. Khrushchev announced the Soviet Union's support of Cuba, and Kennedy set out to counteract the Soviet communist influence in the Western Hemisphere.

A Partnership with Latin America

To strengthen the relationship between the United States and Latin America, Kennedy announced the establishment of the Alliance for Progress. As its name indicated, it was a proposed relationship that promised collaboration on land reform, economic concerns, and social issues. Most importantly, Kennedy anticipated that it would discourage the spread of communism. This was clearly evident to some Latin American representatives, who referred to the alliance as the Fidel Castro Plan.

Opposing the Soviet Presence in the Congo

Kennedy was also concerned with the situation in the Congo. The country had gained its independence from Belgium in 1960, but it was divided by internal conflict. The Soviet Union extended assistance to some of the players in the conflict. The United States, fearing that the Soviets would gain more

HE SAID...

"[O]n your willingness to contribute part of your life to this country, I think will depend on the answer whether a free society can compete. I think it can! And I think Americans are willing to contribute. But the effort must be far greater than we have ever made in the past."—October 14, 1960, Ann Arbor, Michigan ground in Africa if the Congo disintegrated, put its efforts into keeping the country whole. The United States backed the UN decision to send a peace-keeping mission to regulate the conflict, and this was the situation when Kennedy took office. Kennedy supported the UN's mission; in his mind, if the UN were not there, the United States would have to step in and this would mean a direct U.S.-Soviet confrontation.

Reexamining Laos

The civil war in Laos represented another potential area for a confrontation with the Soviet Union. Kennedy's main concern was the prospect of a communist takeover, which threatened to open the door for communist infiltration throughout Southeast Asia. In late March, Kennedy tentatively decided to help preserve Laos's independence. He ordered five hundred marines to the Thai-Lao border. However, nothing immediately came of this plan. Kennedy, as did the Soviets, wanted to remain out of the civil war. Instead, Kennedy directed his attention to a communist threat that was much closer to home.

Chapter 11

THE BAY OF PIGS INVASION

Kennedy hardly had the time to settle into the presidency before his first crisis emerged. The Bay of Pigs invasion was a debacle of Kennedy's own making, but it taught him the importance of carefully choosing his advisors and to rely on his gut rather than the opinions of others. At this early stage of his presidency, he was unsure of his own abilities and overwhelmed by the daunting task of preventing the spread of communism throughout the world.

Considering an Invasion of Cuba

The island nation of Cuba, a mere ninety miles from Florida, concerned Kennedy even more than the complex situation in Laos. In general, he had been supportive of independence in regard to such countries as Algeria, but Cuba needed a more delicate approach. Kennedy had been sympathetic in 1958 when Fidel Castro led the Cuban revolution against the Batista dictatorship. However, once Castro had won control over the country, he joined forces with the communists and severely limited the freedom of Cuba's citizens. As a result, Eisenhower had broken off contact with Cuba and imposed economic sanctions on the country.

THEY SAID...

"I know that imprisonment will be harder for me than it has ever been for anyone, filled with cowardly threats and hideous cruelty. But I do not fear prison, as I do not fear the fury of the miserable tyrant who took the lives of seventy of my comrades. Condemn me. It does not matter. History will absolve me."—Fidel Castro, at his 1953 trial for attempting to overthrow Fulgencio Batista y Zaldivar's dictatorship; he served eleven months of a fifteen-year prison sentence, and the speech made him a national hero.

In addition to the sanctions, the CIA prepared a more aggressive plan of action. At a conference with the agency in late January, Kennedy learned the CIA wanted to prevent Cuba's descent into communism by secretly assisting in the overthrow of Castro's government. The plan involved training and supporting Cuban exiles in Guatemala to overthrow the regime. Once overthrown, the old regime would be replaced with a new provisional leadership that America could support.

Kennedy was unsure about implementing the plot but agreed it was necessary to continue planning. The CIA argued it was an urgent matter that required immediate attention. Fear of Castro's intent to spread communism throughout Latin America and the Caribbean was at the forefront of the agency's concern. Despite these urgings, Kennedy held off on authorizing the plan's implementation.

Overall, Kennedy hoped Cubans themselves would reject communism without U.S. intervention, but the president also had to consider the consequences of either supporting or holding back on the planned invasion. If he left the situation in Cuba as it was, he knew he would certainly face criticism for his failure to put a damper on the spread of communism. Furthermore, there was the issue of the exiles. If the plan was scrapped, the exiles would be free to travel around the country and Latin America, where it was likely they would expose the U.S.-backed attack.

On the other hand, if the plan was implemented and resulted in a failure, Kennedy was likely to pay a political price. As his advisor Ted Sorensen emphasized, there was no way to hide America's role if the invasion was unsuccessful. Even more troubling was the fact that a botched invasion would hurt the reputations of both America and his administration. Kennedy agreed with Sorensen; he believed an invasion in Cuba was inconsistent not only with his belief in a country's right to liberty but also with the founding values of the United States.

Approving the Plan

Although Kennedy remained skeptical about an invasion of Cuba, by early March he was forced to make a decision. The exiles forming the Cuban Brigade were ready to proceed, and the CIA received intelligence that the Soviet Union was planning to provide Castro with jet airplanes, which would give Cuba the advantage over the exiles. Once the jets arrived in Cuba, the exiles would need formal U.S. assistance to defeat Castro's forces.

Sorting Out the Details

Kennedy never considered the possibility of U.S. military assistance. More than anything, he wanted to keep his administration's role secret. The original plan called for the invasion to take place in the town of Trinidad in conjunction with a heavy assault from the hills and the air, but Kennedy was concerned it would be impossible to hide America's involvement. Kennedy voiced his doubts at a March 11 meeting with Allen Dulles, the director of the CIA, and Richard Bissell, the deputy director. He instructed them to formulate a less grandiose plan and insisted that the attack take place at night and without direct aid from the U.S. military.

A few days later, the CIA presented Kennedy with a new plan. The design proposed the invasion take place at the Bay of Pigs near the Zapata area, 100 miles west of Trinidad. The Zapata area was chosen for its airstrip and the natural resources, such as its swamps, which could provide essential defensive cover during combat. Once the invasion began, the CIA anticipated it would inspire a civil uprising within the country. In fact, the success of the plot depended on it, and Dulles and Bissell estimated a quarter of the Cuban people would back the assault. Again, Kennedy stressed that U.S. military involvement was prohibited. The CIA mistakingly believed Kennedy would certainly send in American troops if the success of the invasion was in jeopardy. Furthermore, even the Cuban Brigade was told that American forces would move in if they were losing the battle. On March 15, Kennedy approved the new plan but insisted that he be able to call it off up to twenty-four hours before it started.

THEY SAID...

"Why had he decided to go ahead? So far as the operation itself was concerned, he felt . . . that he had successfully pared it down from a grandiose amphibious assault to a mass infiltration. Accepting the CIA assurances about the escape hatch, he supposed that the cost, both military and political, of failure was now reduced to a tolerable level."

—Arthur Schlesinger, *A Thousand Days*

Doubting the Plan

Even after approving the plan, Kennedy remained skeptical. Dulles and Bissell continued to reassure him, but when the press began reporting about the recruitment of Cuban exiles in Miami, Florida, and about the planned invasion, it appeared that there was no way he could deny U.S. involvement once the plan was put into action. Furthermore, when journalist Joseph Newman reported about the enthusiastic support Castro enjoyed in Cuba, Kennedy had even more doubts about the predicted uprising. The CIA continued to assure him that a civil revolt would take place, but the reports raised serious concerns.

HE SAID...

"There will not be, under any conditions, an intervention in Cuba by the United States Armed Forces. . . . I intend to see that we adhere to that principle and as I understand it this administration's attitude is so understood and shared by the anti-Castro exiles from Cuba in this country."

To top it off, news of the plan had made its way to government officials. Senator William Fulbright, the chairman of the Foreign Relations Committee, heard of the plan and sent Kennedy a memo arguing against the invasion. Fulbright instead suggested that Kennedy implement a policy of containment. Arthur Schlesinger also tried to convince the president not to go ahead with the invasion, but Kennedy had finally come to terms with his decision to push ahead with the plan.

The Invasion: Operation Bumpy Road

The planning of the invasion moved ahead as preparations were made. Kennedy was still adamant that the U.S. military remain out of the assault. To reinforce his stance to the public, at an April 12 press conference, Kennedy reiterated the U.S. position. It was the policy of the government, Kennedy said, to stay out of any internal conflict in Cuba. Later that afternoon, he inquired in a meeting in the Cabinet room whether Cuban exiles were aware that U.S. military assistance would never be forthcoming. Kennedy was assured that they understood.

With the guidelines set, Kennedy was ready to proceed with the planned invasion, scheduled for April 17. He had just received information from a U.S. colonel that the 1,400 Cuban exiles in the brigade were well trained and ready to carry on. Unbeknownst to Kennedy, only 135 members of the brigade were soldiers. The rest included students, professionals, and peasants. They were inexperienced in battle, but they were ready for revenge.

An Unsuccessful Air Strike

Two air strikes were to take care of Castro's air power before the invasion commenced. On April 15, eight B-26s, flown by Cuban pilots, set out for Cuba from Puerto Cabezas, Nicaragua. They bombed three airfields, and all but one pilot returned to Nicaragua. The missing pilot landed in Key West due to engine trouble. His arrival in the United States put a damper on the CIA's elaborate cover story, which called for a ninth pilot to arrive in Miami and claim he had defected from the Cuban military and was responsible for the air strikes. The ninth pilot arrived as scheduled, but the presence of the missing pilot was a strong indication that America was involved.

Calling Off the Attack

With the unanticipated second plane in Key West, questions began to emerge. Adlai Stevenson, the U.S. Ambassador to the United Nations, unintentionally made matters worse when he told the UN General Assembly that the United States was not involved in the air strike. The press began poking holes in the story.

Kennedy and his advisors started to rethink the rest of the plan. A second air strike was planned to coincide with the ground beachfront invasion on April 17, but Secretary of State Dean Rusk became certain it was a terrible idea. He determined the plan could only work if it appeared that the planes were coming from the beach airstrip. Since there was no way to make this happen, the only course of action was to call off the second air strike. On April 16, Rusk contacted Kennedy and expressed his concern. A worried and depressed Kennedy agreed and immediately called off the air attack.

FACT

Cuban exile Miró Cardona was waiting in Miami for word of Castro's defeat. Cardona planned to step in as provisional president. Cardona had been a lawyer and professor at the University of Havana and an early supporter of Castro. During the early Castro regime, he was appointed the ambassador to the United States. He defected after Castro advanced his communist agenda.

Failure in Cuba

The ground invasion began badly when Cuban forces discovered the invaders on the beachfront before sunrise and destroyed the ship harboring the communication equipment and ten days' worth of ammunition. Castro thwarted the anticipated uprising by arresting 200,000 potential troublemakers. Cuban jets outgunned the brigade's obsolete B-26s, and Soviet-supplied tanks bore down on the invaders on the beach.

On the night of April 18, Kennedy met with his advisors. He agreed to permit unmarked U.S. Navy jets to cover the B-26s in a landing of supplies. If the B-26s were subjected to an air attack, the navy jets could defend them. By this time, the Cuban pilots were exhausted, and several of them declined to participate in the mission. In their place, civilian American pilots agreed to the assignment. Once more, everything went wrong.

Due to the difference between Nicaraguan and Cuban time zones, the B-26s arrived at the Bay of Pigs before the navy jets and four American pilots were killed. Kennedy declined any further direct U.S. intervention. Fighting continued until April 21. In the end, sixty-eight members of the Cuban brigade had died and the rest were captured and imprisoned.

The Burden of Defeat

Kennedy felt guilty about the Cuban exiles who had lost their lives and those who were captured by Castro's forces. He had miscalculated the potential success of the plan and sent them into danger. It was a difficult failure to accept.

Accepting Personal Responsibility for the Invasion

Nevertheless, Kennedy had to put his feelings aside to deal with the backlash. As commander-in-chief he took full responsibility for implementing the botched invasion. Even though the CIA had pushed the plan and it had widespread approval among his advisors, Kennedy alone had to take the blame. In speeches, he reiterated that he supported the Cuban brigade's cause and his conviction that the people of Cuba truly wanted freedom.

Besides taking credit for the disaster, Kennedy decided to make sure that Republicans would back him. First, he spoke with Richard Nixon, who agreed to lend his support. Next, he met with Eisenhower at Camp David where he was given the friendly advice to make sure that in the future all other similar endeavors were successful. Kennedy humbly took the advice, and Eisenhower issued a press statement that he supported Kennedy.

Facing Worldwide Criticism

Although Kennedy had managed to win the favor of powerful Republicans, winning over critics and the press was a near impossible task. The domestic press condemned him for his poor handling of the crisis.

These criticisms, although hurtful, were less of a concern then the ones printed in newspapers throughout the country and around the world. "Not much time remains for the education of John F. Kennedy. In his first great crisis, he bungled horribly," printed the *Charleston News and Courier*. The criticism in the international press was similarly scorching. Prior to the Bay of Pigs invasion, Kennedy had enjoyed respect for his ability as a competent leader in foreign affairs. His image was tarnished after the invasion. The *Frankfurter Neue Presse* stated that Kennedy was "politically and morally defeated."

Despite the bad press, Kennedy somehow survived. A Gallup poll taken at the end of April found Kennedy had an 83 percent approval rating. Furthermore, 65 percent of respondents believed it was inappropriate to send American troops to Cuba in an effort to overthrow Fidel Castro. Even more surprising was a separate Gallup poll that revealed 61 percent of the public agreed with how the president handled the Cuba situation.

HE SAID...

"The Cuban people have not yet spoken their final piece. . . . Meanwhile we will not accept Mr. Castro's attempts to blame this nation for the hatred which his onetime supporters now regard his repression."

The Lessons of Cuba

Although Kennedy had the support of a large segment of the American people, he knew there were valuable lessons to be learned from the Bay of Pigs fiasco. On April 21 he established a task force to uncover exactly what had happened. Critics questioned the objectivity of the task force, two members of which had been instrumental in the plan for the Bay of Pigs.

THEY SAID...

"He saw it as an episode, not as a cataclysm; and he was sure that the hope and confidence generated by the rest of the ninety days were entirely sufficient to absorb this error, if it were not repeated. He set quietly to work to make sure that nothing like the Bay of Pigs could happen to him again."

—Arthur Schlesinger, *A Thousand Days*

Nevertheless, the task force carried on with its investigation, focusing on what went wrong during the military operation. It determined the biggest mistake was underestimating Castro. He was organized and prepared, and the first air strike had failed to destroy his T-33 jets. In addition, he quickly neutralized the threat of civil unrest by containing potential adversaries. The task force also focused on future plans regarding Cuba. On June 13, its report summed up that any future goals should revolve around Castro's defeat. The report stayed away from expanding on any future plans.

After Kennedy had time to analyze the situation, he came to the conclusion that the press deserved some of the blame for the botched invasion. The press had reported about the raid before it occurred, and Kennedy believed this was how Castro learned of the attack. He needed the press, but at the same time, they sometimes made his task as president more difficult.

Kennedy learned some personal lessons from the incident. Both Allen Dulles and Richard Bissell had occupied their positions prior to his presidency, and their plan regarding Cuba only furthered his belief that the men he brought into the administration should become his closest and most trusted advisors. After the Bay of Pigs, Kennedy made sure that Bobby Kennedy and Ted Sorensen took part in his most important decisions. Furthermore, he called for changes within the CIA. Within a year, both Dulles and Bissell had been forced to resign.

Chapter 12

PROMOTING THE CAUSE OF FREEDOM

Kennedy was passionate about freedom, but he resisted advancing civil rights in the United States. Instead, he was preoccupied with keeping the world free from communism. He was realistic and knew he could never convert the Soviet Union to democracy, but he was optimistic that the United States and the Soviet Union could live together peacefully. This hope for peace nearly came to an end when a crisis over Berlin escalated to an almost uncontrollable level.

The Freedom Rides

Civil rights leaders were disgruntled over Kennedy's reluctance to propose civil rights legislation. Kennedy achieved smaller measures like the Area Redevelopment Act, but civil rights activists were unimpressed. In answer to their protests, Kennedy could only say that it was an inopportune time.

Forcing the Issue

In 1960, the Supreme Court ruled in *Boynton v. Virginia* that segregation in interstate travel was unconstitutional, but in 1961 blacks were still relegated to substandard restrooms and restaurants at bus and train terminals. Leaders of the Congress of Racial Equality planned an interracial Freedom Ride for the spring of 1961 to force the federal government to uphold the Supreme Court ruling.

FACT

The KKK was originally a social fraternity organized in 1866. One year later, it became a parliamentary force dedicated to thwarting the establishment of Republican governments in the south during Reconstruction. By 1871, the KKK had faded away but it reemerged as a strong force at various times, including World War I and the civil rights era.

The Freedom Riders set out on Greyhound and Trailways buses on their journey from Washington, D.C., to New Orleans. They encountered relatively little resistance until they reached Alabama on May 14. Mobs led by the Ku Klux Klan attacked the Freedom Riders and firebombed one of the buses. Local law enforcement failed to offer protection.

The next morning, news of the violent attack was plastered across the front pages of newspapers across the country. Bobby Kennedy and the Justice Department had been notified of the Freedom Rides before they began, but it was news to the president. The administration was just starting to recover from the Bay of Pigs fiasco, and Kennedy was preparing for a trip to Europe to meet with

Khrushchev for the first time. He was dismayed with this latest negative publicity for the country. His asked his trusted civil rights aide Harris Wofford to influence his "goddamned friends" to call off the Freedom Ride. Wofford had no power over the riders and was at a loss to do anything to affect the outcome.

Protecting the Riders

The riders were determined to continue, but they soon learned from Bobby Kennedy that no bus driver was willing to drive. It also appeared that more violence would result from continuing the rides. Radio broadcasts announced a foreboding statement made by Alabama Governor John Patterson: "[T]he citizens of the state are so enraged that I cannot guarantee protection for this bunch of rabble-rousers." The Freedom Riders decided to call off the ride and fly from Birmingham to New Orleans for a concluding celebratory rally scheduled for May 17. The airport, however, proved even less safe than the bus. Bomb threats trapped the riders inside. Bobby sent his assistant John Seigenthaler to help the stranded riders. The situation was resolved and the group reached New Orleans in time for the rally. But it wasn't over. A group of ten dedicated riders decided to resume the rides. They left from Nashville and reached Birmingham on May 17.

FACT
President Kennedy made his first state visit outside the country between May 16 and May 18, 1961. He went to Ottawa, Canada, to press Canadian legislators on their hesitance to join the Organization of American States and their opposition to the U.S. plan to position nuclear weapons in Canada. Canadian Prime Minister John Diefenbaker did not budge on the issues, and Kennedy left after making an appeal to Parliament.

When the ten riders reached Birmingham, they were swiftly taken into custody and arrested. Officials insisted the riders were being jailed for their own protection, and they did not remain in custody. Police Commissioner Bull Connor escorted the group to the Alabama-Tennessee border and left them there, warning them not to come back. They did. They drove to Birmingham and tried to catch a bus to Montgomery.

This latest newsworthy disaster put an already uneasy Kennedy in an even worse mood. Early in the morning, still dressed in his pajamas, he met in his bedroom with Bobby, Burke Marshall, and Byron White to discuss how to proceed. They decided it was unwise to nationalize the Alabama National Guard. Instead, Governor John Patterson was recruited to protect the riders. At first, he was an unwilling participant, even evading Kennedy's calls. In the end, Bobby threatened that if Patterson refused to protect the Freedom Riders, federal troops would. This was enough to get Patterson's attention.

THEY SAID...

"We can't act as nursemaids to agitators. . . . You see, they [are] always seeking the help of the police to protect them, but they are the first to criticize the police when the police are unable to protect them. And you just can't guarantee the safety of a fool, and that's what these folks are, just fools."

—Governor John Patterson

Next, Bobby had to find a driver for the bus. When the bus company supervisor in Birmingham claimed that a bus driver was unavailable, Bobby angrily demanded the supervisor call someone, even Mr. Greyhound himself. Bobby's tactics worked, and on May 20, under the protection of state troopers, the riders began their journey to Montgomery. When they arrived in Montgomery, state troopers withdrew their protection. As the riders emerged from the bus, they were attacked by a white mob that beat them with clubs, bats, and chains.

Bobby immediately contacted his brother, who made the decision to send federal marshals for protection. Martin Luther King Jr. was on his way to Montgomery to speak at Ralph Abernathy's First Baptist Church, and Patterson warned he wasn't sure if he could protect King. King arrived on May 21 and was escorted by marshals to the church. As King spoke to the crowd of more than 1,000 inside, a white mob slowly encircled the building. Federal marshals were stationed outside, but the mob managed to break some windows with rocks.

THEY SAID...

"Oh, there are fists, punching. A bunch of men led by a guy with a bleeding face are beating them. There are no cops. It's terrible. It's terrible. There's not a cop in sight. People are yelling, 'Get 'em, get 'em.' It's awful."

—John Doar, giving a live eyewitness account of the scene in Montgomery to Bobby Kennedy

In the meantime, tear gas was used to hold off the mob until the National Guard arrived. King and the participants remained trapped inside the church, and even the National Guard could not calm the mob enough to let the worshipers leave the church until the early morning hours of May 22.

THEY SAID...

"Kennedy knew better than to echo former President Truman's remark that the Freedom Riders ought to stay home. . . . But he was irritated by their tactics and preoccupied with planning his coming trip to Europe; they had already changed his agenda and produced an intervention in the South he had hoped to avoid."

—Harris Wofford, *Of Kennedys and Kings*

HE SAID...

"We stand for freedom. That is our conviction for ourselves—that is our only commitment to others. No friend, no neutral and no adversary should think otherwise. We are not against any man—or any nation—or any system—except as it is hostile to freedom."

Bobby Kennedy hoped that this was the last of the rides. But on May 24, the riders continued their crusade. When they were arrested in Jackson, Mississippi, Bobby publicly requested in an NBC interview that the rides have a cooling-off period while he worked on securing the release of those arrested. James Farmer of the Congress of Racial Equality, the group that organized the rides, responded that blacks had spent the last few hundred years cooling off, and "[i]f we got any cooler we'd be in a deep freeze." King stood behind Farmer's position and also refused to support a suspension of the rides.

Refusing to Publicly Condemn Discrimination

The president began to feel the pressure to make a statement in support of civil rights. He met with activist and actor Harry Belafonte, who urged him to speak out publicly in support of the Freedom Rides. Harris Wofford believed the president needed to address the nation on the moral issue of discrimination. Wofford even appealed to Kennedy's strong interest in foreign affairs and the positive effect it could have in that area.

Kennedy, however, remained strongly opposed to such an action. He still believed that he had done as much as he could possibly do, especially after May 29, when Bobby Kennedy announced he had submitted a petition to the Interstate Commerce Commission requesting the creation of regulations forbidding segregation in interstate travel facilities. If this was not enough, asked Kennedy, what more could he do to please civil rights proponents?

A Second State of the Union Address

Despite the Freedom Rides, Kennedy remained focused on international affairs, specifically keeping the world free from the spread of communism. He decided to deliver a mid-year State of the Union Address. Kennedy entitled his May 25, 1961, speech "Special Message to the Congress on Urgent National Needs."

The address began with a statement of the importance of promoting freedom—freedom from communism, not freedom from racial prejudice. Kennedy asked for an additional $2 billion tacked onto the current military budget of $2.4 billion. The money would pay for more weapons, more marines, and the creation of bomb shelters.

Next, Kennedy addressed the need to surpass the Soviets in space exploration. Landing a man on the moon, according to Kennedy, was imperative in the face of Soviet space advancements. This had not always been Kennedy's stance on the space program. In fact, he had contemplated discontinuing the National Aeronautics and Space Administration (NASA), but with his vice president a strong backer of the program, he had decided otherwise. Yuri Gagarin of the Soviet Union had become the first person to orbit Earth in April, and Kennedy decided the American space program was more crucial than ever. Kennedy informed Congress that in order to beat the Soviet Union in space, NASA would need $7 to $9 billion. Kennedy's remarks were met with enthusiastic applause.

President Kennedy, Jacqueline Kennedy, and Vice President Johnson watch a television broadcast of the liftoff of astronaut Alan Shepard on the first U.S. manned suborbital flight.

Photo credit: Cecil Stoughton, White House/John F. Kennedy Presidential Library and Museum, Boston

Meeting with President de Gaulle in France

Kennedy embarked on his first trip to Europe as president of the United States at the end of May 1961. He arrived in Paris to spend some time with France's popular leader, President Charles de Gaulle, before meeting with Khrushchev.

The meeting with de Gaulle was important. De Gaulle was intent on making France a world power, and Kennedy was concerned with his desire to acquire nuclear weapons. The French president was no longer satisfied with protection from the United States; he did not trust the Americans to keep their word on protecting Europe from communism. De Gaulle requested that the United States provide France with the technology needed to develop a defense system.

Receiving a Royal Welcome

Kennedy and Jackie arrived in Paris on May 31. He had antici-pated a somewhat hostile welcome from de Gaulle, but de Gaulle, well known for his insistence on speaking French to foreign guests, uncharacteristically greeted him in English. The red carpet at the airplane door, the roses, and the escort of fifty uniformed police officers on motorcycles underscored the importance of the event.

As they left Orly Airport, the Kennedys were greeted by crowds lining the streets in hopes of catching a glimpse of the American president and his beautiful wife. The First Lady's presence in France contributed to the warm reception. Jackie spoke fluent French, and de Gaulle enjoyed her company and noted her charm. She also intrigued the French press, which referred to her as a "queen." Even Kennedy noted the attention Jackie received, commenting at a press luncheon that he was the "man who accompanied Jacqueline Kennedy to Paris."

The Meeting with de Gaulle

Kennedy, however, held his own when it came to de Gaulle. Although he was young in comparison to the seventy-year-old de Gaulle, the elder statesman soon realized that Kennedy was well prepared for their meeting. If de Gaulle had thought he could exploit Kennedy's youth to get him to accept his proposal for shared military power in Europe, he soon realized he was mistaken. Kennedy gave de Gaulle the same answers Eisenhower had, assuring the French leader that the United States would defend France from an attack by the Soviet Union.

Their discussion moved on to the topic of West Berlin. This was Kennedy's real concern. Kennedy proposed that he make some concessions with the Soviets on West Berlin as long as the three powers continued to have military access. De Gaulle, however, disagreed. He believed that there was no need to negotiate with the Soviets. He asserted that the Soviet Union wanted to avoid war as much as the United States did, and a U.S. presence in West Berlin was crucial.

QUESTION
How did the Berlin dispute between the Soviets and the three allies arise?

After World War II, the Soviets, in control of East Berlin and East Germany, created a communist government. The United States, Great Britain, and France occupied West Berlin and West Germany and helped establish a democratic government. In 1952, East Germany closed off access to West Germany, but escape to the west was still possible through West Berlin.

The Assassination of Rafael Trujillo

Kennedy's meeting with de Gaulle was going well until he received information that the Dominican Republic's dictator, General Rafael Trujillo, had been assassinated. When Kennedy became president he had learned of a CIA plot to kill Trujillo; Eisenhower had already approved the shipment of weapons by the CIA to the dissidents who planned the assassination. After the Bay of Pigs fiasco, Kennedy was hesitant to take any part in another potentially horrific plan. Nevertheless, the plan and the weapons were already in place.

When Kennedy heard of it, the assassination had not yet been confirmed by U.S. sources, nor had the information spread to the press. Kennedy preferred to keep it quiet, but White House press secretary Pierre Salinger was not aware that the news was internal. At an evening press briefing, Salinger casually responded to a question regarding Dean Rusk's whereabouts, telling reporters that he was dealing with the situation in the Dominican Republic.

FACT

Thirty-one years before Rafael Trujillo's assassination, the United States had been instrumental in placing him in power in the Dominican Republic. Trujillo owned 60 percent of the country's assets, which were comprised mostly of sugar cane fields. He had enjoyed aid from the United States until it was cut off following his attempt to take down Venezuela's Romulo Betancourt. This led Trujillo into talks with Fidel Castro.

Trujillo's assassination and Salinger's misstep could not have come at a worse time. Nevertheless, de Gaulle and Kennedy continued on as planned. They had dinner together, attended a performance by the Paris Opera Ballet, and continued their discussion. By the end of Kennedy's stay in Paris, he had won over de Gaulle's confidence in America. Although de Gaulle still viewed Kennedy's inexperience as a disadvantage, he saw that the American president represented the new generation of leadership. Kennedy left Paris after three days with a good feeling about his time with de Gaulle.

Meeting with Khrushchev

Kennedy was anxious for his meeting with Khrushchev in Vienna. His priority was Berlin. The Soviets were mulling over the prospect of signing a peace treaty with East Germany. This would create an independent state with the power to take the city under its control and terminate allied occupation.

The First Summit Meeting

It was an important meeting, and Kennedy felt well prepared. On June 3, he arrived in Vienna to crowds of cheering Austrians and made his way to the home of H. Freeman Matthews, the U.S. Ambassador to Austria. Khrushchev arrived at 12:45 P.M. and the two leaders greeted each other with a firm handshake. Photographers captured the image of the short, stocky sixty-seven-year-old Khrushchev next to Kennedy's trim and youthful physique. Kennedy and Khrushchev proceeded inside to the music room.

Their discussion soon turned serious. Kennedy suggested that both nations were responsible to ensure that their competitiveness in the same geographic areas never led to a direct confrontation. Khrushchev jumped at the chance to reprimand Kennedy. He asserted that communism was a viable system that, just like democracy, had a right to develop. Kennedy responded that it was the Soviets who were trying to destroy America's influence. A combative Khrushchev acknowledged very little of Kennedy's response and instead asserted that ideas could not be suppressed. As for the spread of communism, according to the chairman, he could give no guarantee that it would stop at the Soviet borders.

THEY SAID...

"In the past, U.S. Presidents . . . have never fared too well in face-to-face meetings with Soviet dictators—even when the U.S. was dealing from strength. There was no doubt that Jack Kennedy, his New Frontier policies currently in a state of some disarray, was taking a chance. But Kennedy felt confident that he could look Khrushchev squarely in the eye and effectively warn him that despite recent reverses, neither the President nor the U.S. could safely be pushed around."

—*Time* magazine, May 26, 1961

Kennedy and Khrushchev emerged from the meeting for lunch. Although the chairman had done most of the talking, Kennedy needed a break. The discussion had gone badly for the president, who could hardly get in a word. The two men sat down to lunch together, and the press glimpsed them getting along marvelously.

When they returned to the music room, Kennedy tried to reiterate his earlier point that confrontation was unproductive for each side. The possibility of a nuclear war, he asserted, was something both countries should work to avoid. Khrushchev quickly took control of the conversation, alleging that it was America who was responsible for intervening in conflicts in other countries. He proceeded to give Kennedy a long list of various countries subject to American intervention. Kennedy managed to elicit an agreement to later negotiate a settlement on Laos. Both sides agreed on the importance of a cease-fire in Laos and agreed to a neutral Laos.

FACT

During an Austrian state dinner, Jackie Kennedy mentioned to Khrushchev that one of the dogs involved in the Soviet space program had had puppies. She expressed an interest in having a puppy, and two months later a small dog name Pushinka entered the Kennedys' lives.

Kennedy reflected on the day's discussion and angrily concluded that Khrushchev had treated him "like a little boy." Even his staff was surprised by Kennedy's poor performance. They had warned Kennedy that the chairman was explosive, but they had believed that when it came to the topic of communism, Kennedy was equipped to hold his own in the debate. They could only trust that the following day's meeting would turn out better.

The Second Summit Meeting

On June 4 at 10:15 A.M., Kennedy arrived at the Soviet Embassy for his second meeting with the feisty chairman. This time Kennedy wanted to put to rest the debate over communism and capitalism, stating that neither of them would be convinced to switch sides. He got right down to business with the discussion about a ban on nuclear testing. Khrushchev assured Kennedy that the Soviets had no plans to become the first to resume the testing that had ended three years before, but that an agreement to a treaty which would subject them to UN

HE SAID...

"Mr. Khrushchev and I had a very full and frank exchange of views on the major issues that now divide our two countries. I will tell you now that it was a very sober two days. There was no discourtesy, no loss of tempers, no threats or ultimatums by either side. . . . No spectacular progress was either achieved or pretended."

inspections was out of the question. Khrushchev would consider a test ban treaty if it included a general disarmament agreement and a provision for the UN's leadership to become a three-pronged directorate with a communist, a Westerner, and a neutral chairman.

Finally, the subject of Berlin came up. Khrushchev was clearly angered by the topic. East Berliners and East Germans had been fleeing to West Berlin to seek a better future away from communism. Khrushchev wanted to put a stop to the flight. Also on his mind was the possibility of a U.S.-backed unified Germany, which he was staunchly opposed to. Khrushchev announced his intent to sign a peace treaty with East Germany, which would terminate U.S. access to Berlin. Once signed, any violation of it would be interpreted as an act of aggression.

Kennedy explained that Western Europe was vital to U.S. national security. If the United States abandoned West Berlin, it would also abandon Europe. Kennedy protested that the peace treaty was contrary to the 1945 agreement between the four allies, which granted them all access to Berlin. America would not accept the agreement. If the United States wanted to start a war over the matter, responded Khrushchev, then it was Kennedy's choice. He

HE SAID...

"The signing of a peace treaty is not a belligerent act. . . . However, a peace treaty denying us our contractual rights is a belligerent act. . . . The U.S. is committed to that area and it is so regarded by all of the world. If we accepted Mr. Khrushchev's suggestion, the world would lose confidence in the U.S. and would not regard it as a serious country."

planned on signing the treaty at the end of the year, regardless of how Kennedy felt about it.

On that note, the meeting came to an abrupt end. After lunch and a ceremony the men parted ways; but it was temporary. Kennedy was concerned about their last exchange regarding Berlin and requested a ten-minute meeting with the chairman. Kennedy reiterated that the treaty was not the issue, but he was worried that the termination of the occupation rights in West Berlin would cause friction. Khrushchev stood firm on his decision to sign the treaty. It was up to the United States to choose whether or not to start a war over it. The Soviet Union was prepared to defend itself against American attack.

The Berlin Crisis

Kennedy knew that Khrushchev had defeated him. He felt the faulty Bay of Pigs invasion had given the chairman the idea that he was inexperienced and stupid. Overall he had come into the discussion believing that reason and compromise would win out, but Khrushchev had been unwilling to budge from his position. Kennedy had a hard time believing that the chairman really intended to go to war over Berlin; nevertheless, wars, he knew, had been waged over far less, and he was aware that the situation was serious.

After Vienna

When he returned to Washington on June 6, Kennedy addressed the American people and congressional leaders about the situation in Berlin. He was clear in his televised address about its gravity, and he read excerpts of the talks to the congressional leaders. Four days later, Khrushchev decided to test the waters. He released an aide-mémoire, which defined his position on signing a treaty with East Germany. On June 15, in a televised address to his country-men, Khrushchev urged the adoption of the peace treaty. The situation worsened when Walter Ulbricht, the leader of East Germany, announced that he planned to eliminate U.S. access to Berlin.

THEY SAID...

"I 'feel in my bones' that President Kennedy is going to fail to produce any real leadership. The American press and public are beginning to feel the same. In a few weeks they may turn to us. We must be ready. Otherwise we may drift to disaster over Berlin—a terrible diplomatic defeat or (out of sheer incompetence) a nuclear war."

—Harold Macmillan, prime minister of Great Britain, as quoted in *President Kennedy*

Doubts about Kennedy's Leadership

Kennedy was unmoved by either declaration. Although Berlin was constantly at the forefront of his concerns, he remained silent. His debilitating back problems and a bout with a sore throat and a fever kept him out of the public eye. His silence, however, was of little comfort to the press, who interpreted it as disengagement with the situation. At a press conference on June 28, Kennedy only stated that the threat of cutting off access to West Berlin was a serious one. When asked about the U.S. plan of attack, Kennedy declared that plans were still under consideration. In truth, there was a battle of ideas going on in the administration. On one side were those who advised the president to seek negotiation and military preparation; others advocated intimidation with a military buildup.

Kennedy's July 25 televised speech renewed the American public's faith that the president was determined to fight to preserve its rights. In the address, he stated that the United States was ready to defend its legal rights in West Berlin. In preparation, Kennedy announced that he planned on requesting an additional $3.25 billion from Congress. The American public was pleased with his stance. Kennedy was surprised by polls that showed 60 percent of the public believed that the end result was war—not negotiations—if the Soviets refused to back down.

The Erection of the Berlin Wall

Khrushchev publicly responded to Kennedy's speech with his own threats. Kennedy, predicted the chairman, was going to be the last president of the United States. Behind the scenes, Khrushchev advised negotiation in an effort to play both sides. Nevertheless, Khrushchev did not wait for negotiation or nuclear war. On August 13, 1961, East Germany erected barriers, which eventually became a wall, between East and West Berlin. Although the wall caught the Kennedy administration by surprise, Kennedy had wondered beforehand why Khrushchev had not considered a border.

Sending Support to West Berlin

The appearance of the Berlin Wall prevented the flow of humanity from East to West Berlin, but it also averted a potential showdown between the Soviets and Americans. The situation was not quite over. West Berlin wanted U.S. military reinforcements in the city. Kennedy decided to send additional troops, and he also dispatched Johnson. The vice president flew to West Germany's Bonn airport on August 18, where he was greeted by an excited crowd. He assured the gathering that America was committed to fulfilling its obligation to Berlin. The following day, Johnson

HE SAID...

"When I ran for the presidency of the United States, I knew that this country faced serious challenges, but I could not realize—nor could any man realize who does not bear the burdens of this office—how heavy and constant would be those burdens."

watched as the 1,600 American troops who filed into West Berlin were welcomed with flowers and tears.

Johnson's trip lifted the heavy mood in West Berlin, but Khrushchev viewed the trip and display differently. On August 30, he announced that nuclear testing would resume. Kennedy was angered by this declaration. He called Khrushchev a liar for having told him at the second summit meeting that the Soviet Union would not begin any more nuclear tests. Nevertheless, letters and intermediaries on both sides conveyed a desire for negotiation over the following months.

HE SAID...

"So long as the communists insist that they are preparing to end by themselves unilaterally our rights in West Berlin and our commitments to its people, we must be prepared to defend those rights and those commitments. We will at times be ready to talk, if talk will help. But we must also be ready to resist with force, if force is used upon us. Either alone would fail. Together, they can serve the cause of freedom and peace."

Kennedy still wanted to ensure that Khrushchev never forgot U.S. nuclear superiority. In a speech to the UN on October 21, Deputy Defense Secretary Roswell Gilpatric declared the superiority of U.S. power. On October 23, Khrushchev had a message for the president—the detonation of a thirty-megaton nuclear bomb. Kennedy believed that he had little choice but to renew U.S. testing.

Chapter 13

PROTECTING THE AMERICAN PEOPLE

Kennedy weathered both domestic and international crises in his first eight months in office. The Soviets' refusal to agree to a test ban treaty led to the resumption of U.S. testing, and a potential communist takeover in South Vietnam led to the reluctant decision to send American advisors to the faltering country. At home, the nation's well-being was tested by steel companies who wanted to raise prices and by segregationists who wanted to stop integration.

Operation Mongoose

Even with all of the chaos surrounding Berlin, Kennedy had not forgotten Fidel Castro. In November 1961, he initiated a covert CIA-sponsored operation to take down Fidel Castro from within Cuba.

Assassination plots had been contemplated during the latter part of Eisenhower's presidency, and Kennedy now considered it too. Bobby Kennedy recruited CIA operative Edward Lansdale to head the operation. The attorney general made deposing Castro a personal crusade, and the Kennedy administration spent millions of dollars on the program, which included building a spy base in Miami.

President Kennedy confers with Attorney General Robert Kennedy.

Photo credit: Robert Knudsen, White House/John F. Kennedy Presidential Library and Museum, Boston

In a November 1961 discussion with reporter Tad Szulc, the president asked the *New York Times* journalist point-blank what he would think of an American-sponsored attempt on Castro's life. Szulc, who had an intimate knowledge of the island nation and its leader, replied that it was an action that would in all probability do nothing to change Cuba. Szulc's notes from the meeting indicate Kennedy was opposed to killing Castro and he was only entertaining the thought because he was under immense pressure to give the order.

THEY SAID...

"My idea is to stir things up on island with espionage, sabotage, general disorder, run & operated by Cubans themselves with every group but Batistaites & Communists. Do not know if we will be successful in overthrowing Castro but we have nothing to lose in my estimate."

—Bobby Kennedy, in his notes from a November 1961 meeting

Nuclear Testing and Civil Defense

In November 1961, it became clear that the Soviets had no intention of discontinuing nuclear testing. Their detonation of a fifty-megaton bomb and the performance of atmospheric tests were unmistakable evidence of their stance on a test ban treaty. Nevertheless, Kennedy was hesitant to resume testing, but the pressure to do so was mounting. Gallup polls showed that Americans overwhelmingly supported it. In addition, the Joint Chiefs of Staff, Congress, and the Atomic Energy Commission all wanted the United States to resume testing.

Promoting Civil Defense

With the possibility of nuclear war, Kennedy believed that it was important for the nation to become prepared. He enthusiastically supported a civil defense and fallout shelter program. In a September letter published in *Life* magazine, Kennedy advised readers on survival tips. The article entitled "You Could Be Among the 97% to Survive If You Follow Advice in These Pages" was an unrealistic assessment of the likelihood of survival. Kennedy's science advisers informed him that his analysis would provide false hope, but Kennedy insisted that as long as some were saved, it was worth it.

Despite the unlikely success of the program, Kennedy urged governors to take civil defense seriously and instructed the Pentagon to create a pamphlet discussing the steps to take for survival. In its draft form, its suggestions—just like Kennedy's article—were unrealistic. Even more troubling, only the affluent were able to build fallout shelters, and newspapers reported on the buildup of

HE SAID...

"Today, every inhabitant of this planet must contemplate the day when this planet may no longer be inhabitable. Every man, woman, and child lives under a nuclear sword of Damocles, hanging by the slenderest of threads, capable of being cut at any moment by accident or miscalculation or madness. The weapons of war must be abolished before they abolish us."

weapons among New Jersey and California suburbanites who were preparing to fend off nearby city dwellers from using their shelters.

Finally, Kennedy heeded his advisors' cautionary words. After he met with nuclear scientist Edward Teller, he was at last convinced that his program was doing more harm than good. According to Teller, planning for a nuclear war was much more complicated. He advised Kennedy that a viable program required digging deeper shelters to accommodate the bigger Soviet bombs. With that, Kennedy quietly left the civil defense program alone. The Pentagon brochure was revised to provide a more realistic outlook of surviving a nuclear bomb and its distribution was less significant than had been planned.

Deciding to Resume Testing

Kennedy preferred the continued halt, but he could not bear the thought of standing still while the Soviets moved forward in nuclear weapons technology. He hoped to gain British prime minister Harold Macmillan's support when the two leaders met in Bermuda in December 1961, but Macmillan was also reluctant to resume nuclear testing. The Kennedy administration continued to push Macmillan, and in March Kennedy made a televised announcement that U.S. nuclear testing would resume on Christmas Island instead of Nevada unless the Soviets agreed to a nuclear test ban treaty. The Soviets immediately rejected the proposal, labeling it "completely unacceptable." Kennedy hoped the testing would demonstrate to the Soviet Union the superiority of American nuclear power and increase the pressure to negotiate a test ban treaty.

Providing Aid to South Vietnam

The Eisenhower administration had instituted a policy supporting South Vietnam's campaign against communist North Vietnam, but a South Vietnamese defeat was emerging as a dangerous possibility. Kennedy was committed to Eisenhower's policy, but he wished to avoid sending in U.S. troops, despite suggestions from advisors who insisted that a military intervention could succeed with careful planning.

Supporting a Financial Aid Policy

Kennedy promised enough financial assistance to South Vietnam's Ngo Dinh Diem to expand Diem's army from 170,000 to 200,000 troops. Official estimates in the summer of 1961 noted an alarming increase in the Viet Cong's guerilla forces, but Kennedy's advisors were confident that Diem could hold off the communists with 200,000 troops for the present.

FACT

The Viet Cong, also known as the National Front for the Liberation of South Vietnam, were guerilla troops supported by North Vietnam and their South Vietnamese sympathizers. Their name, which means Vietnamese Communist, was given to them by the Diem regime.

Kennedy preferred that U.S. military forces remain outside of the conflict. He feared that in the end it would turn into a long and drawn-out battle. In addition, on prior occasions he had advocated independence for nations, and to intervene militarily would cast America as a country committed to neocolonialism rather than freedom.

The Taylor Report

In the fall of 1961, General Maxwell Taylor visited Vietnam and issued a report to the president in favor of intervention. The Joint Chiefs, the CIA, and the State and Defense departments supported the plan. It recommended the implementation of an emergency plan; more specifically, it urged the United States to supply military assistance to South Vietnam if the strife continued. It recommended that the United States engage in a limited partnership with South Vietnam. The Vietnamese forces were responsible for defeating the Viet Cong, but U.S. forces could partner with the Vietnamese to instruct them on how to win the war. The report recommended that between 6,000 and 8,000 combat and logistic troops be assigned to the cause. Overall, the Taylor report concluded, the United States must remain present in order to fend off communism and demonstrate America's commitment to halting its spread.

The report's opponents argued that Diem himself was part of the problem and chances for success were slim as long as he remained in power. Diem was significantly unpopular and had already survived one coup attempt in November 1960, and his corruption and repressive measures contributed to the instability within his regime. Taylor's report had touched upon these issues but favored keeping Diem in power in hopes that U.S. influence would convince Diem to make changes in the way he governed.

Agreeing to Send U.S. Advisers to Vietnam

Kennedy still preferred financial aid as opposed to military support. Secretary of State Dean Rusk agreed with Kennedy that it was up to the Vietnamese to fight their own battle, and Kennedy found support from four other allies: Senate Majority Leader Mike Mansfield, economic advisor John Kenneth Galbraith, Undersecretary of State George Ball, and Averell Harriman, the assistant secretary of state for Far Eastern affairs. All of them agreed it would be disastrous to send troops. Ball advised Kennedy that doing so would be "a tragic error."

Nonetheless, Kennedy did not want to risk giving up territory to the communists. At a November 11 meeting, Kennedy emphasized that sending troops was a last resort. In the end, he concluded that sending advisers was the best course of action. The resulting contingency plan called for sending U.S. forces to support the South Vietnamese without joining in direct combat—except in the case of a communist military intervention. On November 15, Kennedy sent a message to Diem committing to a joint effort. The United States promised military equipment and increased personnel and requested that military decisions be made jointly.

HE SAID...

"We have increased our assistance to the government—its logistics; we have not sent combat troops there, although the training missions that we have there have been instructed if they are fired upon to—they would of course fire back, to protect themselves. But we have not sent combat troops in the generally understood sense of the word."

In theory, Kennedy's plan that U.S. forces remain out of combat could work. However, the reality was that the Vietnamese forces were unequipped to handle the Viet Cong without direct instruction on antiguerrilla combat tactics. American advisers often accompanied Vietnamese forces and even participated in combat. Furthermore, because South Vietnamese pilots were unable to fly the newest types of planes, American pilots often flew them instead.

Denying U.S. Involvement

In spite of Washington's warning to Diem to only give the press routine access regarding military operations, war correspondents quickly realized that American troops were more involved than the White House had let on. On January 12, 1962, American advisers participated in their first combat mission against the Viet Cong. In Operation Chopper, American pilots transported 1,000 South Vietnamese troops to a Viet Cong stronghold near Saigon. The secrecy and the restriction on press access aroused suspicion.

Nonetheless, at a press conference on January 15, Kennedy denied that American troops were involved in combat when reporters pressed him.

The presence of 3,500 U.S. troops in Vietnam lent little support to Kennedy's claim. Additionally, combat operations with names like "Sunrise" could hardly hide the fact that U.S. involvement was more than just advisory. These Americanized names were a clear indication to the press that the United States was behind the planning, not the South Vietnamese. American officers were also openly discussing their involvement in planning combat operations. Consequently, the press felt free to report that American participation was not simply continuing but was increasing in magnitude.

Pressuring the Steel Companies

On January 11, 1962, Kennedy delivered his state of the union address. In it, he stressed the importance of focusing on a strong economy. America was an example to the rest of the world that a free economy could also be a stable economy. The economy was in a fragile position, so Kennedy took great interest in the rise in steel prices. Steel prices had consistently risen, but a 40 percent increase in the Wholesale Price Index, the index used to measure the change in the price of commodities prior to its sale in the retail market, between 1947 and 1958 was a direct result of the unorthodox rise in steel prices. In comparison to the average increase of other prices, steel prices had climbed at a much faster rate. Kennedy believed a further rise in steel prices could threaten overall price stability. When Walter Heller, the chairman of the Council of Economic Advisors, informed him that an increase in steel prices could result in a rise in inflation and an economic slowdown, Kennedy quickly took note.

Background on the Steel Industry

After Kennedy learned of an upcoming renegotiation between steel companies and the Steelworkers Union, he quickly went to work securing the cooperation of the parties. Kennedy feared that a sharp rise in steelworker wages would threaten the stability of the economy. In the past, increased steel prices often coincided with wage increases. In fact, it was U.S. Steel's president Benjamin Fairless in 1948 who openly confessed that higher employment costs called for increased steel prices in order to meet the new cost of business.

However, a wage increase would most likely come after a strike. It was anticipated that a strike by steelworkers would result in a half a million workers walking off the job. Without the workers, steel production, a critical cornerstone of the American economy, would come to a crippling halt. Steel was in high demand and was used in such areas as the defense industry and by automobile and appliance manufacturers. "Steel," Walter Heller explained to Kennedy, "bulks so large in the manufacturing sector of the economy, that it can upset the applecart all by itself."

For Kennedy, it was a matter of national interest, and he hoped that the steel industry would place the interest of the nation above its own. In September 1961, he had sent out letters to the union and the steel companies asking them not to raise prices and seeking their cooperation in negotiating a reasonable wage increase. In October, Kennedy was content when the price of steel remained the same. He had another victory when U.S. Steel began negotiation with the union. A deal was made on April 6, 1962. No wage increase was agreed upon, but steelworkers would enjoy an increase in their pension contributions. Within days, the other steel companies also adopted similar contracts.

A Crisis in the Steel Industry

Kennedy was immensely pleased that a strike had been averted and that national interests had won out. Nevertheless, it was only a temporary victory. On April 10, he received an unexpected visitor to the White House. Roger Blough, the chairman of the board at U.S. Steel, delivered devastating news. U.S. Steel had just released a press statement that it planned to raise the price of steel by 3.5 percent. Kennedy was shocked and unable to contain his anger. He felt that he had been double-crossed. Blough's only response was that the company had never agreed to keep prices the same.

HE SAID...

"[A]t a time when restraint and sacrifice are being asked of every citizen, the American people will find it hard, as I do, to accept a situation in which a tiny handful of steel executives whose pursuit of private power and profit exceeds their sense of public responsibility can show such utter contempt for the interests of 185 million Americans."

In a matter of hours the situation worsened. Five other steel companies announced their intent to raise prices. In a public statement on April 11, Kennedy condemned the steel companies for their lack of commitment to the nation's best interest. When Blough decided to respond with his own press conference the next day, Kennedy inundated reporters with hard questions to ask him. Blough was subjected to questions regarding the motivation for not raising prices under the Republican administration and was also grilled about why he never denied the prior news reports that an agreement had been reached not to raise prices.

Kennedy took further action against the six defiant steel companies. The government had contracts with U.S. Steel and Lukens Steel to provide $5.5 million in steel for the Polaris submarines. He immediately gave the order to Lukens, which remained among the steel companies that had not yet raised prices. It was decided to place pressure on the five other steel companies that intended to increase prices; 9 percent of steel's total business came from the U.S. government, so the government's remaining steel orders would go to the six companies that refused to raise prices.

Next, Bobby Kennedy became involved, his interest piqued by a news story in the *Washington Star* that indicated U.S. Steel had pressured Bethlehem Steel to raise its prices. Bobby believed this provided evidence of illegal price fixing. He ordered the collection of evidence—both personal and professional—from the homes and offices of steel executives, and FBI agents arrived at steel executives' homes in the middle of the night on April 12.

Blough was the last to falter under government pressure. On April 13, beginning with Inland Steel, all of the steel companies informed the White House of their decision to refrain from price increases. Blough was the toughest holdout. That same day, he relayed a message to the president through an intermediary that he was ready to deal. Blough believed he had enough leeway to enact a partial increase, but Kennedy responded that any increase was unacceptable and Blough relented. In a press statement, Blough announced that the price increase was no longer in effect.

Kennedy's victory, however, soon turned sour. The press pounced on the tactics the Kennedy administration had used against the steel companies. *Time* wrote that the president's method of handling the steel situation highlighted just how powerful the Washington police state could be. *U.S. News & World Report* labeled the government's actions and outlook as "quasi-Fascism," and the FBI's early-morning visits to the homes of steel executives led the *Los Angeles Times* to compare Kennedy with Mussolini.

THEY SAID...

"The recent display of dictatorial power by President Kennedy has made us realize that freedom in its largest sense is at stake. The Republican party is the last and only remaining bulwark."

—John W. Bricker, former Republican Governor of Ohio and U.S. Senator, as quoted in *A Thousand Days*

Kennedy was most upset by a cartoon in *The New York Herald Tribune* that depicted Pierre Salinger reporting to the president that Khrushchev praised his actions in the steel crisis. This cartoon was so upsetting that Kennedy canceled his subscription. But even this ended badly for Kennedy when cartoonists and comedians attacked him for doing so. Kennedy could do little but respond to the criticism with humor. What mattered to him most was that he had success-fully prevented an economic disaster.

Revitalizing the Domestic Economy

With the bad press behind him, Kennedy decided to focus on the domestic economy. On May 28, the stock market collapsed. Early in 1962, Kennedy had made a goal to lower the unemployment rate, and with the latest glitch in the economy, he set out to find a way to promote economic growth. He determined a tax cut was the best way to address the issue. He proposed to Congress that corpora-tions receive a 40 percent tax cut and that individuals with taxable income in the mid-$30,000 range receive a 50 percent reduction. Today, $30,000 is equivalent to nearly $200,000.

Kennedy's proposed plan found little support from economists or the public, who were staunchly opposed to a national debt. Only 19 percent agreed with Kennedy's plan, while 72 percent overwhelm-ingly believed it was a dreadful proposal, but Kennedy defended his position. At a Yale University commencement ceremony, he pro-claimed that Americans were held back by an old myth that deficits create inflation. The president argued that debt could create economic growth. Kennedy's argu-ments did little to persuade Congress to pass his tax cuts. When they adjourned for the summer break, opposition to it was strong.

Kennedy appealed to Wilbur Mills of the House Ways and Means Committee, but to no avail. Mills told the president it would take a recession to bring Congress

HE SAID...

"It is hard as hell to be friendly with people who keep trying to cut your legs off. . . . There are about ten thou-sand people in the country involved in this—bankers, industrialists, law-yers, publishers, politicians—a small group, but doing anything they can to say we are going into a depression because business has no confidence in the administration."

around. Kennedy also sought support from business leaders. During various receptions he inundated them with information about his tax cut plan and its benefit over the current outdated economic plan. The audience was much more receptive than Mills had been.

Although Kennedy realized that he had little hope of his tax cut passing until 1963, his Trade Expansion bill was a promising resolution to the potential devaluation of the dollar from the gold drain. The bill would give him the power to negotiate lower tariffs with European countries that were part of the Common Market and it would potentially increase U.S. exports. Kennedy believed this bill would help the economy by decreasing unemployment and by helping the national economy overall. Congress agreed and passed the bill in October.

Protecting James Meredith

In January 1961, James Meredith, a student at the all-black Jackson State College, applied for admission to the University of Mississippi. His admission was promptly denied. Meredith took his grievance to the NAACP legal defense team, which filed a lawsuit on his behalf. After making its way through the lower courts, the U.S. Supreme Court heard the case. On September 10, 1962, the Court handed down its decision affirming Meredith's right to attend the university.

FACT
Two days after Kennedy was sworn in as president, James Meredith, inspired by Kennedy's inaugural speech, decided that as his contribution to democracy he would apply for admission to the University of Mississippi. On February 7, 1961, James Meredith wrote the Justice Department requesting that it exert its influence in protecting his rights. He did not receive a response.

Negotiating James Meredith's Admission
Despite the Supreme Court ruling, Mississippi governor Ross Barnett was determined to block Meredith's admission. State legisla-

tors chimed in with a bill that prohibited the admission of a student to a state school if the applicant had been convicted of a crime. Clearly, the bill was aimed at Meredith, who had been convicted of false voter registration.

Kennedy hoped that the situation would end quickly and quietly. Barnett, however, wanted to maintain his popularity. Bobby Kennedy began negotiations with the governor on September 15. Bobby told the governor that the president intended to enforce the Supreme Court ruling. Although Barnett did not want the incident to devolve into violence, he was hardly cooperative. Not even threats of the loss of federal aid influenced him.

Meredith, accompanied by federal marshals, attempted to register at the university but was repeatedly prevented from doing so. The situation escalated. Segregationists from around the state flocked to the campus, and Barnett feared violence. On September 29, President Kennedy spoke to the governor directly. They agreed on a plan to sneak Meredith onto the campus, but Barnett reneged. Kennedy acted. He federalized the Mississippi National Guard and ordered U.S. Army troops to Memphis.

THEY SAID...

"I am a graduate of the University of Mississippi. For this I am proud of my country—the United States of America. The question always arises—was it worth the cost? . . . I believe that I echo the feeling of most Americans when I say that 'no price is too high to pay for freedom of person, equality of opportunity, and human dignity.'"

—James Meredith, in a letter to Robert Kennedy, September 1963

The next day, Bobby Kennedy informed Barnett that the president would address the nation and announce that his decision to mobilize the Mississippi National Guard rested partially on Barnett's failure to keep his word. Barnett protested and assured Bobby that he would cooperate as long as the president didn't mention their agreement. It seemed everyone would get their way: Meredith would be on campus and Barnett could save face with his constituents by protesting he had nothing to do with it. That night Kennedy told the nation that Meredith was safely on the campus.

Unbeknownst to Kennedy, Barnett had relieved the state highway patrol of their duty to protect Meredith. Only 500 marshals remained against a mob of 2,000 people surrounding the campus. The mob attacked the marshals with bricks, guns, and bottles. By the end of the night, 160 marshals had been injured. Two men—one a French journalist—were killed. To quiet the situation, Kennedy was forced to send in the federalized National Guard and order the army to move in from Memphis. The military presence finally brought the situation under control before dawn on October 1. That morning, Meredith finally registered.

Unfortunately for Kennedy, the situation had ended neither quickly nor quietly, and it was more bitter than sweet for civil rights activists. The Kennedy administration had acted to uphold James Meredith's rights, but Kennedy still had not spoken out against the immorality of segregation. Kennedy himself was soon consumed with a greater threat to national security—Soviet weapons in Cuba.

HE SAID...

"Americans are free, in short, to disagree with the law but not to disobey it. . . . If this country should ever reach the point where any man or group of men by force or threat of force could defy the commands of our court and our Constitution, then no law would stand free from doubt, no judge would be sure of his writ, and no citizen would be safe from his neighbors."

Chapter 14

THE CUBAN MISSILE CRISIS

After the end of the Berlin crisis, Kennedy was optimistic that the worst of his dealings with the Soviets was finally over. He thought Khrushchev wanted peace. However, when the Soviet Union moved missiles and troops into Cuba, Kennedy realized he had been gravely mistaken. With Cuba so close to the United States, he knew he had to handle the situation carefully. Any misstep would result in his worst fear—a nuclear war with the Soviet Union. For thirteen days in October 1962, the world watched two superpowers face off.

Rumors of Soviet Missile Buildup in Cuba

By mid-1962, Soviet and U.S. relations over Berlin remained unresolved and the successful negotiation of a test ban treaty continued to be elusive. The situation with the Soviet Union remained stagnant, but Kennedy persisted in his belief that a test ban treaty was on the horizon until early August, when CIA director John McCone informed him of the imminent threat of a Soviet-backed weapons buildup in Cuba.

Early Intelligence

The information initially emerged from intelligence gathered from mail intercepted from Cuba. Several letters discussed the arrival of Russian ships carrying military men and unidentifiable objects. It was unclear, but McCone believed that Soviet SA-2s, also known as surface-to-air-missiles (SAMs), were now on Cuban soil.

McCone sent Kennedy a memo on August 13. In it, he stated his belief that the Soviets were doing more than just providing Cuba with the weaponry for defense. McCone was suspicious that the Soviets were in the process of installing ballistic missiles with nuclear warheads. This concerned McCone deeply. He knew intermediate-range ballistic missiles (IRBMs) stationed in Cuba could easily hit Washington. Nonetheless, McCone was only speculating, and officials in the State and Defense departments quickly disregarded his memo.

QUESTION

What is the difference between SAMs and IRBMs?

SAMs are missiles that are launched from the ground into the air to destroy aircraft. An IRBM is a ballistic missile that can be launched from the ground or from a submarine to a stationary target.

While Kennedy didn't know the specifics of Soviet involvement in Cuba, he did learn the Soviet presence in the country was more active than at any other time. In July, thirty Soviet cargo ships docked in Cuba and unloaded troops, military vehicles, and unidentifiable crates. In August, fifty-five more ships arrived. According to the CIA, 5,000 Soviet troops occupied vacated villages. Additional evidence collected from photographs taken from an August 29 spy plane flight over Cuba showed the presence of SAM missile sites and the construction of a launching pad.

Mounting Pressure in Washington

Kennedy hardly had time to absorb the information when Republican senator Kenneth Keating announced in an August 31 congressional speech that Cuba was harboring Soviet missiles. Worse, he put pressure on Kennedy to take action to resolve the situation.

Kennedy was outraged with Keating's public statement. He knew the CIA was responsible for the senator's concise assessment of the situation. More than anything, he was upset that this latest battle with Khrushchev was coming so close to the November congressional elections. Furthermore, he was being cast as a "do-nothing" president, and this forced him to address the Cuba situation publicly.

On September 4, Kennedy issued a press statement he hoped would calm the public. In it, he emphasized that while there was evidence of the presence of Soviet defense missiles and Soviet military technicians, there was no evidence of offensive missiles or the presence of Soviet combat troops. He ended the statement by reiterating the U.S. commitment to preventing Cuba from spreading its ideology "by whatever means may be necessary." The same day, Robert Kennedy met with Soviet ambassador Anatoly Dobrynin, who assured him the Soviets were helping the Cubans develop defensive technology and had no plans to install offensive weapons.

Buildup to October

All the while, Kennedy clung to the hope that Khrushchev had been telling the truth in April 1961 when he declared his interest was not in Cuba. Two days after Kennedy's press statement, Khrushchev sent his assurance that nothing would occur before the elections. Kennedy, too, was eager to avoid any complications during this important time. The two leaders traded messages in a carefully worded dance of diplomacy. Each man stressed that though his overwhelming desire was peace, any sign or threat of aggression from the other would trigger a reaction.

FACT

In the months leading up to the Cuban missile crisis, U.S. intelligence showed the presence of Soviet military troops in Cuba. Analysts estimated the Soviet force in Cuba numbered a few thousand. In reality, 40,000 Soviet troops were stationed in Cuba at the operation's height, a fact that was not disclosed until some thirty years later.

Congress Weighs In

Kennedy's optimism extended to his belief that the Soviet Union would be extremely unlikely to dare to install nuclear missiles right under America's nose. Not everyone agreed with Kennedy. Republican and Democratic senators clamored to know what Kennedy planned to do to counter the growing threat. Democratic senators warned that if Kennedy failed to exert some sort of military force, he could look forward to standing alone in his position.

Kennedy's woes over Cuba became worse after his old friend, poet Robert Frost, returned from a trip to Russia, where he had met with Khrushchev. At a press conference, the aged poet unwittingly cemented Kennedy's soft stance when he told the press of Khrushchev's remark that modern liberals were "too liberal to fight." Once again, Kennedy was cast as a weak and indecisive president.

The President Responds

Kennedy responded to the pressure by holding a press conference on September 13. "First of all, it is Mr. Castro and his supporters who are in trouble," he declared, categorizing the recent flurry of military activity in Cuba "a frantic attempt to bolster [Castro's] regime." The president noted that while Soviet-Cuban collaboration was not unusual, the United States continued to monitor the situation closely and it did not pose a serious threat to the United States or its allies. Kennedy made it clear that he would take action if the Cubans obtained offensive weapons. He confirmed reports that days earlier he had issued a request to Congress for 150,000 army reserve troops to active duty.

Confirming the Threat

Congress was not satisfied. The Senate passed a resolution on September 20 sanctioning the use of force against Cuba if Cuba showed any signs of aggression. The same day, the House of Representatives passed legislation cutting off aid to countries that continued to trade with Cuba.

By September 21, the CIA received strong evidence that there were offensive weapons in Cuba. A report identified a truck convoy carrying missiles to an airport in Havana. Kennedy ordered the dispatch of U-2 spy planes to fly over Cuba to gather more evidence, but the weather did not cooperate and it was October 14 before the planes could get a clear shot. The October 14 photos showed there were four medium-range ballistic missile sites (MRBM) and two IRBM sites, either completed or under construction, and twenty-one medium-range nuclear-capable bombers. This time, the evidence was conclusive: the Soviet Union was supplying Cuba with dangerous offensive weapons.

The Beginning of the Thirteen Days

Kennedy viewed the photos on the morning of October 16. He recognized how grave the situation was, and he felt betrayed by Khrushchev. He had believed Khrushchev wanted peace, had believed the Soviets when they said they were not building offensive bases in Cuba. But now he was faced with hard evidence that he had been lied to, and it was a blow to him.

The potential for nuclear war hinged on how Kennedy handled the situation, and he needed his most trusted advisors to help find a resolution to the situation. He called Bobby first and then ordered a late morning meeting in the Cabinet Room with thirteen advisors.

He left the rest of his daily schedule intact so as not to arouse suspicion. It was imperative that the Soviets remain unaware that Kennedy knew of the offensive weapons in Cuba.

Kennedy first wanted to know why the Soviets had placed missiles in Cuba. Speculation centered around three possibilities: a convenient launching site for short-range missiles in close proximity to the United States, a challenge to U.S. nuclear superiority, and a bargaining chip over Berlin. Whatever the reason, most important to the group was how to proceed next.

THEY SAID...

"I now know how Tojo felt when he was planning Pearl Harbor."

—Bobby Kennedy, on a note scrawled to his brother during the early hours of the Cuban missile crisis

There was never any question of allowing the missiles to remain on Cuban soil. By the end of the meeting, Kennedy specified four possible ways to address the situation: an air strike against the missile sites, a general air strike, a blockade, or an invasion on Cuba. His preference initially was to eliminate the missiles with an air strike, but the meeting ended without a resolution. Kennedy ordered the U-2 flights to continue and asked his advisors to reconvene in the Cabinet Room at 6:30 P.M.

THEY SAID...

"As soon as he was convinced that [the evidence] was conclusive, he said that the United States must bring the threat to an end: one way or another the missiles would have to be removed. . . . Privately he was furious: if Khrushchev could pull this after all his protestations and denials, how could he ever be trusted on anything?"

—Arthur Schlesinger, A Thousand Days

Further U-2 flights confirmed the existence of four more medium-range missiles, but none of them were operational, and there was no evidence that there were any nuclear warheads in Cuba. Kennedy and his advisors struggled to reach a consensus on a plan of action. Kennedy was concerned about the fallout from conducting an air strike without warning. UN Ambassador Adlai Stevenson confirmed Kennedy's apprehension. Stevenson advocated finding a peaceful resolution. He asserted that if Kennedy should proceed with an attack, it could result in dire consequences over Berlin. He urged Kennedy to try diplomacy before resorting to military measures.

THEY SAID...

"To start or risk starting a nuclear war is bound to be divisive at best and the judgments of history seldom coincide with the tempers of the moment."

—UN Ambassador Adlai Stevenson, in an October 17 letter to President Kennedy

By October 18, Kennedy received new photos showing IRBM launching sites. Analysts speculated that there were sixteen to thirty-two ready to launch missiles. Nevertheless, Kennedy still had concerns that the public would fail to understand the necessity of an air attack without enough evidence to justify it. Only military experts were equipped to decipher the data, so they would be of no use in convincing the public. The president was concerned that military action would lead to a worldwide public outcry. The Joint Chiefs wanted to move forward with an invasion, but when Undersecretary of State George Ball suggested that an attack without warning was comparable to Pearl Harbor, Kennedy moved even further away from such a plan.

Instituting a Blockade

After two meetings with advisors and a meeting with the Soviet foreign minister Andrey Gromyko on October 18, Kennedy was leaning more toward a blockade. Gromyko assured Kennedy that the Soviet Union was helping Cuba arm itself defensively, no more. Minutes after the meeting ended, Kennedy scratched his head in disbelief that Gromyko could make such a statement.

Nevertheless, Kennedy knew the photos told another story. Without a final decision, Kennedy met with the Joint Chiefs on the morning of October 19. They still favored a massive air strike with a possible invasion afterward. The discussion focused on Kennedy's concern that an attack would lead to a Soviet blockade on Berlin, or worse, cutting off allied access altogether. General Maxwell Taylor understood his concern but believed that without military action, America's credibility would suffer. General Curtis LeMay was also unsympathetic to Kennedy's concerns. LeMay thought military action was the most appropriate response; the international community would consider a blockade weak. Kennedy emerged from the meeting even more discouraged than he had been.

THEY SAID...

Bobby Kennedy "thought it would be very, very difficult indeed for the President if the decision were to be for an air strike, with all the memory of Pearl Harbor and with all the implications this would have for us in whatever world there would be afterward. For 175 years we had not been that kind of country. A sneak attack was not in our tradition."

—Leonard C. Meeker, record of Ex Comm meeting, October 19, 1962

At 10:35 A.M. Kennedy left for a weekend of campaigning in the Illinois cities of Cleveland, Springfield, and Chicago. In the meantime, Ex Comm, as Kennedy's National Security Council became known during the crisis, met all day at the State Department. They broke off into two committees, one supporting an air strike and the other in favor of a blockade. When they met back, they decided on a course of action. They recommended the president institute a blockade with the option of air strikes to follow if the Soviets failed to remove the offensive weapons. Discussions continued, and the next morning Bobby called the president and suggested that he return early. Kennedy feigned illness and arrived back at the White House at 1:30 P.M. on October 20.

Kennedy continued to meet with his advisers throughout the weekend. Updated intelligence showed that eight MRBM missiles were equipped to fire immediately. Kennedy favored a blockade, or as he preferred to call it, a quarantine. The blockade would be followed by a mandate for the removal of the missiles. If Khrushchev failed to respond, only then would an air strike take place. It had been a hard decision, and Kennedy's consideration of the potential loss of life from an air strike had influenced his reasoning for a blockade. Now with the decision made, Kennedy hoped that the nation would stand behind him when he announced his decision on Monday, October 22.

Informing the Nation

Before giving his evening speech, Kennedy sought to gather support from other government officials and to silence the press. The *Washington Post* and the *New York Times* were on to the Cuba missile story. Kennedy called and asked the newspapers to halt their stories until after his speech.

To shore up political support, Kennedy spoke with Eisenhower, who liked the idea of an invasion but believed a blockade was more suitable. On the evening of his scheduled speech, Kennedy met with congressional leaders. He was disappointed and angry to learn that they overwhelmingly favored an invasion rather than a blockade, but he stood behind his decision.

Kennedy had one more thing to do before he gave his speech. One hour before his address, he handed the unsuspecting Soviet Ambassador a letter to give to Khrushchev. In it he reiterated to the chairman his previous warning that the United States would protect itself and its allies should "certain developments" take place in Cuba. Since long-range missile bases had been erected, the United

"HE SAID...

"I call upon Chairman Khrushchev to halt and eliminate this clandestine, reckless, and provocative threat to world peace and to stable relations between our two nations. I call upon him further to abandon this course of world domination, and to join in an historic effort to end the perilous arms race and to transform the history of man."

States would eliminate the threat.

At 7 P.M., Kennedy began his address to the nation. He informed the 100 million American viewers that the presence of Soviet IRBMs in Cuba could hit most major U.S. cities. The buildup was unjustified, and it required action. A quarantine would prevent the further transport of military equipment to Cuba, and if the threat should continue, then military action was justified. In addition, asserted Kennedy, he would consider any missile launched from Cuba into the Western Hemisphere to be an attack on the United States by the Soviet Union, and he would be forced to retaliate. After seventeen minutes Kennedy was done with his speech.

FACT
A Gallup poll taken on October 23 showed 84 percent of Americans who were aware of the blockade supported it; 4 percent opposed it. The same poll showed that around 20 percent of respondents thought the blockade would result in another world war.

The international community rallied around the United States. The UN unanimously passed a resolution in favor of the U.S. response. European allies declared their support for the blockade and promised support if war did break out. The only question was how the Soviet Union would respond.

Negotiating a Resolution

That night as the president spoke, nearly sixty U.S. warships proceeded toward Cuba, where they prepared to carry out the quarantine plan once the president gave the order. Khrushchev's response was not promising. A resolution seemed far off, and the possibility of a war increased.

THEY SAID...

"I must say frankly that measures indicated in your statement constitute a serious threat to peace and to the security of nations. The United States has openly taken the path of grossly violating the United Nations Charter, [the] path of violating international norms of freedom of navigation on the high seas, the path of aggressive actions both against Cuba and against the Soviet Union."

—Khrushchev, in a letter to Kennedy, October, 23, 1962

Garnering Support for U.S. Policy

With Khrushchev's position clear, Kennedy had just one last hope. He expected the support of the Organization of American States would provide him leverage. Dean Rusk had left for an early-morning meeting with the group, and he returned in the late afternoon with good news. Members had voted unanimously to condemn the Soviet Union, and they had even supported a resolution for the immediate removal of missiles from Cuba.

The support of the OAS prompted Kennedy to order the blockade to begin the next morning, October 24, at 10:00 A.M. Kennedy wrote to Khrushchev to alert him that the blockade was going to be instituted. He asked that Soviet vessels observe the blockade and stressed his concern that both sides exercise caution.

The U.S.-Soviet Confrontation

The blockade began on October 24, and the situation looked grim. Substantial progress had been made in completing the missile launching sites in Cuba. In addition, Soviet ships large enough to transport missiles were on their way to Cuba with submarine escorts. As the president was being briefed, new intelligence informed him that Soviet ships approaching Cuba had stopped their procession and reversed course. This was promising, but Kennedy knew the crisis was not over.

THEY SAID...

"These few minutes were the time of greatest worry by the President. His hand went up to his face & covered his mouth and he closed his fist. His eyes were tense, almost gray, and we just stared at each other across the table. Was the world on the brink of a holocaust and had we done something wrong?"

—Robert Kennedy

That night he received word that two Soviet ships were only miles away from the blockade. Bobby Kennedy sat across from him as the two awaited word on the situation; finally, they learned the Soviet ships had stopped advancing toward Cuba.

Kennedy was correct in his assessment that disaster was still near. Late that night, he received a letter from Khrushchev. The chairman was clearly angry. Khrushchev refused to order his ships to observe the blockade or back down when it came to protecting their rights. The chairman insisted Kennedy was out of line in enforcing a quarantine, and he was convinced the United States would respond the same way the Soviets were if their roles were reversed.

Kennedy's response was more concise but no less forceful. The president summarized the events leading up to the present situation. It was Khrushchev, asserted Kennedy, who had made false statements regarding the buildup of offensive weapons in Cuba, and the United States had been forced to act to counter the threat.

The next morning resulted in the passage of two Soviet ships through the quarantine. One was an oil tanker and the other was a passenger ship, and neither was suspected of carrying nuclear weapons. On the president's orders, neither ship was boarded. Even more eventful was Adlai Stevenson's performance at a UN Security Council meeting initiated by Cuba. Stevenson and Soviet ambassador Valerian Zorin exchanged heated words over the existence of offensive weapons in Cuba.

Stevenson presented damning photographic evidence of the presence of offensive missile sites in Cuba, and the Soviet ambassador ineffectively questioned their authenticity. For the rest of the delegates, Stevenson's evidence was convincing.

THEY SAID...

"[T]he actions of the United States with regard to Cuba constitute outright banditry or, if you like, the folly of degenerate imperialism. Unfortunately, such folly can bring grave suffering to the peoples of all countries, and to no lesser degree to the American people themselves[.] . . . Therefore, Mr. President, if you coolly weigh the situation which has developed, not giving way to passions, you will understand that the Soviet Union cannot fail to reject the arbitrary demands of the United States."

—Khrushchev, in a letter to Kennedy, October 24, 1962

Khrushchev Seeks a Resolution

Thus far, the quarantine had been effective. Soviet ships with military equipment had reversed course prior to reaching the U.S. quarantine. When Kennedy met with Ex Comm on October 26, the concern had shifted to the continued construction of missile sites in Cuba. The president concluded that if the situation were not resolved within forty-eight hours, a new course of action would have to take effect.

Khrushchev was also working toward a peaceful way out of the situation. KGB agent Aleksandr Fomin approached ABC journalist John Scali. He asked Scali to find out from his contacts at the State Department whether the United States might agree to a deal: the

Soviets would dismantle the missile sites as long as the United States promised not to invade Cuba. Word of the deal eventually reached Ex Comm, and Dean Rusk instructed Scali to tell Fomin the United States might consider such a proposal.

THEY SAID...

"Do you, Ambassador Zorin, deny that the USSR has placed and is placing medium- and intermediate-range missiles and sites in Cuba? Yes or no? Don't wait for the translation. Yes or no? . . . You have denied they exist. I want to know if I understood you correctly. I am prepared to wait for my answer until hell freezes over."

—Adlai Stevenson, UN Security Council meeting, October 25, 1962

It was a hopeful proposition, but Kennedy had every reason not to trust Khrushchev. That night, Kennedy received a rambling letter from the Soviet chairman. The next morning, a revised copy of Khrushchev's letter was published in the press. The second letter demanded an additional concession from the United States: the removal of Jupiter missiles from Turkey.

THEY SAID...

"Armaments bring only disasters. When one accumulates them, this damages the economy, and if one puts them to use, then they destroy the people on both sides. Consequently, only a madman can believe that armaments are the principal means in the life of society. . . . If people do not show wisdom, then in the final analysis they will come to a clash, like blind moles, and then reciprocal extermination will begin. Let us therefore show statesmanlike wisdom."

—Khrushchev, in a letter to Kennedy, October 26, 1962

The new terms confused Kennedy and his advisors, but Kennedy needed to decide on a response quickly. The Joint Chiefs were urging him to order an air strike; Cuban missile sites were almost complete, and that morning an American pilot had been killed when his plane was shot down.

In the end, Bobby Kennedy counseled his brother to ignore the terms of Khruschev's second letter. The president telegrammed Khrushchev that the United States would end the quarantine and promised not to invade Cuba. Kennedy accepted these terms in exchange for the dismantling and removal of offensive weapons from Cuba. Only after this agreement was reached would a discussion ensue over the Jupiter missiles in Turkey.

In addition to sending his letter via cable, he sent Bobby to deliver it to Dobrynin. Bobby, under the president's order, informed Dobrynin that failure to accept these terms would lead to military action. In addition Bobby assured Dobrynin that the president was committed to removing the missiles in Turkey after the current crisis was over but warned that this information was not to become public.

FACT

Kennedy was unsure whether Khrushchev would accept his offer. He secretly had a second proposal drafted by Columbia University dean Andrew Cordier stating that he was willing to remove the Jupiter missiles from Turkey in exchange for missile removals in Cuba. Dean Rusk revealed this fact to the public for the first time in 1987.

Kennedy's proposal got Khrushchev's attention. Less than twenty-four hours later, he accepted the offer. On October 28, American news outlets reported that war with the Soviet Union had been averted. A formal agreement was announced on November 20. Offensive missiles were shipped out of Cuba and Khrushchev agreed to remove all IL-28 aircraft within thirty days. Once again,

Kennedy had diverted a crisis with the Soviet Union, and Khrushchev expressed an interest in negotiating with the United States to ensure there would be no more near misses. It brought Kennedy one step closer to his goal of signing a nuclear test ban treaty with the Soviet Union.

Chapter 15

BALANCING DOMESTIC AND FOREIGN AFFAIRS

As Kennedy recovered from the Cuban missile crisis, he turned his attention to domestic matters. The civil rights movement gained ground, and the president took notice. When violence against protestors in Birmingham, Alabama, hit the front pages of newspapers around the world, Kennedy threw his support behind the creation of civil rights legislation. In foreign affairs, he worked toward cementing relations with West Germany, but it was a test ban treaty with the Soviets that mattered most.

Racial Tension in Birmingham

Kennedy emerged from the Cuban missile crisis as a well-regarded statesman. His popularity soared. A Gallup poll showed his approval rating at a remarkable 74 percent, 12 points higher than his prior approval rating. In November 1962, he made tax reform his biggest priority. This commitment was reflected in his 1963 State of the Union Address. "I am convinced that the enactment this year of tax reduction and tax reform overshadows all other domestic problems in this Congress. For we cannot for long lead the cause of peace and freedom, if we ever cease to set the pace here at home," the president declared. Kennedy announced he would seek the passage of a bill giving $13.5 billion in tax cuts to individuals and corporations.

Focusing on Civil Rights

The State of the Union address contained only a passing reference to civil rights—"surely in this centennial year of Emancipation all those who are willing to vote should always be permitted"—but 1963 was the year in which Kennedy became a champion of the civil rights movement.

As Kennedy waited for the unlikely passage of his tax cut bill, he paid particular attention to civil rights. In November 1962, he had issued an Executive Order that integrated federal public housing, but he knew more was necessary. In addition, in February, he declared that the cause of equal rights for black citizens would continue until it was fulfilled, and he urged Congress to take action against discrimination. Specifically, he proposed legislation that would tackle discriminatory voter registration practices, he advised the implementation of the U.S. Supreme Court decision desegregating public schools, and he supported the passage of legislation barring discrimination in public places. In the end, though, Kennedy accomplished nothing. While he offered support for antisegre-

HE SAID...

"While we shall never weary in the defense of freedom, neither shall we ever abandon the pursuit of peace."

gation laws, he neither proposed anything specific nor took a clear public stance against discrimination. This was especially apparent when he declined to follow the recommendation of the Civil Rights Commission to suspend federal funds to Mississippi, which had become one of the nation's most violent and egregious violators of civil rights.

Overall Kennedy believed that in comparison to prior administrations, he had achieved significant gains for blacks. Despite the administration's voting rights lawsuits, civil rights leaders were pressing him for much more. They wanted legislation to end discrimination in places of public accommodation. While the president may have failed to see the significance of his stance on civil rights, Bobby Kennedy knew exactly why it was important. He wanted to get an early start on preparing for the presidential election, and he realized that his brother's failure to do enough for civil rights could result in a loss.

The Birmingham Campaign

On April 3, 1963, Martin Luther King Jr. and the SCLC initiated a campaign to desegregate stores and secure black employment in Birmingham, Alabama. Support from the black community was sparse, but it received a boost when King was arrested. His imprisonment once again drew the president into the civil rights fray. King received legal counsel, but his lawyers' access to him was severely limited. Coretta King requested Bobby Kennedy's assistance. Days later, the attorney general let her know he had arranged a phone call with her husband.

The president hoped that the Birmingham campaign would die out. King, on the other hand, had been released from jail and was doing everything he could to ensure that it continued. The lack of protestors was hurting the campaign, so King relented on a proposal to allow high school students to participate. On May 3, 1,000 students proceeded from the Sixteenth Street Baptist Church toward downtown. Birmingham's police commissioner, Bull Connor, had set up a blockade of buses, police cars, fire engines, and K-9 units to impede their procession. When the students refused to stop, they were sprayed with fire hoses and attacked by police dogs. Photographers and television crews captured the brutal images. Kennedy was sickened by the image in the *New York Times* of a police dog attempting to bite a young bystander in the stomach.

Over the years, King had become a media-savvy civil rights leader. He wanted federal intervention, and he used the press to secure it. He appealed directly to Kennedy through the media, urging the president to take a stand against segregation. He baited the president by stating that the administration would have intervened if the protestors had been white.

FACT

When King was arrested, a letter from a group of white ministers was published in the *Birmingham News*. It criticized the protest and called for its termination. King responded in what is now famously known as his "Letter from Birmingham Jail." Although he wrote it in jail and smuggled it out through his attorney, it was not published until mid-May.

Now more than ever, Kennedy had to respond. The photos had been published for the world to see and he feared that America's reputation would suffer if the violence continued. Burke Marshall and Joseph Dolan of the Justice Department went to Birmingham to help negotiate an agreement between activists and local businesses. Although Kennedy believed that the federal government was powerless in the situation—which, after all, involved no federal violations—he knew something had to be done. By May 8, negotiations had resulted in substantial progress. He announced in a news conference that protests were suspended while the negotiations continued. Kennedy believed he was doing all he could. Not everyone agreed with this assessment. When a paper the next day quoted Erwin Griswold, a member of the Civil Rights Commission, as saying that Kennedy had failed to use all of the power available to him, he was furious.

> ## THEY SAID...
> "When things started happening down here, Mr. Kennedy got disturbed. For Mr. Kennedy . . . is battling for the minds and the hearts of men in Asia and Africa . . . and they aren't going to respect the United States of America if she deprives men and women of the basic rights of life because of the color of their skin. Mr. Kennedy knows that."
>
> —Martin Luther King Jr., as quoted in
> *President Kennedy: Profile of Power*

Unbeknownst to Kennedy, Bull Connor was still at work. When a judge handed down an order for King's incarceration for his prior arrest, Connor happily took King into custody. King had a choice of serving jail time or paying a $2,500 bond. He chose to remain in jail. In response, civil rights leader Fred Shuttlesworth prepared to lead a protest. This threatened to dissolve any progress toward an agreement, so Bobby Kennedy immediately contacted Shuttlesworth and convinced him to wait. Within hours, A. G. Gatson, a wealthy black Birmingham businessman, paid King's bond.

On May 10, Birmingham's storeowners and black leaders reached an agreement. It included a provision to integrate drinking fountains and restrooms within thirty days and lunch counters within sixty days.

The Bombings in Birmingham

It appeared to Kennedy that Birmingham had been a victory. Just as he was settling in at Camp David, near midnight on May 11, bombs soared through the windows of King's empty room at the Gatson Motel and the Birmingham home of A. D. King, Martin Luther King Jr.'s brother. No one was hurt; earlier that day Martin Luther King had left Birmingham to return to his home in Atlanta. Black residents swarmed the streets, angry that the bombing of the motel occurred right under the noses of the Alabama state troopers. Police officers were assaulted with bricks and bottles. Kennedy awoke to the news early Sunday morning.

HE SAID...

"This Government will do whatever must be done to preserve order, to protect the lives of its citizens, and to uphold the law of the land. . . . The Birmingham agreement was and is a fair and just accord. It recognized the fundamental right of all citizens to be accorded equal treatment and opportunity."

Kennedy returned to Washington and met with advisors. He first wanted to know what King intended to do. Burke Marshall called King, who was preparing to return to Birmingham and settle the community. Although King was resolved to quiet the situation without troops, Kennedy did not want to take any chances. He federalized the Alabama National Guard and placed army troops near Birmingham on alert. Once again, Kennedy addressed the nation. In a five-minute speech that night, he urged an end to the violence and attested to his commitment to upholding the law.

Supporting Civil Rights

The Birmingham situation finally convinced Kennedy of the necessity of proposing a civil rights bill. He realized that without legal teeth behind the civil rights movement, situations like Birmingham would inevitably continue to occur—and they did. When sit-in demonstrations began on May 28 in Jackson, Mississippi, the press reported that lunch-counter protestors were brutalized by white mobs. This underscored the necessity for civil rights legislation, but the path would not be easy.

Alabama's Governor George Wallace planned to stand in defiance of a court order. At issue was the enrollment of two black students in the segregated University of Alabama. Wallace repeatedly vowed that he would block the students' enrollment. Bobby Kennedy had tried without success to get Wallace to relent. In an effort to counter Wallace, the Justice Department secured a court order prohibiting his interference—but not his presence on the university campus.

FACT

Wallace became an outspoken segregationist after he lost his run for governor of Alabama in 1958. He realized that to win he had to take more than a moderate stance on segregation. Four years later, he emerged a zealous segregationist. In 1982, when he was again elected governor, he had undergone another complete turn-around in his attitude toward blacks.

The Kennedy administration tried to find a way to turn Wallace's uncooperative attitude to their own advantage. Bobby's initial attempt to influence *Newsday* to run a story about Wallace's "nervous disability" failed. Instead, the Kennedys agreed to allow a film crew to follow them as they handled the crisis on June 11. Wallace also agreed, and his standoff with the Kennedy administration was captured on film. As Wallace had promised, he blocked the university doorway. Nick Katzenbach, the deputy attorney general, requested that he move, and Wallace responded with a statement about his opposition to the interference of the federal government. Wallace only stepped aside when Kennedy federalized the National Guard. It was a victory for Kennedy, who was pleased that the school was integrated without violence.

Proposing Civil Rights Legislation

Kennedy decided it was time to introduce civil rights legislation. At 8:00 P.M. on June 11, with only part of a speech in front of him, Kennedy addressed the nation. He combined the remarks from his prepared text with a contemporaneous discussion about the moral issue of segregation. Kennedy asserted that segregation was wrong, and it was unfair for blacks to have to fight for their rights. He called for legislation that would make desegregation of public facilities and public schools not merely the law but the reality as well. Kennedy wanted Congress to find a way for the federal government to enforce desegregation and voting rights.

Kennedy presented his civil rights legislation to Congress on June 19. The right to vote would extend to any citizen with a sixth-grade education and all public places would have to be desegregated. He requested that the attorney general receive substantial power over court-ordered public school desegregation cases.

The proposed civil rights bill was a progressive step toward the elimination of discrimination and segregation. All the same, King and civil rights leader A. Philip Randolph decided to put pressure on Congress to pass the bill with a March on Washington for Jobs and Freedom. Kennedy had already encountered enough opposition from some legislators, and he worried about how Congress would respond to the march. He immediately met with King, Randolph, and other civil rights leaders. He explained to them that the march could jeopardize the passage of the bill. King, however, refused to budge. Kennedy reflected that the bill might not pass, and his strong support of it might endanger his own reelection.

Mastering Foreign Affairs

For the moment, Kennedy had done all he could in regard to civil rights. All he could do was wait and see whether Congress would pass the bill. In the meantime, there were still pressing foreign affairs matters that required his attention. In late 1962, Kennedy had decided to forgo further development of the Skybolt, an air-launched ballistic missile. Its cost of $2.5 billion, he decided, was a waste of money since the Polaris submarine and the Minutemen missiles provided sufficient defense. Since President Eisenhower had promised to supply the

HE SAID...

"We face, therefore, a moral crisis as a country and as a people. It cannot be met by repressive police action. It cannot be left to increased demonstrations in the streets. It cannot be quieted by token moves or talk. It is a time to act in the Congress, in your state and local legislative bodies and, above all, in all of our daily lives."

Skybolts for British nuclear warheads, Kennedy had to break the news to Prime Minister Macmillan. With the turnaround, Britain's plan for independent nuclear might was potentially shattered.

The Nassau Agreement

Kennedy knew Macmillan was disappointed. More than that, he realized that such a huge departure from the previous administration's agreement threatened relations with Britain. Consequently, he struck a new deal with Macmillan at a meeting in Bermuda on December 18, 1962. According to the Nassau Agreement, the two nations would work together in the creation of nuclear submarines equipped with Polaris missiles. These submarines would be part of a multilateral force of the North Atlantic Treaty Organization (NATO), but Britain was authorized to use them for its own protection under conditions of extreme distress.

Kennedy sensed the necessity of offering the same agreement to France, but de Gaulle had other plans. He believed it was unwise to rely entirely on U.S. protection, and he thought the British agreement with the United States was evidence of Britain's preferred alignment. In January 1963, de Gaulle made a startling disclosure. France intended to block Britain's admission into the European Economic Community (EEC). Furthermore, in February, as France moved away from its allies, it formed a new alliance with West Germany that allowed the Germans to be less dependent on the United States and NATO. France planned to develop nuclear weapons and now wanted to be on an equal footing with the United States in NATO.

QUESTION
What was the purpose of the European Economic Community?
The EEC, renamed the European Community in 1993 and also known as the Common Market, was created by the Treaty of Rome in 1957 by the participating countries of Belgium, France, West Germany, Italy, Luxembourg, and the Netherlands. Its goal was to achieve economic unity through its trade policies.

Visiting West Germany

This, of course, concerned Kennedy. He feared that France's fall-out with the United States made Europe even more prone to Soviet influence. To test the waters between the United States and Germany, Kennedy decided to take a trip to Europe in the early spring of 1963. Kennedy was concerned about the new alliance between France and Germany, and German chancellor Konrad Adenauer's plan to step down within the year caused Kennedy to fear that the worst for Europe still lay ahead. On June 22, hours after meeting with King and civil rights leaders about the March on Washington, Kennedy boarded his plane for the six-hour trip to Europe.

When he arrived in Bonn, Germany, Kennedy could not help but get excited over the enthusiastic welcome. Crowds chanted his name and waved American flags. When he spoke to a large audience in Bonn, they went wild with his remarks about U.S. commitment to their freedom and safety.

The enthusiasm was no less when he arrived in West Berlin. He spent four hours touring Berlin, and he had the opportunity to stand on a guard platform and look over the Wall at the deserted streets of East Berlin. This was a disturbing sight for Kennedy. Next, he addressed the 150,000 people who crowded around the platform in the City Hall. Just like the audience in Bonn, they too went wild when he spoke about freedom versus communism. Kennedy's statement, "Today, in the world of freedom, the proudest boast is 'Ich bin ein Berliner' (I am a Berliner)," received enthusiastic applause. Kennedy arrived back in Washington from his trip, satisfied with Germany's enthusiasm over American support.

HE SAID...

"My stay in this country will be all too brief. But in a larger sense, the United States is here on the continent to stay so long as our presence is desired and required; our forces and commitments will remain, for your safety is our safety. Your liberty is our liberty; and any attack on your soil is an attack upon our own."

Making the Case for Peace

After the Cuban missile crisis, Kennedy believed more than ever that a test ban treaty was a necessity. In addition, it appeared that Khrushchev was ready to talk. In several public statements, he commented that an end to nuclear tests was urgent. But when Kennedy entered into the Nassau agreement with Macmillan, Khrushchev interpreted this as an impediment to any kind of agreement with the United States in spite of Kennedy's assurance that he was committed to working out an accord. Moreover, early in 1963, talks had reached a sticking point when there was a disagreement about the number of on-site inspections. Khrushchev believed that three or four were adequate, while Kennedy insisted on eight to ten.

Talks continued despite the rocky start, and now both Macmillan and Kennedy urged Khrushchev toward an open discussion. Khrushchev finally agreed to begin talks in July with American and British representatives. On June 10, at the American University in Washington, Kennedy spoke of peace, mutual tolerance, and the need for a new outlook and respect for the Soviet Union.

Initially, the speech failed to elicit substantial attention from either the press or the American public. Weeks later, nearly 2,000 letters—mostly supportive—arrived at the White House. Khrushchev's response pleased Kennedy. The Soviet Union printed his speech in its entirety and broadcast it on the radio.

HE SAID...

"I also believe that we must reexamine our own attitude—as individuals and as a Nation—for our attitude is as essential as theirs. And every graduate of this school, and every thoughtful citizen who despairs of war and wishes to bring peace, should begin by looking inward—by examining their own attitude toward the possibilities of peace, toward the Soviet Union, toward the course of the cold war and toward freedom and peace here at home."

Khrushchev praised Kennedy's speech as the best from an American president since Roosevelt was in office. Khrushchev seemed even more ready to deal and announced that the Soviet Union would agree to the establishment of a direct hot line between Washington and Moscow.

Negotiating a Test Ban Treaty

On July 14, 1963, U.S. representative Averell Harriman arrived in Moscow to meet with Khrushchev and Britain's Lord Hailsham. It was the beginning of the negotiation for a test ban treaty. Khrushchev was still opposed to submitting to inspections but was open to a discussion on the matter. By July 25, a limited test ban agreement had been reached. Testing underwater, in the atmosphere, and in space were banned, although underground testing could continue. Secretary of State Dean Rusk, Soviet Foreign Minister Andrey Gromyko, and British Foreign Secretary Lord Home signed the treaty on August 5.

President Kennedy delivers his radio and television address on the Nuclear Test Ban Treaty.

Photo credit: Abbie Rowe, White House/John F. Kennedy Presidential Library and Museum, Boston

Negotiating the treaty with Khrushchev was the easy part. Kennedy needed Congress to approve it. Moreover, he would also need to convince the American public that the limited treaty was in the best interest of the country. Kennedy went to Capitol Hill to rally support and then took his appeal directly to the public. On the evening of July 26, he made a televised speech. In it he emphasized that a nuclear war would result in the death of millions of people around the world. Because of this, the United States and the other nuclear powers had an obligation to prevent the spread and testing of weapons. Kennedy emphasized peace over all other options.

Kennedy's speech was a forceful proclamation. By September, polls showed that 81 percent of Americans approved of the treaty. Kennedy knew that success would come by quickly moving it along through Congress. Now with the public behind the treaty, senators originally opposed to it were hard pressed to deny its passage. On September 23, the Senate approved the Limited Nuclear Test Ban Treaty by a vote of eighty to nineteen. Kennedy ratified the treaty on October 7.

President Kennedy signs the Limited Nuclear Test Ban Treaty.

Photo credit: Robert Knudsen, White House/John F. Kennedy Presidential Library and Museum, Boston

Chapter 16

THE LAST DAYS
OF CAMELOT

After the successful negotiation of a test ban treaty, Kennedy pushed ahead with his next agenda. Creating a strong space program that would land a man on the moon, reevaluating U.S. involvement in Vietnam, and his last push toward the passage of his civil rights legislation were his primary administrative concerns during the fall of 1963. More than ever, though, he increasingly felt the pressure to begin campaigning for reelection. This concern took him to Dallas, Texas.

Promoting the Space Program

Although Kennedy finally obtained a test ban treaty, the competition with the Soviet Union was far from over. The Soviets had successfully launched the first orbit around Earth in 1961, and Kennedy was intent on having the United States do the same. In 1962, he proudly congratulated John Glenn after Glenn became the first American to orbit the earth. Nevertheless, Glenn's accomplishment came after the Soviet Union's achievement. Kennedy set his sights on something bigger; he wanted to be the first country to send a man to the moon. The Apollo project would cost $40 billion, but Kennedy believed it was well worth it.

Not everyone agreed with Kennedy. NASA's Jim Webb put less importance on landing a man on the moon and more emphasis on gaining an understanding of space. Other critics argued that the large Apollo budget should go toward medical advancements and the revitalization of cities. Even Eisenhower gave his opinion. He believed that instead of focusing on placing a man on the moon, the space program should further the goal of military advancements. Not even talk of discontinuance of the Soviet moon project could persuade Kennedy to forgo his objective. If anything, polls throughout the world reflected the belief that the Soviets were more advanced, and this made Kennedy even more determined to surpass Soviet advancements in space.

HE SAID...

"First, I believe that this nation should commit itself to achieving the goal, before this decade is out, of landing a man on the moon and returning him safely to earth. No single space project in this period will be more impressive to mankind, or more important for the long-range exploration of space. . . ."

Revisiting the Cuban Situation

Although the Cuban missile crisis had ended well, that was not the last of Cuba. Still at issue for Kennedy was what to do about Castro. In January

1963, Operation Mongoose was replaced by the Interdepartmental Coordinating Committee. For the military, assassination was always an option, but with the upcoming election, Kennedy strove to stay away from another blunder regarding Cuba. Although Kennedy ordered the creation of an invasion plan should it become necessary in the future, overall he preferred to tackle the situation differently.

President Kennedy aboard the "Honey Fitz," off Hyannis Port.

Photo credit: Cecil Stoughton, White House/John F. Kennedy Presidential Library and Museum, Boston

In November 1963, an opportunity for resolution with Cuba presented itself. Castro declared that he would like to come to an agreement with the United States. His conditions for an accord encompassed the termination of the economic embargo and the end of U-2 flights over Cuba. These were conditions that Kennedy refused to accept, but he was interested in entering into talks. With Kennedy's approval, William Attwood, the former ambassador to Guinea, took on the cause for the president.

Attwood began his discussion with Carlos Lechuga, the UN ambassador for Cuba. Attwood suggested that talks begin in secret at the United Nations. Castro responded with an invitation for secret negotiations with an American representative to commence in Cuba

HE SAID...

"In the final analysis, it is their war. They are the ones who have to win it or lose it. We can help them, we can give them equipment, we can send our men out there as advisers, but they have to win it, the people of Vietnam, against the Communists."

instead. On November 12, 1963, Kennedy, in turn, suggested to Attwood that Castro send a representative to the United States. In addition, Kennedy wanted to know whether Castro intended to break ties with the Soviet Union. On November 18, Castro responded that the invitation to come to Cuba was still open, and upon Attwood's request, he promised to send an agenda.

Keeping a Handle on Vietnam

Just like in Cuba, little progress had been made toward a resolution of the situation in South Vietnam. American advisers, which in 1963 numbered a little over 16,000, were still involved in the war. Moreover, Kennedy was subjected to reports and questions from the press about the death of American troops in combat. By May 1963, Kennedy wanted to pull troops out of Vietnam. His preference for a pull-out was also influenced by Diem's brother's public proclamation in a *Washington Post* interview that there were too many military advisers. According to O'Donnell and Asian expert Mike Mansfield, although Kennedy agreed and wished to completely withdraw American troops, he feared that a withdrawal prior to the election could possibly result in his loss.

Kennedy's distress over Vietnam was furthered in May and June when the Buddhist majority demonstrated against Diem's repressive tactics. Diem's continued stance against the Buddhists only furthered Kennedy's belief that the United States should disassociate itself from the South Vietnamese government. Additionally, in August Diem's destruction of pagodas urged Kennedy in a new direction. Just like with the Bay of Pigs, he considered a coup. Once again,

Kennedy wanted no evidence of U.S. involvement. Although he agreed to the plan, when word reached the U.S.-backed Vietnamese generals charged with executing the mission, they were unprepared to carry it out.

Without the prospect of a successful coup, there was very little left for Kennedy to do about Vietnam. His military advisors were in constant disagreement over the war. He received varied reports from advisors that ranged from great progress to a dismal outlook. By fall, Kennedy was finally able to make a decision about the U.S. involvement. When McNamara and Taylor returned from a trip to Vietnam, they had several helpful observations. They believed that a successful coup was only a slight possibility and discouraged active promotion of a new government. They also suggested that most troops could be withdrawn by the end of 1965. In the meantime, they suggested the withdrawal of 1,000 troops. On October 31, at a news conference, Kennedy announced that he planned to withdraw 1,000 troops by the end of 1963.

President Kennedy, Secretary McNamara, and General Taylor meet at the White House.

Photo credit: Robert Knudsen, White House/John F. Kennedy Presidential Library and Museum, Boston

Pulling U.S. troops out of Vietnam provided Kennedy with a hopeful outlook in this regard, but overall, the prospects for Diem's winning the war were bleak. At the same time, anti-Diem forces were ready to make their move. On November 1, the generals launched a coup. Diem and his brother were eventually seized from their hideout in a Catholic church and assassinated. At first Diem's death was attributed to a suicide, but Kennedy knew otherwise.

When Kennedy heard the news, he was distraught. He had wanted a change in the government, but he did not want it to end with Diem's death. The damage had been done, and Kennedy was left with the knowledge that his administration was somewhat responsible. Its encouragement of a coup, believed Kennedy, gave it the responsibility to assist the newly established government in spite of his desire to withdraw from the war.

FACT

It was later learned that the generals had asked the CIA to transport Diem and his brother out of the country. The CIA informed the generals that it would take twenty-four hours to do so. The generals responded that they were unable to wait that long.

The March on Washington

Since Kennedy was unable to convince King and the other civil rights leaders to call off the March on Washington, he publicly announced his support on July 17. Nevertheless, he remained apprehensive. He was most concerned with the possibility of violence, which he knew would quickly eliminate any chance his bill had in Congress. He put Bobby in charge of working with the planners, and it was agreed to hold the demonstration at the Lincoln Memorial. Nearby stores were scheduled for closure, and the rally was intended to last three hours. In case there was a controversial speech, the sound system could lose power in a matter of seconds.

President Kennedy and his brothers, Attorney General Robert F. Kennedy and Senator Edward M. Kennedy, August 28, 1963.

Photo credit: Cecil Stoughton, White House/John F. Kennedy Presidential Library and Museum, Boston

A Successful Demonstration

It seemed that every potential problem was planned for. However, when August 28, 1963, arrived, Patrick Cardinal O'Boyle, who was scheduled to deliver the invocation, threatened to leave. At issue was the wording of a speech by John Lewis, the president of Student Nonviolent Coordinating (SNCC). As opposed to King's well-seasoned SCLC, the SNCC was composed of students, whose youthful passion was often interpreted as more militant. The twenty-three-year-old Lewis planned to advocate marching through the South like Sherman did, and he threw in a few unsavory remarks about cheap political leaders and the pursuit of a scorched-earth policy. While these words were upsetting to O'Boyle, Kennedy focused on Lewis's comment that he would not support the civil rights bill. Initially Lewis stood firm in his plan to deliver the speech, but with only minutes until the program was scheduled to begin, he finally relented. The speech was revised, and Lewis's controversial language was omitted. In addition, he would proclaim that although he supported the bill, he did so with reservations.

> ## THEY SAID...
> "[Kennedy's] attempt to find a middle ground made him less effective in a fight that required unqualified expressions of faith in the righteousness of the cause. Since civil rights—more so than any other national issue confronting him—raised fundamental ethical questions, he certainly could have made it the one great domestic moral cause of his presidency."
>
> —Robert Dallek, *An Unfinished Life*

As the rally began, Kennedy, just like many other Americans, sat down to watch the day's proceedings. The event began with O'Boyle and proceeded with speeches by A. Philip Randolph, Roy Wilkins of the NAACP, Whitney Young of the Urban League, and John Lewis's revised speech. It was King, however, whom Kennedy was waiting to hear, so when he stepped to the podium, Kennedy watched with anticipation. King began his speech, but in the middle he departed from his planned address. Instead, he was moved to deliver a speech that he had given on several other occasions. As Kennedy watched, King made his most memorable and powerful statement. "I have a dream," he declared. It was a dream of brotherhood and the end of discrimination and segregation. He finished his speech with a proclamation that it was his belief that one day blacks and whites would sing together the words of an old spiritual, "Free at last, free at last, thank God Almighty, we are free at last."

Meeting with Civil Rights Leaders

Kennedy was impressed and pleased with the March. "He's damned good," he proclaimed about King. Violence was absent and the presence of senators at the rally gave him confidence that if anything, the March would help gain support for the bill. Within an hour after the March ended, Kennedy met with the leaders of the event. When King arrived, Kennedy greeted him with the statement "I have a dream" and a head nod.

President Kennedy meets with the leaders of the March On Washington.

Photo credit: Cecil Stoughton, White House/John F. Kennedy Presidential Library and Museum, Boston

Kennedy wanted to discuss the bill's support in Congress. The prospect of its passage without strong Republican support was not likely, he commented. He could only agree with Randolph who stated that a "crusade" was necessary in order for its passage.

An Objectionable Compromise on Civil Rights

Kennedy believed that while a crusade was certainly helpful, a limited civil rights bill would gain the support of hardliners. More than ever, with his reelection campaign near, Kennedy wanted to put the civil rights issue in the foreground temporarily. To that end, on October 23 he reached an agreement for a compromise bill with House leaders. The new bill made substantial changes to Kennedy's initial civil rights legislation. The public accommodation clause would apply to everything except retail stores and personal services, voting rights applied only to federal elections, a Fair Employment Practices Commission was no longer part of the bill, and the EEOC was limited in its power.

On November 20, Kennedy's compromise bill passed the Judiciary Committee. Next, the bill would have to pass the Rules Committee. Its chairman, a segregationist, stood ready to prevent its introduction to the House floor. Although the passage of his bill was in serious jeopardy, Kennedy headed off to Texas on November 21.

Assassinated in Texas

Kennedy was intent on winning reelection. In March 1963, a poll showed 74 percent of respondents believed that he would win. Nevertheless, he did not want to leave anything to chance. With the passage of his weakened civil rights bill pending, Kennedy wanted to work especially hard at ensuring the Southern vote. He decided to go to Texas, where civil rights had become a divisive issue that affected his popularity with voters and many local party leaders.

Kennedy and Jackie arrived in San Antonio, and he dedicated the Aerospace Medical Center. He proceeded to Houston for a dinner for Representative Albert Thomas. At each stop, he was welcomed by crowds of people. It was a surprising turnout, since his approval rating in Texas had fallen to 50 percent, a 26 percent decrease from 1962. That night, Jackie and Kennedy traveled to Fort Worth to spend the night. When Kennedy awoke the next morning, a crowd of supporters had already gathered outside his hotel.

President and Mrs. Kennedy deplane from Air Force One at Love Field, Dallas, Texas.

Photo Credit: Cecil Stoughton, White House/John F. Kennedy Presidential Library and Museum, Boston

Nevertheless, Kennedy knew that Texas was going to be a difficult state to win. That morning, the *Dallas Morning News* had reported some less than welcoming news. Its front-page story was entitled: "President's Visit Seen Widening State Democratic Split." The story reported that Kennedy had failed to take a hard stand against communism. Kennedy arrived at the Love Field airport, where he and Jackie slid into the backseat of an open limousine. The car proceeded through the downtown area destined for a luncheon in which he was scheduled to speak.

Waiting for Kennedy's procession was Lee Harvey Oswald. He was well traveled, having lived in Russia for several years, and he had visited Cuba during Castro's dictatorship. Oswald worked along the downtown route of Kennedy's procession at the Texas School Book Depository in the Dealey Plaza building. With all of the preparations made for the president's visit, Oswald knew ahead of time that Kennedy would travel along this route. When the time finally arrived, Oswald waited for a sighting of Kennedy from a sixth floor window in the building. Around 12:30 P.M., when Kennedy arrived in his view, he fired three shots from his rifle. The second one hit Kennedy in the back of the neck, and the third struck him in the back of the head. Kennedy was rushed to the Parkland Memorial Hospital where he was pronounced dead at 1:00 P.M.

The Nation Mourns

Americans were shocked at Kennedy's senseless murder. He had provided hope and inspiration to millions. As the nation mourned, Jackie was determined that her husband be remembered. She decided that rather than bury him in Brookline, Massachusetts, as the press had announced, his final resting place would be at Arlington National Cemetery. Arlington was an appropriate choice. Kennedy had visited the cemetery two years before on Armistice Day. He gave a moving speech about peace, freedom, and war. It was tragic that man's ability to find new ways to kill each other had "far outstripped his capacity to live in peace with his fellow man."

President Kennedy's body lies in state in the East Room of the White House.

Photo credit: Abbie Rowe, White House/John F. Kennedy Presidential Library and Museum, Boston

Jackie modeled her husband's funeral on Abraham Lincoln's. Professor John Robertson of the U.S. Civil War Centennial and the Library of Congress director David Mearns were charged with researching the details of Lincoln's funeral. The actual gravesite also had to be chosen. There were three choices. Bobby recommended that out of the three, the most accessible to Americans was the one positioned on a slope just below Arlington House. Among the last details, Jackie decided that an eternal flame should mark his gravesite.

FACT

Jackie's idea for an eternal flame came from France's flame that marks the gravesite of the Unknown Soldier in Paris. The flame over the tomb in the Arc de Triomphe has come to memorialize the soldiers who died in both world wars.

The funeral began on November 25 at 3:00 P.M. Before the ceremony a convoy traveled from the White House to St. Matthew's

Cathedral. At the gravesite, navy and air force jets and Air Force One flew over. The Irish Guard stood nearby the grave as Cardinal Cushing performed the service. A flag was presented to Jackie, and she, along with Bobby, lit the eternal flame.

Procession to St. Matthew's Cathedral.

Photo credit: Abbie Rowe, White House/John F. Kennedy Presidential Library and Museum, Boston

Burial ceremony for President Kennedy.

Photo credit: Abbie Rowe, White House/John F. Kennedy Presidential Library and Museum, Boston

Conspiracy Theories

Jack's death devastated Bobby. Although their age had separated them as children, Jack's political career drew them together. Bobby had become one of his most trusted advisors. In the months after his brother's death, he found it difficult to accept that the assassination was the result of a single gunman. He came to believe that it was the work of Castro, the CIA, the Mafia, or Jimmy Hoffa. Bobby was not alone in his doubts. At first, Johnson believed that Kennedy's murder was the result of a revenge killing for the death of Diem, but he later came to believe that Castro was responsible.

FACT

Johnson created the Warren Commission to investigate the Kennedy assassination. It took nearly a year to analyze evidence and hear testimony from hundreds of witnesses. It released its report in September 1964, announcing its findings that Lee Harvey Oswald acted alone in the assassination.

Oswald's Murder

Just as Bobby and Johnson doubted that Oswald was solely responsible, the American people were not convinced. Although the September 1964 Warren Commission concluded that Oswald alone was responsible, the account was not enough to quiet doubts. What advanced the conspiracy theories even more was the surprising killing of Oswald.

On November 24, as he was being transferred to the county jail, an armed man in the crowd pulled out a gun and shot Oswald. It was both shocking and disheartening for many Americans, who wanted to know exactly why Oswald had shot the president. With Oswald's death, speculation arose that his murder was part of a conspiracy cover-up. One month after Kennedy's death, this belief was reflected in a poll that showed 52 percent of Americans believed in some sort of conspiracy theory.

THEY SAID...

"It's always seemed to me that John F. Kennedy's assassination marked a watershed in the history of America—and the world. . . . I've often wondered what the world would be like if those shots had not rung out in November 1963. I tell myself that much of the chaos we've experienced during the last forty years might not have happened, but of course, we'll never know."

—Leonard Maltin, as quoted in *"We'll Never Be Young Again"*

Film Footage

This belief was in part spurred along by the film footage of Kennedy's assassination. The video recording, which was taken by an amateur filmmaker, was played and replayed to the point that many no longer believed the Warren Report's conclusions. The footage, according to many, indicated that there was another shooter. The film showed that when the bullet struck Kennedy in the back of his skull, his head moved backward. From this analysis of the footage, a belief emerged that the shooter was positioned in front of the limousine on a grassy knoll.

The Rockefeller Commission

In 1975, President Ford established the Rockefeller Commission to look into activities related to the CIA, which overlapped with Kennedy assassination theories. The Rockefeller Commission, headed by Vice President Nelson Rockefeller, was also interested in the way Kennedy's head and body moved when he was shot. The commission's report focused in part on whether President Kennedy could have been shot by an assassin positioned in front of the limousine. The commission concluded that the movement of Kennedy's body when shot was consistent with the entry of a bullet from his rear or above him and to his right. "[I]f any other bullet struck the President's head," stated Dr. Cyril H. Wecht, one of three doctors to extensively examine the autopsy photos and x-rays, "whether before, after, or simultaneously with the known shot, there is no evidence for it in the available materials."

The Rockefeller Commission also tackled the issue of CIA involvement. One theory alleged that E. Howard Hunt of the CIA and Frank Sturgis, a former participant in government sponsored anti-Cuban activities, were directly involved in the assassination on behalf of the CIA. This theory emerged in 1974, two years after both men participated in burglarizing the Democratic National Committee headquarters in the Watergate scandal. It was based on the belief that Hunt and Sturgis could be identified as two of the men in press photographs of six to eight vagrants taken into custody by the police after being found loitering in freight cars a half mile from the site of the assassination. The commission, however, was unable to substantiate the presence of either man in Dallas or confirm their identities in the photos.

The second theory alleged that the CIA was in some way connected to Lee Harvey Oswald and Jack Ruby. It was alleged that Hunt and Sturgis had ties with Oswald and Ruby because all men shared the common link of Cuba; each of them at one time had been involved in activities related to Cuba. The commission ruled out this theory. They could find no credible evidence to indicate that either man knew Oswald or Ruby.

Further Investigations

In 1979, another investigation began. This time, the Report of the Select Committee on Assassinations of the U.S. House of Representatives came to another conclusion. The committee concluded that while Oswald had fired three shots, two of which struck the president, there was a high probability that a second shooter may have fired at the president. The report also found that Kennedy's assassination was probably the result of a conspiracy. However, the committee was unable to identify those involved, but they did rule out the CIA, the Cuban government, anti-Castro Cuban groups, the Soviet Union, the FBI, the Secret Service, and organized crime. As for organized crime and anti-Castro groups, the committee noted that while as a group they were ruled out, individual members may have been involved. The committee's report, although it ruled out several conspirators, did manage to keep the conspiracy theories alive with its analysis.

To this day, conspiracy theories about Kennedy's death abound. In 1992, less than one-third of respondents polled believed the Warren Commission's conclusion. When Oliver Stone released his 1991 movie, *JFK*, a renewed batch of conspiracy theories emerged. Most likely, there will always be speculation as to whether Oswald plotted and carried out Kennedy's assassination alone.

Chapter 17

THE PERSONAL SIDE
OF JOHN F. KENNEDY

After Kennedy's death, new facts have emerged about his life. His short term as president was filled with more than just the battles he took on to protect the country. He secretly wrestled with the physical pain brought on by serious medical ailments. His marriage and family life seemed happy, but Kennedy was also caught up in illicit affairs with various women.

JFK and Jackie

By all accounts, Jack and Jackie appeared perfectly matched. They were both good looking and came from wealthy families. As Lem Billings would later say, just the names—Jack and Jackie—were so similar that it seemed as if it were meant to be. In addition, not many women from Kennedy's long stream of relationships had managed to capture his attention long enough for him to consider marriage. But Jackie, with her obvious beauty and sophistication, intrigued him. This was evident from their first meeting; Jackie proved to be a tough opponent when they played a series of word games. Kennedy was used to winning, but Jackie emerged the victor. It was the beginning of their relationship.

Part of what attracted Kennedy to Jackie was her superior social skills. However, after he was elected president it became evident that she preferred to stay out of the public view and wanted to focus on raising their children. She defined her position early on in Kennedy's term. She proclaimed that she was a wife and a mother, but not a public official. She clarified to the White House social secretary that she would not attend lunches or teas or give speeches.

President and Mrs. Kennedy leave for a trip to Pakistan and India.

Photo credit: John F. Kennedy Presidential Library and Museum, Boston

Jackie, however, wanted a little bit more than time with her family, and Kennedy soon learned the cost of his wife's happiness. She had expensive tastes in all things, especially clothing. She quickly exceeded Kennedy's annual presidential salary of $100,000 in 1961 and 1962. In addition, she surpassed the White House entertainment budget, and Kennedy was forced to cover the cost with personal funds. Kennedy's concern for reining in Jackie's spending came to a head when he received the tally for her expenditures at department stores, which totaled $40,000. When he asked her what she had spent it on, she could offer no explanation. Jackie disagreed with her husband's decision to donate his salary to charity.

THEY SAID...

"From the beginning there was a playful element between them. Jackie gave him a good match: that's one of the things Jack liked. But there was a serious element too. Who was going to win?"

—Lem Billings, as quoted in *The Kennedys: America's Emerald Kings*

An Unfaithful Husband

Finances were hardly all that separated Jackie and her husband. His philandering continued after they were married and even when he became president. Jackie most certainly knew about his affairs. On one occasion, when she found a woman's panties in her pillowcase, she asked Jack to find out who they belonged to since they were not her size. For the most part, while Kennedy put little effort into hiding his philandering from Jackie, he was also unconcerned about media exposure. While the mainstream press resisted the temptation to publish information about his philandering, other less reputable media outlets were not so reserved. Nevertheless, Kennedy was rarely concerned that these stories would receive serious attention.

J. Edgar Hoover's Surveillance

There was at least one person who was paying attention to Kennedy's sexual life. FBI director J. Edgar Hoover was keeping close tabs on the president and had a steady stream of information coming in about his affairs. It was common for Hoover to send

Bobby the latest information he had uncovered. It wasn't purely for Bobby's sake that Hoover sent this information. In fact, Hoover had his own personal interest in mind—the preservation of his power.

One such liaison that Hoover learned about was Kennedy's relationship with Judith Campbell, later Exner. Kennedy was introduced to Campbell by Frank Sinatra during his candidacy for the Democratic presidential nomination. At the same time, Sinatra also introduced Campbell to mobster Sam Giancana, and they too began an affair. In 1961, Hoover learned of Kennedy and Campbell's affair from wiretaps placed on Mafia leader John Roselli's phone. The FBI learned that Campbell frequently called the White House and spoke with Kennedy's personal secretary, Evelyn Lincoln, who was charged with making the arrangements for her visits. With this information, Hoover went to Bobby and informed him that his brother was engaged in a relationship with a woman who was involved with mobsters. In March 1962, Kennedy broke off relations with Campbell and in May, upon Bobby's advice, he severed all ties with Sinatra.

FACT

Kennedy's affair with Judith Campbell Exner remained a secret until members of the Republican Party leaked the information to the press in 1975. In 1977, Campbell published the book *Judith Exner: My Story,* which was an account of her relationships with Kennedy and Sam Giancana.

Hoover also knew of another of Kennedy's affairs. This time it was with Ellen Rometsch, a twenty-seven-year-old German-born call girl. Bobby Baker, the Senate secretary to the Democrats, was responsible for their introduction. Although it was a short-term fling, Rometsch became a frequent visitor to the White House for naked pool parties during the spring and summer of 1963. On July 3, Hoover informed Bobby that Rometsch might be a spy. On August 21, Bobby had her deported back to West Germany.

This, however, failed to put an end to the matter. One month later, Bobby Baker, who frequently paired call girls with senators, came under the scrutiny of the Senate Rules Committee, which was investigating whether he was involved in unethical financial transactions. Rather then face scrutiny from his colleagues, Baker resigned on October 7. In the meantime, Bobby Kennedy came to an agreement with Baker for his silence about Rometsch. Nevertheless, on October 26 the *Des Moines Register* reported the story about Rometsch and "some prominent New Frontiersmen from the executive branch of Government."

THEY SAID...

"The President came in all excited about the news reports concerning the German woman and other prostitutes getting mixed up with government officials, Congressmen, etc. He called Mike Mansfield to come to the office to discuss the playing down of this news report."

—Evelyn Lincoln, as quoted in *An Unfinished Life*

In response, Bobby quietly arranged for a meeting between Hoover and Senate leaders Mike Mansfield and Everett Dirksen on October 28. Bobby wanted to make sure that the Senate refrained from investigating the Romestch matter. At the meeting, Hoover reported that there was no evidence to suggest that Rometsch was a German spy. Further, he noted that the FBI investigation had turned up interesting evidence that Baker had provided call girls to numerous senators, and he had the list of names to prove it. The meeting had the desired result. When the investigation into Baker's activities continued, Rometsch was never brought up.

Although Kennedy escaped the revelation of his tainted private life on this occasion, many details would come out after his death. In November 1975, a Senate subcommittee, which was charged with investigating the CIA's assassination plots, uncovered the details of Kennedy's affair with Campbell. Although it comprised just a small footnote, which was buried deep into the report, it was nevertheless exposed. In addition to the affair with Campbell, it was revealed that during Kennedy's administration, the CIA had given the go ahead for Sam Giancana, Campbell's other sexual liaison, to carry out a plot to kill Castro. These two revelations of sex and mobster dealings tainted Kennedy's reputation.

The Other Women

Kennedy also had an affair with Jackie's press secretary Pamela Turnure. Turnure was a twenty-three-year-old who received the job upon Kennedy's urging. She was inexperienced, having never worked in a press position, but Kennedy urged Jackie to hire her. Jackie did as he wished, and he continued on with his three-year relationship with Turnure.

At the same time, Kennedy was having an affair with reporter Ben Bradlee's sister-in-law, Mary Pinchot Meyer. It began in early 1962 after Kennedy propositioned her at a White House reception in December 1961. Meyer was from a political family and Kennedy found solace in their relationship because of her understanding of his political trials. From 1962 to 1963, she visited the White House at least thirty times. The affair was exposed in 1976. Kennedy also had affairs with the White House secretaries he called "Fiddle" and "Faddle," and with numerous other women.

Kennedy and Marilyn Monroe

Kennedy's alleged sexual relationship with actress Marilyn Monroe has received the most interest in recent years. Evidence that they had an affair is inconclusive, but Kennedy did seek to squash rumors that he had a sexual relationship with Monroe. The rumors began when Monroe, wearing a well-fitted rhinestone gown, sang a suggestive rendition of "Happy Birthday" to Kennedy at Madison Square Garden in May 1962. This was one of the only times that Kennedy was concerned with putting a stop to gossip about his womanizing. On his behalf, he sent William Haddad of the Peace Corps to inform editors that the stories were untrue.

It did not help that Monroe was part of the problem when it came to the rumors. She talked to anyone who would listen about her relationship with Kennedy. According to Monroe, she and Kennedy had spent time together at a beach house in Santa Monica and at various hotels. While it is unclear whether theses allegations are true, there is concrete evidence that she did call the White House on numerous occasions.

Kennedy's Children

Jack and Jackie had three children together. Caroline Bouvier Kennedy was born on November 27, 1957, John Fitzgerald Kennedy Jr. was born on November 25, 1960, and their last child, Patrick Bouvier Kennedy, was born on August 7, 1963. Patrick was born five weeks premature at the Otis Air Force Base on Cape Cod. His small frame weighed only four pounds, ten ounces. As was common for premature babies, Patrick was born with respiratory distress syndrome. His condition was untreatable, and he died on August 9, 1963.

President Kennedy and his family.

Photo credit: Robert Knudsen, White House/John F. Kennedy Presidential Library and Museum, Boston

President Kennedy and his family, Hyannis Port.

Photo credit: Cecil Stoughton, White House/John F. Kennedy Presidential Library and Museum, Boston

Caroline Kennedy

When Kennedy died, Caroline had just turned six years old. There is one timeless image of Caroline playing in her father's office at the White House while he looks on that has become one of the most memorable shots of her. While there were numerous other pictures taken at the White House, for the most part, she has shied away from the kind of publicity that being a Kennedy has typically brought.

President Kennedy and daughter Caroline aboard the "Honey Fitz" off Hyannis Port, Massachusetts.

Photo credit: Cecil Stoughton, White House/John F. Kennedy Presidential Library and Museum, Boston

Caroline, however, did not immediately retreat from publicity or politics. Upon the urging of Ted Kennedy, she got a taste of the political system when she worked as an intern in his Senate office. But Caroline preferred a less public position. After graduating from Harvard University, she began her career working at the Metropolitan Museum of Art in New York. During this

HE SAID...

"I have been presented with this donkey by two young ladies down there for my daughter. My daughter has the greatest collection of donkeys. She doesn't even know what an elephant looks like. We are going to protect her from that knowledge."

time, she met her future husband Edwin Schlossberg. After years of dating, they married while she was attending Columbia Law School. She graduated in 1988, and gave birth to their first child shortly thereafter. Two other children followed.

In 1989, Caroline was instrumental in the creation of the Profiles in Courage Award, given annually to public officials who fit the definition of courage in John F. Kennedy's book of the same name. She edited *Profiles in Courage for Our Time*, a collection of fifteen essays on modern politicians, and coauthored the 1991 book, *In Our Defense: The Bill of Rights in Action*.

Over the years, Caroline has increasingly stepped out into the public eye. She became a board member for the Citizens Committee for New York City in 1997 and became the president of the John F. Kennedy Library Foundation in Boston. One year later, she became active in a Washington campaign against an initiative that threatened to end affirmative action in that state. More recently, from 2002 to 2004, she took on the role of chief executive for the Office of Strategic Partnerships for the New York City Department of Education. Caroline now serves as the director of the NAACP Legal Defense and Educational Fund and the Director of the Commission on Presidential Debates.

John F. Kennedy Jr.

One of the most famous photos of John F. Kennedy Jr. was taken on his third birthday as he saluted the carriage carrying his father's casket. The American public adored him and anticipated that John Jr. might inspire the nation and carry on his father's legacy. But Jackie wanted her children to grow up as normally as possible and limited the media's access to them while they were young.

President Kennedy and his son, John F. Kennedy Jr., at the White House.

Photo credit: Cecil Stoughton, White House/John F. Kennedy Presidential Library and Museum, Boston

Although many Americans knew what they wanted John to do, John himself had other plans after he graduated from Brown University in 1983. He helped the poor in India and tried theater. He then entered New York University Law School and graduated in 1989. It took three attempts for him to pass the New York state bar, and the press scrutinized his failures. Meanwhile, John worked for the Manhattan district attorney's office. In 1993, he became dissatisfied with practicing law and resigned from his position. In 1995, he launched the magazine *George*. With this new venture he had the opportunity to interview both politicians and notable public figures.

All the while, he was heralded as one of America's most eligible bachelors. In 1988, *People* magazine named him the "sexist man alive." His bachelor status ended when he married Carolyn Bessette in 1996. The union resulted in intense press coverage for the young couple. Bessette was irritated by the scrutiny, but the press ignored John's appeals for privacy. Her comings and goings and a well-publicized fight between the couple in New York's Central Park received notable coverage.

On July 16, 1999, John, Carolyn, and Carolyn's sister were reported missing after their plane disappeared en route to Hyannis Port. Their bodies were later discovered submerged in the waters along the Massachusetts coast.

Lifelong Medical Problems

John F. Kennedy was plagued by health problems for much of his life. In 1934, doctors diagnosed Kennedy with a condition called colitis. Colitis causes inflammation in the lining of the colon. This inflammation results in the development of ulcers in the lining of the large intestine and is responsible for effectively eliminating the cells that line the colon. As a result, Kennedy experienced frequent diarrhea since the colon was forced to empty more than usual.

QUESTION
What is the cause of colitis?
Doctors are unclear about the exact cause of colitis, but it is believed that the condition is the result of the immune system's reaction to the presence of a virus or bacteria. This, in turn, causes the inflammation in the lining of the colon.

To treat Kennedy's colitis, he was given a steroid treatment beginning in 1937. One year later, he began suffering from back pain. According to biographer Robert Dallek, Kennedy's back condition and stomach ulcer were a result of the steroid treatment. Dallek asserts that Kennedy's erratic use of steroids caused not just his back and ulcer conditions, but was also the likely cause of his Addison's disease. Another explanation is that Kennedy's Addison's disease could have been inherited, especially since his sister Eunice also suffered from the condition.

Although Kennedy was receiving the necessary treatment for his medical conditions when he became the president, he still suffered from the side effects. Abdominal problems, diarrhea, and back pain plagued his daily existence. Kennedy's medication included daily injections of codeine and procaine for pain, and cortisone to treat his Addison's disease. It was the back pain that gave him the most problems. At times the pain was so intense that simple acts of walking up or down the stairs and bending caused great discomfort. To lessen the pain and strengthen his back, he wore a back brace and often needed the assistance of crutches to walk.

President Kennedy.

Photo credit: Robert Knudsen, White House/John F. Kennedy Presidential Library and Museum, Boston

Over time, Kennedy increasingly focused less on the pain and more on the possibility that his health condition would eventually be uncovered to the public. Around the same time that Johnson told the press that Kennedy had Addison's disease, Kennedy's bag of medication was misplaced. This occurrence led to increased security measures in regard to his medical condition. Once he was president, his medical records were hidden safely away in a vault and the several doctors who treated him for other ailments were often in the dark regarding the entire extent of his medical condition.

By the end of his life, Kennedy had made substantial progress in alleviating his ailments. When one of his several doctors informed him that if he continued on with his pain treatment, he could expect to one day end up in a wheelchair, Kennedy began intense exercise therapy. With a new regimen of swimming, his pain decreased and he became much more mobile than he had been.

Kennedy's View on a Free Press

When Kennedy became president, he quickly discovered that it was going to be a battle to keep the press on his side. One of the first notable negative brushes with the press occurred after the failed Bay of Pigs invasion. Kennedy believed that the failure was partly caused by the press. In April 1961, he told the press at the American Newspaper Publishers Association that they should consider abstaining from printing certain information "in the interest of national security." Needless to say, the press was unenthusiastic about the idea. When Kennedy later met with a group of editors and publishers who wanted to discuss his recommendation, he admitted that the freedom of the press was essential to democracy.

The value Kennedy placed on a free press was once again jeopardized by his irritation with the coverage of the Vietnam conflict. Several press stories reported that progress was slow, contradicting Diem's reports.

HE SAID...

"[T]here is a terrific disadvantage not having the abrasive quality of the press applied to you daily, to an administration, even though we never like it, and even though we wish they didn't write it, and even though we disapprove, there isn't any doubt that we could not do the job at all in a free society without a very, very active press."

253

Furthermore, they alleged a conflict between U.S. military advisers and Diem's military. Such reports caused Kennedy to believe that the press was not just unfair to his administration, but that many reporters were in search of a controversial story at any cost.

In response, he decided that the best way to prevent the leaks was to place restrictions on their sources. He instituted a rule that his officials were forbidden from engaging in solo meetings with reporters in regard to Vietnam. If they did, it was expected that they provide a written report about the discussion. Of course the media was upset by this rule, but Kennedy believed that this restriction was necessary in order to protect highly sensitive information. Although the leaks continued, the press could hardly ignore what they believed was the president's attempt to keep them in the dark. Overall, while Kennedy knew that the press was essential in a free country, he believed that national security concerns warranted limitations on press coverage.

Kennedy's Catholic Faith

Most historians provide little account of Kennedy's faith. It is typically believed that he never took Catholicism seriously. This perception is understandable considering that he rarely displayed public signs of his faith nor did he abide by the tenants of Catholicism regarding sex. However, Thomas Maier, a Kennedy family biographer, sees it another way. According to Maier, even though Kennedy was never considered very religious in comparison with Bobby or his sister Eunice, he was a practicing Catholic. He attended Mass, followed the traditions of the church, and prayed. Lem Billings also confirms this but has stated that Kennedy held a certain amount of skepticism when it came to his religion.

In addition, others who knew him noted that it was not uncommon for Kennedy to side with the Catholic position in regard to a historical conflict. And that, according to Schlesinger, included his distaste for certain anti-Catholic words such as "liberal." By many accounts, Kennedy's faith was something he rarely talked about. As

Ted Sorensen put it, he was a "faithful adherent" and accepted it "as part of his life." As for discussing his faith, Kennedy rarely did.

THEY SAID...

"I don't think he was a dedicated Catholic like his mother and sisters, but he was a good Catholic. I cannot remember in my life when Jack Kennedy didn't go to Church on Sunday. . . . I never, never, never remember in my life Jack's missing his prayers at night on his knees. He always went to confession when he was supposed to."

—Lem Billings, as quoted in *The Kennedys: America's Emerald Kings*

According to Maier, part of Kennedy's hesitancy to speak about his religious belief lay in his concern for his political career. When he ran for president he avoided taking pictures with bishops or nuns. When a *Look* magazine article questioned Kennedy's commitment to Catholicism, Cardinal Cushing immediately wrote a defensive response. He gave Kennedy a copy, but his advisors determined that it would do more harm than good.

There was one occasion that Kennedy allowed the public a glimpse into his religious affairs. While he was president-elect, the world witnessed the well-publicized baptism of John Kennedy Jr. Photographs documented the joyous event, and *Life* magazine made the baptism its cover story. The article captured the baptism that took place at the chapel in the Georgetown University Hospital. Reverend Martin J. Casey presided over the event as Jackie and an elated Kennedy looked on. The public saw a new side of Kennedy, and in fact, it would be one of the only times he was seen publicly practicing his religion.

Chapter 18

JOHN F. KENNEDY'S LEGACY

Without a doubt John F. Kennedy has become one of America's most favorite presidents. Among his greatest accomplishments were his leadership during the Cuban missile crisis and the establishment of the Peace Corps. In contrast to his success, however, the Bay of Pigs invasion and his stance on civil rights showed him at his worst. Yet more than Kennedy's successes and failures, his ability to inspire many Americans to serve their country has been his lasting legacy.

A Global Icon

During his term, Kennedy rose to become one of the world's most prominent and respected leaders. People from all over the world identified with him, and his death elicited an outpouring of grief. U.S. embassies around the globe were packed with people waiting to sign condolence books. In West Berlin, mourners gathered in the square outside city hall where Kennedy had given one of his most memorable speeches mere months before. Behind the Iron Curtain, Khrushchev expressed his heartfelt sympathies, and Soviet television broadcast Kennedy's funeral.

THEY SAID...

"People expressed their grief without restraint, and just about everybody in Guinea seemed to have fallen under the spell of the courageous young hero of far away, the slayer of the dragons of discrimination, poverty, ignorance, and war."

—Dispatch from the U.S. Embassy in Ghana, *A Thousand Days*

The Appeal of JFK

Kennedy served the sixth-shortest presidential term ever, and yet he remains one of the most admired U.S. presidents. Perhaps his popularity is due in part to his tragic death, but this does not explain the fascination completely. Besides Abraham Lincoln, who is also one of the most esteemed presidents, James Garfield and William McKinley were also assassinated, but neither of them commands the level of reverence Kennedy receives. Kennedy's accomplishments pale in comparison to other presidents who accomplished more, so this cannot be the reason for Kennedy's lasting appeal.

Part of the explanation lies in what Arthur Schlesinger believed was Kennedy's appeal—he promised hope. When Kennedy died, for many so did this hope. This explains why it is so often wondered: What if John F. Kennedy had lived?

THEY SAID...

"John Fitzgerald Kennedy in his thousand days gave the country back to its own best self. And he taught the world that the process of rediscovering America was not over."

—Arthur Schlesinger, *A Thousand Days*

Kennedy's Personality

Sixty percent of respondents in one poll considered Kennedy's the most appealing of presidential personalities. Kennedy's use of television displayed his public persona best. He used it to his advantage, clearly displaying his humor, wit, sincerity, and confidence.

Kennedy also enjoyed the image of a sophisticated and well-cultured family man. His public support for the arts and Jackie Kennedy's efforts behind the scenes made the White House a place where creativity was celebrated and encouraged.

Kennedy's image as a father of young children added to the public perception that he was a young and vibrant leader. One particular photo that reflected this public fascination was the image of five-year-old Caroline and two-year-old John playing in the Oval Office as Kennedy looked on.

Kennedy's Popularity

Kennedy inspired the nation in a way that no other president had done. His inaugural address motivated Americans, especially young people, to serve, and this speech is often used to represent what Kennedy stood for.

Kennedy remains one of the nation's most beloved presidents. A 1975 Gallup poll revealed that 52 percent of Americans ranked him first among the presidents. Ten years later, Kennedy still held the number one spot. More recent polls confirm his standing. In 1999, Kennedy tied for second with Ronald Reagan, George Washington, and Bill Clinton. By 2000, however, the public put him right back in first.

> ## THEY SAID...
> "Whatever that Kennedy 'thing' was, I wanted a part of it. I developed an inchoate . . . sense of longing to be connected to something larger and more historic. . . . It made me determined to find a career that could take me closer to the world he inhabited, where world history could play out before my eyes."
>
> —Journalist Jonathan Alter, as quoted in
> *"We'll Never Be Young Again"*

Kennedy's Critics

While the public considers Kennedy one of the greatest leaders, historians have reservations about whether he deserves such notable praise. They point out that Kennedy failed to enact momentous legislation. Although he averted a nuclear war during the missile crisis, created the Peace Corps, and negotiated a test ban treaty, most historians do not believe these accomplishments are enough to make him one of America's greatest presidents. In fact, among the academic community he has been commonly referred to as overrated. In 2000, seventy-eight scholars ranked him at number eighteen out of forty-two presidents, near the bottom of the above-average list.

Kennedy, however, did accomplish one thing no other president had. He confronted the stigma attached to his faith and convinced a majority of Americans that they did not need to be afraid of a Catholic in the White House. With this action, Kennedy broke down political barriers for all minorities, not just Catholics.

No matter what the scholars think of Kennedy, the public has remained steadfast in its fascination. Not even the exposure of his womanizing and his secret health problems could destroy the public's affection for Kennedy.

Preserving Kennedy's Legacy

The admiration for Kennedy is due in part to the work of Jackie Kennedy. She understood what her husband meant to the nation, and it influenced her decision to bury him at Arlington National Cemetery instead of in a more private place. "He belongs to the people," she explained.

Camelot

A week after Kennedy's assassination, Jackie sat down to talk with *Life* magazine reporter Theodore H. White. In the emotional interview, Jackie described one of the things Kennedy enjoyed doing most. At night when he had time to relax, he listened to the recording of the 1960 musical "Camelot," and he especially liked the line "don't let it be forgot that for one brief shining moment there was Camelot." For Jackie, Camelot represented Kennedy's presidency.

QUESTION

What is the original meaning of Camelot and how has it changed?
Camelot originally referred to the legendary King Arthur's court in England in the sixth century. Now the term has come to encompass the definition of an idyllic or peaceful place or situation.

The analogy stuck. *Life* magazine printed the story, and magazines and newspapers seized the name. Eventually the music of "Camelot" was played alongside of photos and television clips of Kennedy, cementing the Kennedy-Camelot association.

John F. Kennedy Space Center

Jackie Kennedy wanted her husband's commitment to space exploration to be remembered. After Kennedy was assassinated, the Launch Operations Center was renamed the John F. Kennedy Space Center in his honor.

The Kennedy Space Center has been instrumental in NASA's success. It has been the launching and landing site for many of NASA's flights, including Apollo 11, the first successful human mission to the moon. It is still an active part of the space program, and visitors are encouraged to take a tour of the center and view public exhibits.

FACT

In 1964, the Department of the Interior renamed Cape Canaveral, Florida, as Cape Kennedy over the protests of local Floridians, who successfully lobbied to have the name changed back to Cape Canaveral ten years later.

John F. Kennedy Presidential Library and Museum

Every president since Herbert Hoover has a presidential library to house the papers, photographs, and other historical artifacts of his term in office. Jackie Kennedy took the lead in implementing her vision for her husband's library. She saw it as a living part of the president's legacy, a place to encourage learning and the free exchange of ideas, not simply a repository for the effects of the Kennedy administration.

I. M. Pei's eye-catching white building sits on the edge of Columbia Point in Boston, Massachusetts, overlooking Dorchester Bay. Completed in 1979, the library's collection includes photographs, original papers, presidential recordings, speeches, and an oral history project comprised of more than 1,100 interviews with those who knew Kennedy.

In addition, it holds the collection of one of America's literary greats. Jackie Kennedy pursued an offer from Mary Hemingway, Ernest Hemingway's widow, to house Hemingway's collection alongside the president's.

FACT

Kennedy applied Hemingway's definition of courage, "grace under pressure," to the statesmen he honored in *Profiles in Courage*. Kennedy and Hemingway respected each other, although they never met. Hemingway was invited to Kennedy's inauguration, but his ill health kept him from attending. He died in 1961.

In 1968, four years after Mary Hemingway had offered to donate her husband's collection, it was finally given to the library. The collection contains thousands of pages of hand-written manuscripts, family photographs, and personal correspondence. The Hemingway Research Room opened in 1980.

Hemingway's collection is not open to the general public, but the John F. Kennedy Presidential Museum allows visitors to journey back to the 1960s and explore the life of the president.

John F. Kennedy National Historic Site

The Kennedy National Historic Site was founded on May 26, 1967, after Congress established Kennedy's birth home in Brookline, Massachusetts, as a site of preservation. The house went through several owners after the Kennedys moved out in 1920. In 1966, the Kennedy family purchased the home and started to restore it. From Rose Kennedy's memory, the home was reconstructed to represent the way it looked when the family lived there. Not all of the objects in the home are original, but Kennedy's bassinet and porringer are among the 152 objects that are.

President Kennedy and Rose Kennedy at the first annual international awards dinner for the Joseph P. Kennedy Jr. Foundation.

Photo credit: Abbie Rowe, White House/John F. Kennedy Presidential Library and Museum, Boston

John F. Kennedy Center for the Performing Arts

The Kennedy Center was a work in progress even before it took on the name of one of America's most popular presidents. President Eisenhower created the National Cultural Center Act in 1958 to promote the arts. Kennedy inherited the program from Eisenhower and advanced it.

FACT

The Center was dedicated to Kennedy for his commitment to the arts. While in office, he conducted fundraising luncheons at the White House to earn money for the Center. Jackie was also instrumental in creating a cultural environment at the White House with the concerts, musicals, and plays that were held in the East Room.

On January 23, 1964, President Johnson signed the John F. Kennedy Act into law, making the center a living memorial. To help get the project underway, Congress allocated $23 million to the construction of the John F. Kennedy Center for the Performing Arts. Private donations were also secured, and in December 1965, construction began in Washington, D.C., near the Lincoln Center. On September 8, 1971, the Center hosted its first performance. Its performances run the gamut from comedy acts to celebrations of classical music. Each year, the center honors five individuals for their contributions to the arts.

Kennedy's Cold War Legacy

The Kennedy administration pursued a two-sided approach toward the Cold War. Kennedy pursued negotiations with the Soviet Union to put an end to the arms race, yet he dedicated military resources to stop the spread of communism in Southeast Asia.

A Committed Proponent of Peace

Kennedy's desire for peace can be traced back to his college days. His initial stance on World War II—that negotiation was possible—clearly reflects his desire for harmony over discord. This was a naïve perspective in regard to World War II, but it represented his early idealism. By the time he became president, Kennedy would describe himself as an "idealist without illusions." Kennedy's idealism and realism, combined with his commitment to peace, helped him react in the turbulent 1960s.

The Cuban missile crisis tested his resolve. It was the

HE SAID...

"Unless we are willing to take the leadership in the United States, next week as well as next year, unless we are willing to channel more of our ideas and our programs and delegate power to that body in the fight for peace, then we may expect to see the last great hope of peace swallowed up in the oceans of indifference and hate."

first time America had come so close to nuclear war with the Soviet Union. With the Soviet threat in Cuba, Kennedy found that Congress and many Americans favored a military strike rather than a blockade. Kennedy, although prepared to protect the United States, more than anything wanted a nonmilitary resolution. Rather than use military force to resolve the situation, he chose a safer, less deadly method: a blockade. In the end, this approach and Kennedy's diplomacy when dealing with Khrushchev ended the crisis without bloodshed. The crisis was a wake-up call to both sides, and it helped push negotiations for the historic nuclear test ban treaty along.

Vietnam

Kennedy subscribed to the "domino theory"—if communism gained a foothold in one developing nation, others around it would inevitably follow suit. Such a situation could have grave political and economic consequences, especially in Southeast Asia. The United States was intent on preventing the Asian communist powers, China and the Soviet Union, from exporting their views to democratic parts of the region.

The Eisenhower administration had taken the first steps toward the Vietnam War, and Kennedy continued on the same path. He

HE SAID...

"To renounce the world of freedom now, to abandon those who share our commitment, and retire into lonely and not so splendid isolation, would be to give communism the one hope which, in this twilight of disappointment for them, might repair their divisions and rekindle their hope."

made two crucial decisions: he drastically increased the number of U.S. military advisors in the region and he supported the overthrow of the Diem government in November 1963. Kennedy did not live long enough to do more, but the increased U.S. military involvement in Vietnam after his death has affected the view on his policy. Johnson claimed to have based his Vietnam policy on Kennedy's. Schlesinger and other Kennedy advisors argue Kennedy never would have escalated the conflict as much as Johnson did and that Kennedy was in fact seriously considering reducing the U.S. military presence. Speculation on what would have happened if Kennedy had lived is impossible. The conflict worsened, and Kennedy undeniably contributed to U.S. involvement in the region.

Alliance for Progress

Kennedy attempted to control the spread of communism through the creation of the Alliance for Progress. The program promised to promote democracy in Latin America through social reforms in such areas as education, land reform, healthcare, technology, and science. It "is an alliance of free governments," Kennedy stated to a group of Latin American representatives at the White House on March 13, 1961, "and it must work to eliminate tyranny from a hemisphere in which it has no rightful place." Ultimately, however, even though Kennedy had originally promised $20 billion and several Latin American countries, excluding Cuba, agreed to supply $80 billion over ten years, the administration's focus on Vietnam offset the success of this program and the original amount promised. The program was dismantled in 1973.

Kennedy's Legacy on Civil Rights

Kennedy promised freedom to the world, but he was more cautious about ensuring equal rights in the United States. Although he expressed his commitment to civil rights to leaders such as Martin Luther King, he was slow to act. Kennedy was only convinced of the necessity of civil rights legislation after violence broke out in the South, and he was willing to eliminate parts of his civil rights bill in order to secure its passage.

Kennedy's leadership in the civil rights arena was hesitant at best, but he laid the groundwork for the civil rights measures his successors carried out after his death. Less than a year after Kennedy's assassination, Lyndon B. Johnson signed the Civil Rights Act of 1964 into law. The bill was monumental. Among its provisions, it struck down laws that allowed segregation in public places, it gave power to the federal government to enforce school desegregation, and it established a Commission on Equal Employment Opportunity.

Johnson did what it appeared Kennedy was unable to do, and he did it without stripping the bill of its most important measures. The combination of Kennedy's vision and Johnson's skill as a politician led to the passage of legislation that secured rights for all Americans.

THEY SAID...

"To me, one of President Kennedy's greatest achievements was inspiring a generation of Americans to serve their country. He believed that each person in our society can make a difference, and that everyone should try. His influence reaches across decades because of his extraordinary ability to articulate fundamental principles of democracy, freedom, and patriotism."

—Caroline Kennedy, "Message from Caroline Kennedy"

His Leadership Inspired a Nation

Kennedy's ability to inspire ordinary people to action is perhaps the most enduring part of his legacy. More than 187,000 volunteers have joined the Peace Corps, and countless others followed Kennedy's example in the political arena.

Clearly, Kennedy was imperfect both in his personal life and as president but perhaps he fulfilled the nation's need for a president who exuded confidence in a time when it seemed that democracy might be unable to withstand the threat of communism and the arms race. From his first day in office to the negotiation of the test ban treaty, Kennedy's most pressing goals were to keep Americans safe and democracy strong. More than that, he brought something unique to the presidency in his call for unselfish duty. Maybe it was exactly this plea that has made him an appealing and long-standing favorite among Americans.

John F. Kennedy, White House, Oval Office.

Photo credit: Cecil Stoughton, White House/John F. Kennedy Presidential Library and Museum, Boston

Appendix A

JOHN F. KENNEDY'S SIBLINGS

The Kennedy family has seen their fair share of misfortune. The tragic death of Joe, Kathleen, Jack, and Bobby has led to the belief by some that the family is cursed. Although it seems that tragedy exerts a strong hold on their lives, more than anything it is because of the family's wealth and fame that their misfortune has received particular attention. More important than the tragedy has been the common thread for all of the Kennedy children. Whether through politics or nonprofit organizations, the family's wealth has provided them with innumerable opportunities to serve.

Joseph Kennedy Jr.

Joseph P. Kennedy Jr. was born on July 25, 1915. He shared his father's intense drive for success. At Harvard, he too was invited to join the Hasty Pudding Club, and he also received an invitation to join the elite Spee Club. By most accounts, his drive for success was his most memorable quality.

THEY SAID...

"Yet, for all the difficulty between the two brothers, they shared a common vitality and an essential closeness. . . . After Joe's death, Jack would confess that in all his experience, he didn't know anyone with a better sense of humor or anyone with whom he would 'rather have spent an evening or played golf or in fact done anything.'"—Doris Kearns Goodwin, *The Fitzgeralds and the Kennedys*

In 1938, Joe graduated *cum laude* from Harvard. He decided to attend law school, which he anticipated would prepare him for a political career. One year after he entered Harvard Law School, he decided to run for delegate to the 1940 presidential convention. His grandfather John Fitzgerald was still up to his old tricks and advised Joe that he could fix the election in his favor through a contact. Joe Sr. was strongly opposed and encouraged his son to vie for the seat by campaigning. Joe did as his father wished, and when voting day arrived it was evident that he had run a successful campaign. He came in second, winning one of the two delegate seats.

When it came time to vote at the convention in July 1940, Joe emerged as a young politician able to hold his own. During the campaigning, he had promised to support and cast his vote for Jim Farley. However, when the convention got underway, Roosevelt suddenly decided to run for a third term. Initially, Farley, the Democratic Committee chairman, had widespread support from the delegates, but with Roosevelt's announcement many switched sides. Roosevelt was intent on a unanimous victory, but Joe was one of the delegates who stood in the way. He refused to change his vote from Farley. He reasoned that since he had committed to vote for the chairman, he would keep his pledge. When the votes were finally cast, Joe stood true to his word. Although he was among the minority, he made his father proud that he had stood up for his convictions. His actions, too, caught the attention of the public.

HE SAID...

"Joe refused his proffered leave and persuaded his crew to remain on for D-day. . . . He felt it unfair to ask his crew to stay on longer, and they returned to the United States. He remained. For he had heard of a new and special assignment for which volunteers had been requested which would require another month of the most dangerous type of flying."

A political career, however, would have to wait. In May 1941, before entering his final year of law school, he signed up to join the navy as a pilot. After training at a navy air base in Quincy, Massachusetts, he was sent to Jacksonville, Florida, for more instruction. After ten tough months of preparation, Joe graduated in May 1942. Following his training to fly a B-24 Liberator, Joe was stationed in the English Channel where he was charged with making routine flights over the area.

More than anything, Joe was drawn to excitement. In July 1943 when he heard about a dangerous assignment in the English Channel and the Bay of Biscay, he quickly volunteered for the mission. He wrote his father about the assignment, but Joe Sr., far less enthusiastic, cautioned him not to push his luck. Nevertheless, this caution came too late. Joe had already committed to the mission, and on August 12, 1944, after checking his flight plans and plane, he was all set to go. Joe and a copilot took off from the airfield. At first it seemed that the mission was proceeding as planned, but ten minutes before its scheduled completion, the plane exploded.

Rose Marie Kennedy

Rosemary, as she was called, was born on September 13, 1918. It became apparent early on that she had special needs. The usual childhood developments of crawling, walking, and speaking occurred much later than usual. Due to her slow development, Rose Kennedy paid particular attention to Rosemary. At first Rose believed that her daughter's slow development was a result of the natural differences in children. When Rosemary was finally tested, however, it was discovered that she was mentally retarded. At the time, there was almost no literature on the condition, nor was there substantial help for caretakers. Most often, it was recommended to place the child in an institution. Nevertheless, Rose and Joe refused to send their daughter away.

Instead, they hired tutors and governesses to care for her. Rosemary learned to read, write, dance, and play tennis, and she was also an active participant in family activities such as sailing. Her participation was in part a reflection of Joe and Rose's desire to keep her condition hidden. Most people, even extended family, were unaware of it. She was presented as the shy, quiet child.

In 1938, when her younger sister Kathleen was presented at court at Buckingham Palace, Rosemary was by her side. Rosemary had spent hours practicing, and when it was all over no one had noticed that she was any different from her sister. In 1939, while Rosemary accompanied her father in England during his ambassadorship, two reporters wrote her a letter requesting an interview. Joe composed a reply for her, and she copied it. In it, she stated that she was studying psychology after having just received a teaching degree. In truth, Rosemary was attending a special school.

By 1942, Rosemary abruptly changed. She had been happy, sweet, and easy to get along with, but suddenly she became prone to violent outbursts. She began screaming, hitting, and swearing. Additionally, she took up the habit of roaming the streets alone in the middle of the night. It was believed that Rosemary was finally feeling the effects of womanhood and that she was frustrated that unlike her siblings, she was unable to accomplish the same level of achievement.

Whatever the reason, Rose and Joe were extremely worried. Joe decided that a prefrontal lobotomy was the best course of action. According to experts, this type of operation would relieve her of the worry she felt but would not interfere with her ability to function. Joe, without telling Rose, had the surgery performed in 1941. When Rosemary emerged, it was clear that something had gone wrong. Her ability to speak was severely impaired and her head, which had once stood erect, tilted to the side.

FACT

The first lobotomy was performed by Dr. Egas Moniz in 1935. Its reported success earned him a Nobel Prize. At the time, it was believed that by drilling a dime-sized hole into the skull and severing the connecting fibers in the front part of the brain, behaviors such as violent episodes and depression could be eliminated.

After the surgery, Joe still told Rose nothing about it. He did inform her that he had placed her in an institution and recommended that she not visit for a while. Rose remained absent from Rosemary's life until Joe had a stroke in 1961. She finally visited her at St. Coletta's, an institution in Jefferson, Wisconsin. It was then that she discovered something was wrong. Not long afterward, she found out the ugly truth of what Joe had done. Rosemary remained in an institution until she died on January 7, 2005.

Kathleen "Kick" Kennedy

Kathleen Kennedy was born on February 20, 1920. Early on, it was evident that Kathleen had a passion for life. She was bubbly, happy, popular, and athletic. Kathleen attended Riverdale County School, Noroton Convent of the Sacred Heart in Connecticut, and spent one year in France attending the Holy Child Convent. While her father served as ambassador, Kathleen lived with the family in England. While there, in addition to her presentment to the court with Rosemary, she also had a very successful debutante ball in May

1938. Among the 300 guests, she had the chance to dance with the prince of Prussia and the Earl of Chichester and Viscount Newport. The most important person she met in England was her future husband, William Cavendish Harrington.

After returning to the United States in 1939, she enrolled at Finch School, located in New York. Kathleen, however, wanted to help Great Britain during wartime. She volunteered for the Red Cross and took charge of organizing luncheons and fashion shows to earn money for injured British seamen. It was a noble cause, but Kathleen soon turned her attention to personal endeavors. In 1941, she began her career at the *Times-Herald* in Washington, D.C. It was there that she had the opportunity to spend time with Jack, who was serving in the navy.

THEY SAID...

"I can still remember how happy Jack was when she came to the convent at Noroton. The first week she was there he insisted we sneak up and visit her, and what fun we had. . . . Kathleen and Jack . . . they . . . loved each other as much as any brother and sister I have ever seen."

—Lem Billings, as quoted in *The Fitzgeralds and the Kennedys*

Kathleen soon found that she could no longer deny her passion to help in the war effort. After receiving training to become a Red Cross volunteer, she returned to London in June 1943. She served as the program assistant for a club that provided food and supplies to officers. Not long after her arrival, she married Harrington in May 1944. After he died in wartime service three months later, Kathleen decided to make her permanent home in London. She too, however, met an untimely death when her plane crashed on May 13, 1948. She was buried in Chatsworth, England.

Eunice Kennedy

Eunice Kennedy Shriver was born on July 10, 1921, in Brookline, Massachusetts. After attending Convent of the Sacred Heart School in Noroton, Connecticut, and Manhattanville College, she attended Stanford University, where she earned a bachelor's degree in sociology in 1943. Eunice's sociology degree was an early indication of her interest in helping others. Shortly after her graduation, she began working on a juvenile delinquency project for the Department of Justice. By 1950, her interest had expanded to include social work. For a year she worked in Alderson, West Virginia, at the Penitentiary for Women.

Eunice's true passion came out after she married Robert Sargent Shriver. She took on the cause that had ailed her sister Rosemary for her entire life. Out of all the Kennedy children, she had been the closest to Rosemary. She understood her and felt a unique bond and responsibility for her. In 1957, she began with her service to the Joseph P. Kennedy Jr. Foundation. She led the foundation in its efforts to discover the cause of mental retardation and in the organization's attempt to promote new ways for society to deal with its mentally retarded populace. One of Eunice's greatest accomplishments was the creation of the Special Olympics in 1968. For her dedication to helping those with disabilities, she has received numerous awards such as the Presidential Medal of Freedom, the Legion of Honor, and the Theodore Roosevelt Award.

Patricia Kennedy

Patricia Kennedy was born on May 6, 1924. By the time she reached Rosemont College where she earned her bachelor's in 1945, it was evident that Patricia had a love of acting. She acted and directed plays, and after she graduated, she obtained a position as an assistant for NBC's production department in New York. She eventually landed a job as an assistant for the Family Theater and Family Rosary Crusade in Los Angeles. In 1954, she married English actor Peter Lawford. They had four children together but divorced in 1965.

Besides an intense passion for acting, Patricia was one of her brother Jack's biggest supporters. She was involved in the teas during his campaign for the House in 1946 and his Senate campaign in 1952. During his presidential campaign, she served as a traveling spokesperson. Just as she had done for her brother John, she would later support her brothers Robert and Edward in their political campaigns. Patricia, however, returned to her passion for the arts. She created the National Committee for the Literary Arts and she began raising money for the arts through fundraisers and charity auctions. Patricia died on September 17, 2006.

Robert Francis Kennedy

Bobby Kennedy was born on November 20, 1925. Bobby, a small and shy child, was both more religious and more obedient than the other Kennedy children. Although he was considered gentle and affectionate, he did possess his father's driving force to succeed. Prior to attending college, just like his older brothers Joe and John, he too wanted to serve in the navy. After serving, he graduated from Harvard University with a degree in government and later received a law degree from the University of Virginia Law School. While attending law school, he married Ethel Skakel in 1950. They eventually had eleven children.

HE SAID...

"I've been criticized by quite a few people for making my brother Bobby attorney general. They didn't realize that I had a very good reason for that appointment. Bobby wants to practice law, and I thought he ought to get a little experience first."

Although he never practiced law, early on Bobby had a passion for justice. When John Kennedy died, Bobby resigned as attorney general and started a campaign to become a New York senator. He won the 1964 election and got right to work. He developed a special commitment to the poor in America and around the world. In an effort to raise the consciousness of the American public, he traveled to ghettos and migrant camps where he got a firsthand look at the conditions they faced. With this knowledge, he spoke out on behalf of the less fortunate.

Bobby's passion went beyond the United States. He traveled to Eastern Europe, Latin America, and South Africa where the lack of political participation caught his attention. He believed that all people were entitled to political freedom. In February 1966, Bobby came to believe that South Vietnam was also entitled to sovereignty. When President Johnson stepped up U.S. involvement in Vietnam, Bobby became a vocal opponent. He urged Johnson to decrease American participation and promoted his belief that a negotiation and the restructuring of the economic and political system in South Vietnam was the most effective strategy.

Besides his interest in Vietnam, Bobby had other goals. Just like his older brother he too wanted to become president. On March 18, 1968, he announced his run for the Democratic presidential nomination. On June 5, he was shot and killed by Sirhan Sirhan at the Ambassador Hotel in Los Angeles after clinching a crucial victory in the California primary.

Jean Ann Kennedy

Jean, the youngest daughter of Rose and Joe Kennedy, was born on February 20, 1928, in Brookline, Massachusetts. She graduated from Manhattanville College with a degree in English. She married Stephen E. Smith in 1956, and they had four children. Just like the rest of her family, when John Kennedy ran for president, she campaigned around the country on his behalf. After helping her brother win, she put her focus into other activities. In 1964, she began serving as a board member for the Joseph P. Kennedy Jr. Foundation. She later served on the board of the John F. Kennedy Center for Performing Arts.

Jean, like her sister Eunice, also had compassion for those with disabilities. In 1974, she created a nonprofit organization, Very

Special Arts, for people with disabilities. The organization was established to help the disabled participate in art and also to provide a forum to showcase their work. In 1993, her book *Chronicles of Courage: Very Special Artists* was published. Jean, however, would change course and follow in her father's footsteps. In 1993, she was appointed by President Clinton to serve as the U.S. Ambassador to Ireland. She served until 1998.

Edward Moore Kennedy

Ted, the youngest of the Kennedy clan, was born on February 22, 1932. He graduated from Harvard with a degree in government in 1956, and from the University of Virginia Law School in 1959. In 1958, he married Virginia Joan Bennett and they had three children together. Not surprisingly, after college he hoped to embark upon a political career. After John Kennedy was elected president, Edward sought the vacant Senate seat left by his brother. In 1962, Ted was elected to the Senate.

On July 18, 1969, Ted was involved in a car accident. While driving home from a party on Chappaquiddick Island, part of Martha's Vineyard, he drove the car off a bridge and into the pond below. As the car submerged underwater upside down, Ted was able to escape.

According to Ted, he tried to rescue his passenger, Mary Jo Kopechne, but was unable to do so. Although there was a house nearby, he returned to the party. He told his cousin and friend what had happened, and they returned to the scene of the accident. No one notified the police.

Ted reported the incident the following morning and it quickly became a newsworthy story. What was most intriguing about the story was the question of why Ted failed to notify the authorities immediately. It was a question that would never receive an adequate answer. In the end, he pled guilty to leaving the scene of an accident and received one year probation.

FACT

On the night of the accident, Ted and his five married friends were partying with Kopechne and five other single women known as the "Boiler Room Girls." The group of women had worked on Robert Kennedy's presidential campaign. According to the men, it was a weekend getaway to thank the women for their help.

Although Ted emerged from the accident nearly unscathed physically, his political career suffered. Many voters were disturbed by his conduct, and in 1980 when he ran for the Democratic presidential nomination against Jimmy Carter, he was defeated. Ted decided to dedicate himself to his work in Congress. Today, he is Chairman of the Senate Health, Education, Labor and Pensions Committee and serves on the Judiciary Committee and the Armed Services Committee. He is now married to Victoria Reggie.

John F. Kennedy with the next generation of Kennedys, August 1963.

Photo credit: Cecil Stoughton, White House/John F. Kennedy Presidential Library and Museum, Boston

Appendix B

TIMELINE

May 29, 1917: John Fitzgerald Kennedy was born in Boston, Massachusetts.

July 1940: Kennedy's book *Why England Slept* is published.

July 23, 1942: Assigned to sea duty during World War II.

July 27, 1942: Begins training at a midshipmen's school in Chicago.

March 28, 1943: Arrives at the Solomon Islands to begin his command of *PT 109*.

August 1, 1943: *PT 109* is split in half by a Japanese destroyer.

August 1, 1943: Kennedy and his crew are rescued.

August 16, 1943: Returns to duty as commander of *PT 59*.

June 23, 1944: Has back surgery at New England Baptist Hospital in Boston.

August 12, 1944: Joe Jr. dies in a failed navy mission.

March 1, 1945: Retires with an honorable discharge from the navy.

April 28, 1945: Writes his first story for the Hearst *Chicago Herald-American* during the United Nations Conference in San Francisco.

November 5, 1946: Elected to the U.S. House of Representatives for Massachusetts.

May 13, 1948: Kathleen Kennedy dies in an airplane crash.

November 4, 1952: Elected to the U.S. Senate.

September 12, 1953: Marries Jacqueline Bouvier at St. Mary's Roman Catholic Church in Newport.

October 21, 1954: Undergoes back surgery. A metal plate is inserted for support.

February 15, 1955: Metal plate is removed from his back.

August 14, 1956: Fails to win enough delegate support for the Democratic vice presidential nomination.

August 23, 1956: Jackie gives birth to a stillborn daughter.

November 25, 1956: Decides that he will run for the Democratic presidential nomination for 1960.

May 1957: *Profiles in Courage* is awarded the Pulitzer Prize.

November 27, 1957: Caroline Kennedy is born in New York.

November 1958: Wins reelection to the Senate.

January 20, 1960: Announces candidacy for president in a press conference.

July 5, 1960: Lyndon B. Johnson announces that he is running for the Democratic presidential nomination.

July 13, 1960: Wins the Democratic presidential nomination.

September 26, 1960: Debates with Nixon in the first televised presidential debate.

November 8, 1960: Wins the presidential election against Richard Nixon.

November 26, 1960: John F. Kennedy Jr. is born.

January 20, 1960: Takes the presidential oath at the inauguration. He becomes the first Catholic elected U.S. president.

March 1, 1961: Signs an executive order creating the Peace Corps.

April 17, 1961: The Bay of Pigs invasion in Cuba begins.

May 4, 1961: The Freedom Rides commence.

June 3, 1961: Meets with Soviet Chairman Khrushchev in Vienna.

August 13, 1961: The Berlin Wall is built between East and West Berlin.

September 22, 1961: Congress passes legislation creating the Peace Corps.

May 28, 1962: The stock market collapses.

August 13, 1962: Learns from CIA director John McCone that the Soviets may have placed offensive weapons in Cuba.

September 4, 1962: States in a press conference that there is no evidence of Soviet offensive missiles in Cuba.

October 14, 1962: Photos reveal that missile sites are being constructed in Cuba by the Soviet Union.

October 24, 1962: Orders a quarantine of Soviet weapon shipments to Cuba.

October 28, 1962: A resolution is reached with the Soviet Union for the removal of the missiles.

May 3, 1963: The civil rights demonstrators in Birmingham, Alabama, are attacked with fire hoses and police dogs.

June 19, 1963: Kennedy's civil rights legislation is presented to Congress.

June 22, 1963: Leaves for trip to Ireland, Italy, England, and West Berlin.

August 7, 1963: Jackie gives birth to five-week-premature Patrick Kennedy. He dies two days later.

September 24, 1963: Limited Nuclear Test Ban Treaty is passed by Congress. Kennedy signs it on October 7.

October 23, 1963: Presents a compromised civil rights bill to the House for acceptance.

October 31, 1963: Announces that one thousand troops will be pulled out of South Vietnam by the end of 1963.

November 21, 1963: Leaves for San Antonio, Texas.

November 22, 1963: Kennedy is shot at 12:30 P.M. by Lee Harvey Oswald while riding in an open limousine in downtown Dallas, Texas. He is pronounced dead at 1:00 P.M.

November 24, 1963: Lee Harvey Oswald is shot by Jack Ruby while being transferred to county jail.

November 25, 1963: Kennedy is buried at Arlington National Cemetery.

Appendix C

BIBLIOGRAPHY AND WEB SITE RESOURCES

Selected Bibliography

Bradlee, Benjamin C. *Conversations with Kennedy*. New York: W.W. Norton & Company, Inc., 1975.

Clarke, Thurston. *Ask Not*. New York: Owl Books, 2005.

Collier, Peter, and David Horowitz. *The Kennedys: An American Drama*. San Francisco, CA: Encounter Books, 1984.

Dallek, Robert. *An Unfinished Life*. New York: Little, Brown and Company, 2003.

Goodwin, Doris Kearns. *The Fitgeralds and the Kennedys: An American Saga*. New York: Simon and Schuster, 1987.

Fries, Chuck, and Irv Wilson. *"We'll Never Be Young Again."* Los Angeles: Tallfellow Press, 2003.

Kennedy, John F. *Profiles in Courage*. New York: HarperCollins Publishers, 1956.

Kennedy, John F. *The Uncommon Wisdom of JFK*. New York: Rugged Land, 2003.

Kennedy, Rose Fitzgerald. *Times to Remember*. New York: Doubleday & Company, 1974.

Maier, Thomas. *The Kennedys: America's Emerald Kings*. New York: Basic Books, 2003.

May, Ernest R., and Philip D. Zelikow. *The Kennedy Tapes*. Cambridge, MA: Belknap Press of Harvard University Press, 1997.

Reeves, Richard. *President Kennedy: Profile of Power*. New York: Touchstone, 1993.

Reeves, Thomas C. *A Question of Character*. New York: Crown Forum, 1991.

Schlesinger, Arthur M. *A Thousand Days*. Boston: Houghton Mifflin, 1965.

Sorensen, Theodore C. *"Let the Word Go Forth."* New York: Laurel, 1988.

Wofford, Harris. *Of Kennedys and Kings*. Pittsburgh, PA: University of Pittsburgh Press, 1980.

Web Site Resources

John F. Kennedy Presidential Library and Museum
www.jfklibrary.org
This site includes photos, a timeline, a White House diary, a virtual museum tour, oral history interviews with Kennedy associates, and a reference center for researching documents housed at the library.

John F. Kennedy National Historic Site
www.nps.gov/jofi
This site provides information about visiting Kennedy's birthplace.

Report of the President's Commission on the Assassination of President Kennedy
www.archives.gov/research/jfk/warren-commission-report
This site contains the 1964 Warren Commission's report on Kennedy's assassination.

Report of the Select Committee on Assassinations of the U.S. House of Representatives
www.archives.gov/research/jfk/select-committee-report
The Select Committee's 1979 report regarding Kennedy's assassination.

American Experience: The Presidents
www.pbs.org/wgbh/amex/presidents/35_kennedy/index.html
This site contains an overview of Kennedy's term as president and a collection of primary sources.

INDEX

Other titles available in the *Everything*® Profiles Series:

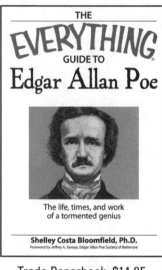

THE

EVERYTHING
GUIDE TO
Edgar Allan Poe

The life, times, and work
of a tormented genius

Shelley Costa Bloomfield, Ph.D.
Foreword by Jeffrey A. Savoye, Edgar Allan Poe Society of Baltimore

Trade Paperback, $14.95
ISBN 10: 1-59869-527-4
ISBN 13: 978-1-59869-527-4

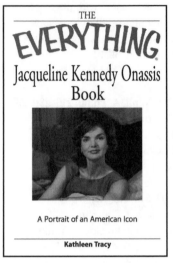

THE

EVERYTHING
Jacqueline Kennedy Onassis
Book

A Portrait of an American Icon

Kathleen Tracy

Trade Paperback, $14.95
ISBN 10: 1-59869-530-4
ISBN 13: 978-1-59869-530-4

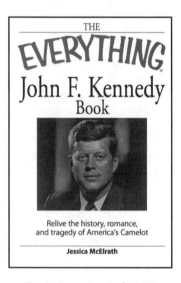

THE

EVERYTHING
John F. Kennedy
Book

Relive the history, romance,
and tragedy of America's Camelot

Jessica McElrath

Trade Paperback, $14.95
ISBN 10: 1-59869-529-0
ISBN 13: 978-1-59869-529-8

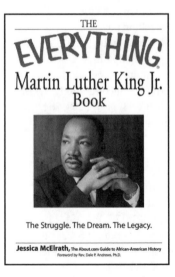

THE

EVERYTHING
Martin Luther King Jr.
Book

The Struggle. The Dream. The Legacy.

Jessica McElrath, The About.com Guide to African-American History
Foreword by Rev. Dale P. Andrews, Ph.D.

Trade Paperback, $14.95
ISBN 10: 1-59869-528-2
ISBN 13: 978-1-59869-528-1

Available wherever books are sold!
Or call 1-800-258-0929 or visit *www. adamsmediastore.com.*